report on BLACKLISTING

I · Movies

JOHN COGLEY

ARNO PRESS & THE NEW YORK TIMES

New York · 1972

129984

Reprint Edition 1972 by Arno Press Inc.

Copyright © 1956 by The Fund for the Republic, Inc.
Reprinted by permission of John Cogley
LC#   79-169349
ISBN   0-405-03915-8

THE ARNO PRESS CINEMA PROGRAM
See last pages of this volume for titles.

Manufactured in the United States of America

report on BLACKLISTING

I · Movies

JOHN COGLEY

THE FUND FOR THE REPUBLIC, INC.

CONTENTS

CONTENTS

Acknowledgment

THIS REPORT would not have been possible without the support of a devoted staff of researcher-reporters. I am particularly indebted to Elizabeth Poe and Paul Jacobs, both of Los Angeles. Edward Engberg and Margaret Bushong, though their efforts were concentrated on the radio-television industry, made many valuable contributions.

James Greene served as secretary for the entire project. He and Michael Harrington, my assistant, deserve a special word of thanks.

I am grateful to all these co-workers, to the Fund for the Republic, which sponsored this study, and to some two hundred interested persons who gave freely of their time for lengthy interviews. The conclusions found in these pages are mine alone. They do not necessarily reflect the judgments of any other person.

JOHN COGLEY

Foreword

MOST AMERICANS ARE CONVINCED that loyalty-security investigations of people working for the government in sensitive positions or seeking key federal jobs are necessary to protect the government from the infiltration of persons who might try to destroy it. But when loyalty tests are applied by private groups to people in private industries — and people are barred from jobs because they are "controversial" — many citizens become alarmed.

The present report (with its companion volume dealing with the radio television industry) embodies the results of a study initiated by The Fund for the Republic in September, 1954, when many Americans had become disturbed by the revelation of blacklisting practices in the radio, television, and motion picture industries.

At the time this study was launched, such blacklisting was a subject of vigorous public controversy, involving civil liberties issues of a serious kind. It raised questions of freedom of thought and speech, of due process, of the protection of the individual against group pressures and of the community against the disloyalty of the individual. It was a controversy in which all participants commonly spoke in the name of the Constitution and civil liberty, but in violently conflicting terms.

Those who advocated blacklisting practices did so on the ground that Communist and pro-Communist infiltration into the entertainment industries represented a serious peril to the American system of law and governance, and therefore to the freedoms which it enshrines. The peril might be direct, through giving Communists access to mass media into which they could introduce subversive propaganda, or which they might even sabotage given the proper circumstances. It might be only indirect, permitting Communist sympathizers to enjoy popular esteem, earning incomes which would help support Communist causes, operating their own black-lists against anti-Communists and promoting the interests of an international conspiracy directed toward the destruction of all liberties. In any case, it was contended, the extirpation from the entertainment industries of proven members of the Communist conspiracy and of all who were considered to have lent it their support or had been indifferent to its dangers (and remained im-penitent) was essential as a protection to American institutions.

Opponents of blacklisting contended that such a policy could only subvert the rights and liberties it sought to protect. Some held that it violated the Constitutional guarantees of freedom of speech and thought, since it destroyed an individual's livelihood on the sole ground of his political beliefs. This raised the issue whether a sympathy with Communism could properly be regarded as a "political belief" or must be taken as proof of complicity in a criminal conspiracy, even though no criminal charge could be brought. Beyond that, many who accepted the view that a con-vinced Communist should be barred from the cameras and micro-phones were disturbed by the methods being used to achieve this result. It was contended that blacklisting resulted in the ruin of many entirely loyal individuals without formal charges, hearings or other safeguards of due process, often on flimsy or mistaken charges and at the dictates of self-appointed censors or pressure groups.

Several things were apparent in this controversy. The major arguments simply did not meet. The facts around which the argu-ments raged were largely unknown. In these issues, plainly of critical importance to all those interested in the preservation of civil liberty, the information necessary to arriving at valid conclu-sions was largely unavailable. It was not even clear whether a blacklisting system actually existed in the motion picture, radio and TV industries. If it existed, it was not known on what principles it worked, who controlled it, how accurate were the criteria it applied in screening Communists and pro-Communists out of the industries, what were the motives which might have contributed to its growth. Beyond the somewhat rough-and-ready disclosures of the various investigating committees, there was little useful data on the nature and extent of Communist influence in the industries; on the effect, if any, which it had exerted on the output; on the extent to which the Communists themselves had engaged in black-listing practices, or on numerous other facts essential to formulating any answers for the issues of civil liberties here involved. The subject was being debated, in short, in a vacuum.

The Fund for the Republic was established as an educational undertaking in the field of civil liberties in the United States. It seemed to its Directors that here were problems of immediate concern and that the Fund could render a useful service toward their solution by ascertaining the facts involved. It asked John Cogley, then Executive Editor of *The Commonweal,* to study and report upon the situation as a whole. This he has done. Mr. Cogley and his associates have interviewed — so far as they found it possible to do so — every important interest concerned. These include executives of the motion picture industry and the radio and TV chains, the advertising agencies, leading advertisers, the theatrical unions, leaders of anti-Communist organizations and others prominent in "listing" or "clearing" individuals, and many producers, directors, actors, writers, reporters, news commentators and agency men.

From the first it was recognized that this was a highly complex question, and Mr. Cogley and his associates have been scrupulous in trying to present all significant points of view. He was given a free hand in the organization of the study and presentation of the facts. While he accepts responsibility for this report as its director and author, the Board of The Fund for the Republic wishes to state its full confidence in the calm deliberation which he has given to its preparation. We believe he has done a thorough job in a very difficult field.

It was recognized that many in the industries are aware of the difficulties raised by blacklisting and have been wrestling earnestly with them. Mr. Cogley has tried to give a detailed picture of a situation as it exists. He has brought in no indictments, and has offered no recommendations. The Board of the Fund for the Republic offers none, believing that progress in resolving the conflicts of interest, viewpoint, and principle involved must and will come in the first instance from the industries affected. But even this progress must ultimately turn upon public knowledge and understanding of the actual situation and its problems. This report seeks only to supply the data on which such knowledge and understanding may be established.

FOR THE BOARD OF DIRECTORS,
THE FUND FOR THE REPUBLIC:
By Paul G. Hoffman, *Chairman*

The 1947 Hearings

AFTER THE MOVIE HEARINGS of the House Un-American Activities
Committee in October, 1947, *Life* Magazine ran a report on them,
with the subhead: *"Congressional committee poses a question: is it
un-American to ask a man if he is a Communist — or un-American
to refuse to answer?"* At the hearings, held in the Caucus Room
of the Old House Office Building in Washington, Representative
J. Parnell Thomas, chairman of the committee, had offered a vigorous
no to the first part of the question: "Any real American would be
proud to answer the question 'Are you or have you ever been a
member of the Communist Party?' — any *real* American!" Thomas
told an uncooperative witness. A group of Hollywood witnesses —
later identified as the Hollywood Ten — had been truculently positive about the second half. "It is absolutely beyond the power of
this committee to inquire into my association in any organization,"
screenwriter John Howard Lawson told the chairman. ". . . It is
unfortunate and tragic that I have to teach this committee the basic
principles of American life."

In those dim pre-Hiss, pre-McCarthy days, *Life's* double-bar-
relled question seemed eminently worthy of debate.

The author of the magazine's report, Sidney Olson, answered
the question this way: "The fact is that Congressional investigating
committees legally have the right to ask a witness anything within
the purview of their investigation. This right has been maintained
in the U.S. courts many times, on the basis in common law that a

1

legislative body does have the power to inform itself sufficiently in order to carry out its duties."*

Alvah Bessie, one of the Ten, argued:

It is my understanding of the first amendment to our Constitution that it expressly forbids Congress to pass any law which shall abridge freedom of speech or of opinion. And it is my understanding of the function of Congressional committees that they are set up by the Congress for the express purpose of inquiring into matters that may lead to the initiation of legislation in the Congress . . . Since the only legislation this Committee could possibly initiate would automatically abridge freedom of speech and opinion, and would therefore be automatically unconstitutional, I have come to the conclusion . . . that this body is totally unconstitutional and without power to inquire into anything I think, believe, uphold, and cherish, or anything I have ever written or said, or any organization I have ever joined or failed to join.

George E. Sokolsky, a man destined to play a key role in the subsequent history of Hollywood, had expressed remarkably similar sentiments some seven years earlier. In his newspaper column for March 25, 1940, Sokolsky wrote:

Civil liberties are always impaired by Congressional committees and by most administrative boards. The fundamental trial by jury, the right of a day in court, the right to be represented by counsel and many other basic civil rights are impaired.

You will say that the Congressional committees only investigate; they do not try. That is, in fact, a false notion. These committees put

---

* *Power to compel pertinent disclosures is implied in the grant of all legislative power to Congress* . . . there is no provision expressly investing either house with power to make investigations and exact testimony to the end that it may exercise its legislative function advisedly and effectively. So the question arises whether this power is so far incidental to the legislative function as to be implied.

In actual legislative practice power to secure needed information by such means has long been treated as an attribute of the power to legislate. It was so regarded in the British Parliament and in the Colonial legislatures before the American Revolution; and a like view has prevailed and been carried into effect in both houses of Congress and in most of the state legislatures (*McGrain* v. *Daugherty* (1927) 273 U.S. 135, 161). *Senate Document No. 99, 83D Congress, 2d Session: Congressional Power of Investigation. 1954.*

a man on a spot, bring in the reporters, camera men, newsreelers and demand to know, yes or no, whether it isn't true that he did so and so. He says that he would like to read a statement proving that he is being maligned and his conduct misunderstood. Nothing doing! You can't read statements! Well, he says, have I done anything that's against the law? That isn't the point. They've given the public the impression they want to give, and the defendant is almost helpless unless he has a good publicity man of his own or he shouts down the Congressmen, who don't like to be exposed to shouts.

What about the civil liberties involved in this technique? What about the civil liberties involved in a squint-eyed brat out of the Harvard Law School chasing around the country demanding to see private letter files and squeaking: "When you talk to me you're talking to the government of the United States"? What are the civil liberties in that proposition?

I should like to get this thing cleared up in some way. I should like to see an answer to the question, "Has a man a right to be a Communist, Republican, Fascist, manufacturer or A. F. of L. labor leader or a farmer who owns his own farm without being subject to New Deal smear?" Perhaps the Republicans and manufacturers will not like the company I join them to. But the technique is used on all of them in the same way.

At the time of 1947 hearings, this view of Congressional investigating committees was widespread in liberal-minded Hollywood, as elsewhere. The film industry was generally antagonistic to the idea of an investigation. In May, 1947, Parnell Thomas complained that the industry seemed unwilling to cooperate with his committee. Later, in an official statement, the Association of Motion Picture Producers asserted that "Hollywood is weary of being the national whipping boy for Congressional committees. We are tired of having irresponsible charges made again and again and again and not sustained. If we have committed a crime we want to know it. If not, we should not be badgered by Congressional committees."

Hollywood stars vied with one another in proclaiming their disdain for Mr. Thomas and his committee. JUDY GARLAND: "Before every free conscience in America is subpoenaed, please speak up!

Say your piece. Write your Congressman a letter! Airmail special! Let the Congress know what you think of its un-American Committee. Tell them how much you resent the way Mr. Thomas is kicking the living daylights out of the Bill of Rights!" FREDRIC MARCH: "Who do you think they're really after? Who's next? Is it your minister who will be told what he can say in his pulpit? Is it your children's school teacher who will be told what she can say in classrooms? Is it your children themselves? Is it you, who will have to look around nervously before you can say what is on your minds? Who are they after? They're after more than Hollywood. This reaches into every American city and town." FRANK SINATRA: "Once they get the movies throttled, how long will it be before the Committee goes to work on freedom of the air? How long will it be before we're told what we can say and cannot say into a radio microphone? If you make a pitch on a nationwide radio network for a square deal for the underdog, will they call you a Commie? . . . Are they going to scare us into silence? I wonder."

In a formal statement signed by 28 Hollywood personalities, the following alleged abuses were noted:

I. The investigative function of the Committee on Un-American Activities has been perverted from fair and impartial procedures to un-fair, partial and prejudiced methods.

II. The reputations and characters of individuals have been smeared and besmirched in the following manner:

a. The Committee on Un-American Activities has been guilty of a violation of the long established Anglo-Saxon-American principles of individual accountability. They have accomplished this by adopting the "mass guilt" principle, i.e., guilt by association. Not only have the subpoenaed witnesses suffered by these methods, but mass lists have been publicized that contained many names of other people. These people were included in lists which have been designated by Committee members and counsel as "subversive," "pinko," "radical," "communistic," "disloyal," "un-American," etc. These people were neither subpoenaed nor given the opportunity to defend their characters.

4

b. The proceedings of the Committee have come to be regarded by the American people as a criminal trial. Nevertheless, American citizens have not been given the American privilege of ordinary self-defense statements and the right to cross-examine their accusers. The accused witnesses have become defendants in fact, have not been allowed the right of obtaining witnesses to testify on their behalf. Neither have they been allowed the full right of professional counsel in the defense of their characters.

c. Moreover, while theoretically the Committee is not supposed to apply punitive measures, because of its procedural abuses, it has punished individuals in a far more damaging way than the assessment of fines or personal imprisonment. They have done this by besmirching and damaging man's most precious possession, his reputation.

The statement formed part of a petition for redress of grievances. It had been presented to the clerk of the House of Representatives by a group of Hollywood celebrities who came to Washington as representatives of the Committee for the First Amendment. It was signed by Robert Ardrey, Larry Adler, Lauren Bacall, Humphrey Bogart, Geraldine Brooks, Jules Block, Richard Conte, Philip Dunne, Melvin Frank, Anne Frank, Ira Gershwin, Sheridan Gibney, Sterling Hayden, Mrs. Sterling Hayden, June Havoc, David Hopkins, Paul Henreid, John Huston, Gene Kelly, Evelyn Keyes, Danny Kaye, Arthur Kober, Marsha Hunt, Robert Presnell, Jr., Henry Rogers, Shepperd Strudwick, Joe Sistrom and Jane Wyatt.

Later, Humphrey Bogart, Lauren Bacall, Jane Wyatt and some of the others described their participation in the hearings as a "mistake." "Roosevelt was a good politician. He could handle those babies in Washington," Bogart told Lillian Ross of *The New Yorker*, "but they're too smart for guys like me. Hell, I'm no politician. That's what I meant when I said our Washington trip was a mistake."

Others in the group now point to the Washington flight as an example of their political naiveté at the time. "I went along," one

5

actress explained not long ago, "because I thought I owed it to the industry. I understood that the Committee was trying to impose censorship on Hollywood and dictate what kind of films we could make. I certainly did not get involved out of any feeling of sympathy for the ten men who behaved so badly on the witness stand. Some of us were under the impression these men would call a press conference and answer the questions they said they refused to answer on principle. We felt terribly let down when they wouldn't."*

The Committee for the First Amendment was organized in Hollywood by producers William Wyler and John Huston and screenwriter Philip Dunne. Dozens of Hollywood personages endorsed the Committee's belief that ". . . any investigation into the political beliefs of the individual is contrary to the basic principles of our democracy. Any attempt to curb freedom of expression and to set arbitrary standards of Americanism is in itself disloyal to both the spirit and the letter of the Constitution." Among them were Norman Corwin, Henry Fonda, Ava Gardner, Paulette Goddard, Benny Goodman, Van Heflin, Katharine Hepburn, John Houseman, Myrna Loy, Burgess Meredith, Gregory Peck, Barry Sullivan, Cornel Wilde and Billy Wilder.

The Committee, *Daily Variety* reported, "plans a backfire against the House Un-American Activities Committee via a drive to battle the top headlines out of Washington each day," adding that its

---

* In a pamphlet called "The Time of the Toad," Dalton Trumbo, one of the Ten, explained why he and his nine associates did not call such a press conference: "Such action, dramatic as it might have been, would have negated all that went before. . . . The accused men made their stand before the Committee to reestablish their right of privacy, not only in law but in fact. . . . Privacy in relation to political opinion means secrecy. What principle, then, is served by defending the right of secrecy in law only to reveal the secret in life?" The same explanation was offered to readers of the New York *Herald Tribune* by Ring Lardner, Jr., another of the Ten. Lardner's statements were specifically endorsed by his colleagues.

But on the witness stand John Howard Lawson, leader of the Ten, had declared unmistakably that although he would not answer any questions about his political affiliations he would "offer my beliefs, affiliations and everything else to the American public, and they will know where I stand."

6

founders "declared themselves to be anti-Communist." In the days following, the Committee for the First Amendment placed advertisements in the trade papers and solicited funds from dozens in Hollywood who, according to one of its founders, "would not have it known that they gave money." The Committee decided to send a delegation to Washington to watch the hearings, to "see whether they would be fair" (and, incidentally, to take some of the newspaper play away from Parnell Thomas and the big-name Hollywood personalities he had summoned as "friendly" witnesses). The group also decided to make coast-to-coast radio broadcasts at which stars would discuss the Constitution and civil liberties.

The Hollywood delegation planned to arrive at the hearing on Monday, October 27, when Eric Johnston was scheduled to testify as a representative of the motion-picture industry. Their appearance, it was felt, would bolster Johnston's testimony. William Wyler recalls that he briefed the group before they left Hollywood. "I told them to stay away from the 'unfriendly' witnesses. I told them that the newspapers would say they were there to defend the Communists, but that they were going to Washington to attack the House Un-American Activities Committee and not to defend any Communists."

But Eric Johnston was not called on schedule. After the Hollywood delegation, in a blaze of publicity, took their places in the hearing room the chairman called John Howard Lawson, who had been named several times during the hearings as leader of the Hollywood Communists. The link did not go unnoticed in the press.

Lawson was an extremely "unfriendly" witness. His behavior on the stand came as an enormous shock to most of the Hollywood visitors. None of them expected him to "cooperate" but they were not prepared for shouting and unabashed insolence. A press conference was held that same afternoon, attended by dozens of newspapermen. At the conference, the Hollywood delegation was hopelessly demoralized when newsmen suggested that their appearance in Washington would be interpreted all over the country as support for Lawson. The next day, after two more unfriendly witnesses were called, the group left Washington. Many of them were utterly disappointed and angry. "We've been had!" they told each other.

The complete collapse of the Committee was hastened by another incident growing out of the Hollywood hearings. A Washington newspaper had reported that Sterling Hayden, one of the stars who made the Washington trip, was a Communist. After William Wyler had called a meeting of Committee members to raise funds so Hayden could sue for libel, it was discovered that there was some truth in the story. (Hayden subsequently testified that he had been a Party member for six months in 1946.)

In the years since, the Committee for the First Amendment has been widely listed as a Communist-front organization. (Membership in it has frequently been a factor in determining employability.) Some of the Committee's founders resent this. "Of course the Attorney General said it was a Communist front, and apparently a front organization is what the Attorney General decides," William Wyler stated recently. "But this was *not* a Communist-front organization. There may have been some Communists in the group, but then there are probably Communists in any organization. The point is, they did not run the Committee, and a Communist-front organization is one that is run by Communists. *We* ran the Committee and we were not Communists."

Wyler believes that the Committee made mistakes. "We attacked the hearings, when the Un-American Activities Committee legally had the right to investigate. We should have had advice from a Constitutional lawyer. We should have attacked the Committee's methods rather than the Committee itself. But J. Parnell Thomas and those terrible proceedings seemed so unconstitutional to us then. I think, though, we had some effect. The Committee observes some civil liberties now."

Soon after the 1947 hearings, Wyler was one of a delegation of

8

three who went to an office maintained by the "unfriendly" witnesses and begged them "to go before a judge, or the press, or something, and answer the questions." But, he says, "We were naive, and of course they wouldn't do it."

The Committee for the First Amendment was not alone in its view of "those terrible proceedings." After two days of the hearings, the New York *Herald Tribune* commented that the testimony so far had "produced exactly what was expected of them." Mr. Thomas' labor, the paper declared, had brought forth "an abundance of unsubstantiated charges, some dizzying," "new definitions of Communism," and "a satisfactory collection of clippings" for the Congressman's own scrapbook. The editorial asserted that "the beliefs of men and women who write for the screen are, like the beliefs of any ordinary men and women, nobody's business but their own, as the Bill of Rights mentions."

At the end of the first week's testimony, *Daily Variety* noted that "the Committee permitted friendly witnesses to read prepared statements, use notes, and ramble widely in offering testimony of strong nature without supporting evidence." The trade paper quoted a letter written to Congress that week by Eric Johnston: "Too often, individuals and institutions have been condemned without a hearing or chance to speak in self-defense; slandered and libeled by hostile witnesses not subject to cross-examination and immune from subsequent suit or prosecution."

It seemed to many at the end of the first week of hearings (when only "friendly" witnesses were heard) that the intention of the Committee was not so much to attack the alleged Communists as to threaten the motion-picture industry itself. The late Paul V. McNutt, once High Commissioner to the Philippines, who had been engaged as counsel for the producers at the hearings, said on October 23: "It became apparent by the chairman's questions that the purpose of the hearing was to try to dictate and control through the device of the hearings, what goes on in the screens of America.

9

It does not require a law to cripple the right of free speech. Intimidation and coercion will do it. Freedom simply cannot live in an atmosphere of fear. The motion-picture industry cannot be a free medium of expression if it must live in fear of a damning epithet 'Un-American!' whenever it elects to introduce a new idea, produce a picture critical of the status quo, or point up through a picture some phase of our way of life that needs improving." McNutt's views of the proceedings were generally shared in Hollywood.

The famous Hollywood Ten were originally 19. When a group of 41 witnesses ("friendly" and "unfriendly") was first summoned to testify about communism in Hollywood, these 19 announced that as a matter of principle they would refuse to answer the Committee's questions. Someone dubbed them the "unfriendly 19," and the name caught on.

In Hollywood there were rumors that the 19 would be banished from work in the film colony because of the stand they were taking. Paul V. McNutt said he advised the industry against instituting such a blacklist since it would be "a conspiracy without warrant of law." Again, after Representative Thomas had been quoted in the press as saying that the producers had agreed to establish a political blacklist throughout the entire motion-picture industry, Eric Johnston, speaking as president of the Motion Picture Association of America, vehemently denied the report. The report was nonsense, he said: he insisted that any statement purporting to quote him as agreeing to a blacklist was a libel upon him as a good American. Johnston made this statement to Robert W. Kenny and Bartley C. Crum, attorney for the 19, on October 18, 1947. He assured the lawyers that Hollywood would never countenance blacklisting.

The movie hearings in 1947 lasted two weeks. As spokesman for the anti-Communist forces in Hollywood, Parnell Thomas had lined up a group of actors and writers, most of them members of the Motion Picture Alliance for the Preservation of American Ideals. The Alliance, a militantly anti-Communist, pro-free enterprise group, was founded in 1944 to combat "the growing impression that this industry is made up of, and dominated by, Communists, radicals and crackpots." Earlier, leaders of the Alliance, at the peril of being branded disloyal to the industry, had endorsed the findings of Senator Jack B. Tenney's California Un-American Activities Committee. Few in Hollywood had any use for Tenney or his Committee. No one was surprised, then, when the Alliance openly welcomed the Thomas investigation. Early in 1947 Congressman John Rankin of Mississippi made a speech in the House in which he claimed that the "old time American producers, actors and writers" were behind the impending investigation and had furnished "evidence" to substantiate charges of Red infiltration. It was generally understood in Hollywood that Mr. Rankin's "old time Americans" were leading lights of the Alliance.

At the time of the Hollywood hearings the Alliance, like the House Committee itself, was particularly interested in film content. One of its prominent members, novelist Ayn Rand (*The Fountainhead*), wrote a "Screen Guide for Americans" which the Alliance published and distributed. The Guide provided a list of "do's" and "don'ts" for moviemakers: "Don't Smear the Free Enterprise System," "Don't Deify the 'Common Man'," "Don't Glorify the Collective," "Don't Glorify Failure," "Don't Smear Success," "Don't Smear Industrialists."

"It is the *moral* (no, not just political but *moral*) duty of every decent man in the motion picture industry," the pamphlet asserted, "to throw into the ashcan where it belongs, every story that smears industrialists as such."

Screenwriter Rupert Hughes, a founder of the Alliance, granted while he was on the stand that there was no open Communist propaganda on the screen. But, Hughes declared, "where you see

11

a little drop of cyanide in the picture, a small grain of arsenic, something that makes every Senator, every businessman, every employer a crook and which destroys our beliefs in American free enterprise and free institutions, that is communistic!"

Mrs. Lela Rogers, mother of film actress Ginger Rogers, testified that "it has been a long time since you could get a good American story bought in the motion-picture industry." But Adolphe Menjou, another Alliance board member, declared that the "vigilance" of the organization had "prevented an enormous amount of sly, subtle, un-American class-struggle propaganda from going into pictures."

Chairman Thomas encouraged these "friendly" witnesses to expand freely on the Communist problem in Hollywood. Among other charges, they claimed that members of the Party had attempted to take over the talent unions and had in fact achieved notable success in the Screen Writers Guild. Communist writers had introduced "communistic" slants in the films they wrote, though there was scant outright Soviet propaganda to point to. Like Mr. Hughes, several witnesses found subversive significance in the fact that bankers and industrialists were cast as "heavies." The wartime films "Mission to Moscow," "North Star," and "Song of Russia" were discussed at length. Miss Rand, herself a Russian emigrée, analyzed the last-named and found it a wholly misleading picture of life in the Soviet Union. Robert Taylor, star of "Song of Russia," told of his patriotic reluctance to play the leading role in it. Mrs. Rogers, who held that there were traces of communism in "Tender Comrade" and "None But the Lonely Heart," declared that she forbade her famous daughter to play the title role in Dreiser's "Sister Carrie," which she described as "open propaganda." But few specific charges against specific films were made.

The Committee actually seemed more interested in films not made than in those written, directed or produced by the alleged Communists in the industry. Again and again, friendly witnesses were asked if they did not agree with the Committee that Hollywood should make more anti-Communist pictures patterned after the anti-Nazi pictures that appeared before and during World War II. The witnesses agreed readily that the field had been neglected. Other questioning led to the conclusion that movie producers had a patriotic duty to soft-pedal "social" themes and make movies that would point up the benefits of free enterprise.

Even while the hearings were being held, Representative Thomas was widely charged with attempting to set up a censorship over films. But one screenwriter, John C. Moffit, stated that the Committee, rather, was "taking steps to end the most dangerous censorship that has ever occurred in the history of motion-picture industry and in the history of American thought." To bolster his claim that Hollywood Communists had kept anti-Soviet material off the screen, Moffitt quoted from an article in the Communist *Worker*, written by Dalton Trumbo:

We have produced a few fine films in Hollywood, a great many of which were vulgar and opportunistic and a few downright vicious. If you tell me Hollywood, in contrast with the novel and the theater, has produced nothing so provocative or so progressive as *Freedom Road* or *Deep Are the Roots*, I will grant you the point, but I may also add that neither has Hollywood produced anything so untrue or so reactionary as *The Yogi and the Commissar, Out of the Night, Report on the Russians, There Shall Be No Night,* or *Adventures of a Young Man.* Nor does Hollywood's forthcoming schedule include such tempting items as James T. Farrell's *Bernard Clare,* Victor A. Kravchenko's *I Chose Freedom,* or the so-called biography of Stalin by Leon Trotsky.

Other friendly witnesses charged that Hollywood Communists conspired to keep "good Americans" unemployed in the studios. The late Sam Wood, a noted director-producer, explained how they did it:

For instance, a man gets a key position in the studio and has charge of the writers. When you, as a director or a producer, are ready for a writer you ask for a list and this man shows you a list. Well, if he is following the Party line his pets are on top or the other people aren't

13

on it at all. If there is a particular man in there that has been opposing them they will leave his name off the list. Then if that man isn't employed for about two months they go to the head of the studio and say, "Nobody wants this man." The head is perfectly honest about it and says, "Nobody wants to use him, let him go." So a good American is let out. But it doesn't stop there. They point that out as an example and say, "You better fall in line, play ball, or else." And they go down the line on it.*

Menjou told the committee that "under certain circumstances a communistic director, a communistic writer, or a communistic actor, even if he were under orders from the head of the studio not to inject communism or un-Americanism or subversion into pictures, could easily subvert that order, under the proper circumstances, by a look, by an inflection, by a change in the voice." The actor however did not believe that a motion-picture worker suspected of communism should be blacklisted in the studios: "He could be very carefully watched; this producer could watch every script and every scene of his script. We have many Communist writers who are splendid writers. They do not have to write communistically at all, but they have to be watched." Nor would Menjou object to Communist propaganda on the screen, provided it was clearly labelled. He agreed with committee member Richard M. Nixon, then a freshman congressman, that "if we refuse to allow a Communist picture to be made and advertised as such we would be falling into the same error that we criticize the Communists for in Russia."**

The friendly witnesses, though rambling and repetitious, made it

---

* Interestingly enough, John Gunther in *Inside U.S.A.* (1947) cited Wood in an example of how bitterly opposed political factions work amicably together in Hollywood: "Sam Wood, boss of the Motion Picture Alliance, directed 'For Whom the Bell Tolls.' But Dudley Nichols, the spearhead for the other side, wrote the script! Even in the most reactionary studio, nobody will be quicker than an MPA-sympathizer to grab off a Russian director, say, or a best-selling novel by a leading antifascist, if the prospect is lucrative enough, since the profit motive is the final arbiter in Hollywood, the ultimate and unanswerable determinant of all behavior."

clear beyond question that they felt Thomas' investigation of Hollywood was long overdue. In turn, the chairman thanked Miss Rand, Mrs. Rogers, Rupert Hughes, Adolphe Menjou, Sam Wood, James K. McGuiness, Morrie Ryskind, Richard Macaulay, Fred Niblo, Jr., and Howard Rushmore, an ex-*Daily Worker* film critic turned Hearst journalist. Thomas commended the patriotism of all and found a good word too for Robert Taylor, Robert Montgomery, George Murphy, Ronald Reagan and Gary Cooper, whose appearances before the Committee had made front-page copy. Director Leo McCarey and Walt Disney rounded out the stellar cast of friendly witnesses.

Jack L. Warner and Louis B. Mayer represented the top Hollywood executives at the hearings. Warner's testimony, while not overly coherent, was vehemently anti-Communist. He denied there was Communist propaganda in the films he produced but admitted readily that in all probability there had been Communists on his studio payroll who tried to get propaganda into the films they wrote. When he detected "slanted" lines in scripts, Warner declared, he had the lines removed, bided his time, and then refused to rehire the offending writers when their contracts ran out. That way he had "cleaned out" his studio. "You have been doing exactly the same thing in your business that we have been attempting to do in

---

** Six years later, after a group of film workers who refused under oath to affirm or deny their alleged membership in the Communist Party — including several of the Hollywood Ten — made an independent motion picture in Mexico, called "Salt of the Earth" (under the sponsorship of the Mine, Mill and Smelter Workers, a union often cited as being Communist-led), Representative Donald L. Jackson, then a member of the House Committee on Un-American Activities, sought to suppress the picture. Jackson sent a telegram to a number of key figures asking "Is there any action that industry and labor in motion picture field can take to stop completion and release of picture here and abroad?"

Roy M. Brewer, then International Representative of the Theatrical Stage Employees Union, and Chairman of the Hollywood A. F. of L. Film Council, offered the services of the Council in helping to suppress the film. The distribution of "Salt of the Earth" was halted after motion-picture projectionists (members of Brewer's union) and theater owners across the country refused to show it.

15

ours," the chairman told the producer, and the latter agreed. But despite the chairman's prodding, Warner could not agree to an industry-wide ban on Communists. In his opinion, Warner testified, it would not be legal for any group of producers to band together to obstruct the employment of other men. He would continue to get rid of writers he suspected of "un-Americanism" but would not join any concerted attempt to blacklist them in the industry.

In secret testimony before the Committee a few months earlier, Warner had named a certain number of Hollywood figures as probable Communists. He seemed reluctant about naming them again in public, so the secret testimony was read back to him. He was asked if he stood by his previous testimony. The producer replied that he didn't know whether the writers he had named were Communists — "but I could tell from what they were putting into scripts that they were un-American." He specifically exempted four of the writers included in his original charge of "infiltration," stating that he had been mistaken about them.

At least three of those cited in this manner by Warner were never again named in all the Hollywood hearings that followed. But even though their names were not included in the long lists published in the House Committee's Annual Reports, they are still unable to work in Hollywood.

One of the men Warner described as Communist propagandists in his secret testimony was Howard Koch, who had been subpoenaed and become one of the 19 "unfriendlies." Warner said that Koch was one of the writers he had fired. After Warner made this claim on the witness stand, Robert Kenny, attorney for the 19, told the press that several of the men Warner said he fired because they were Communists had since been offered jobs in Warner's studio. Koch, for instance, could prove that he sought release from his Warner's contract himself and had paid the studio $10,000 in order to be released. When the hearings were over, Koch announced in a *Daily Variety* advertisement that he was not and had

16

never been a Communist, but that he reserved the right to refuse to answer the Committee if it ever subpoenaed him.

Louis B. Mayer, when his turn came, held that Communist writers could never succeed in influencing pictures made at M-G-M because in that studio scripts were read and reread by executives, producers and editors. On several occasions, Mayer recalled, writers on the M-G-M payroll had been charged with communism but no proof was ever offered. He personally studied the pictures written by these men and could find no slanting. Mayer expressed "contempt" for members of the Communist Party, but as far as their influence at Metro-Goldwyn-Mayer went, the pictures were there to be seen and "they will speak for themselves."

Dore Schary, now studio chief at M-G-M but then an RKO executive, insisted that he would continue to hire performers on the basis of merit alone until such a time as it were proved that they had been personally guilty of subversion or espionage. The chairman asked him: "Therefore, assuming that X is a great artist; assuming also that he is a Communist, you would not hesitate to rehire him?" Schary replied: "I would not hesitate to rehire him if it was not proven that he was a foreign agent. I would still maintain his right to think politically as he chooses." Thomas asked Schary then if he ever heard of Rip Van Winkle and added: "It is the Rip Van Winkle opinion that has been permitting communism to grow throughout the world the way it has."

Two Hollywood union representatives appeared: Roy M. Brewer, of the International Alliance of Theatrical Stage Employees and Motion Picture Machine Operators of the United States (IATSE), and Emmet Lavery, screenwriter, then serving his third term as president of the Screen Writers Guild.

Brewer spoke of Communist activity in the motion-picture trade-union movement. His own union only a few years earlier had received national attention when its president, George E. Browne, along with his personal representative, Willie Bioff, were sentenced to jail sentences and stiff fines, on conviction of extortion and conspiracy. Brewer's IATSE had long been involved in jurisdictional disputes with a rival labor group called the Conference of Studio Unions. On the stand, the IATSE chief described the Conference as Communist and — to the dismay of many knowledgeable movie people — spoke of Hollywood's long inter-union struggle as if it were a simple battle between subversion and patriotic opposition. "We hope . . . that with the help of the committee," Brewer told the chairman, "the Communist menace in the motion-picture industry may be successfully destroyed, to the end that Hollywood labor may be spared in the future the strife and turmoil of the immediate past."

Emmet Lavery (who had been described by Rupert Hughes as "a man whose views are Communist, whose friends are Communists, and whose work is communistic") surprised the Committee by testifying with easy candor. Though a lawyer himself, Lavery said he was not sure of the Committee's right to demand a yes or no answer to the question, "Are you a member of the Communist Party?" But before the chairman got around to the question he volunteered: "Let me break the suspense immediately and tell you that I am not a Communist. I never have been. I don't intend to be." At Lavery's own request his testimony before the California Tenney Committee was read into the record of the House hearing. He had been as unevasive a witness before Tenney as he proved to be before Thomas.

Lavery agreed that Communists might be active in the Screen Writers Guild but pointed out that the Guild accepted members only after they had qualified as screenwriters. "Under our existing contract with the producers and our existing constitution, it would be next to impossible to remove anybody from our Guild for political belief, private political belief or action. . . . If any individual members are guilty of indictable offenses, that are clearly sedition or treason, let a proper complaint be brought to the FBI and an indictment sought by a Federal grand jury and action taken accordingly."

In Lavery's opinion, there was an extreme right and left in his Guild but the vast majority of its members belonged to the "liberal center." Lavery was not afraid of Communist activity in the Guild, he said. Yes, he thought it possible that Communists would try to take over but he did not believe that "in a group of writers it is possible for them to get away with it." So far, Lavery testified, *he* had the upper hand. He did not believe in making political martyrs out of the Communists but thought they should be opposed by open, democratic means.

Screenwriter John Howard Lawson, the first of the uncooperative witnesses to take the stand at the public Washington hearings, established a pattern followed by the nine other "unfriendly" witnesses who were called. Lawson's period on the stand was stormy, disorderly and notably brief. Chairman Thomas, who found it necessary to pound his gavel for order 16 times while Lawson was testifying, was determined that the witness was not going to have the opportunity to "make speeches" and did not permit him to read a prepared statement. "I refuse you to make the statement, because of the first sentence in your statement," Thomas said firmly. "That statement is not pertinent to this inquiry." The first sentence read: "For a week, this Committee has conducted an illegal and indecent trial of American citizens, whom the Committee has selected to be publicly pilloried and smeared."

The rest of the forbidden statement was written in what was later described in *Life* as *"Pravda*-like prose." Lawson declared that the "so-called 'evidence' " at the hearing came from a parade of "stool pigeons, neurotics, publicity-seeking clowns, Gestapo agents, paid informers and a few ignorant and frightened Hollywood artists." He accused J. Parnell Thomas and the "un-American interests he serves" of "conspiring against the American way of life. They want to cut living standards, introduce an economy of poverty, wipe out

19

labor's rights, attack Negroes, Jews and other minorities, drive us into a disastrous and unnecessary war."

In his actual testimony Lawson never succeeded in keeping his voice down and refused to answer any questions bearing on his trade-union or political affiliations. He accused the Committee of threatening and intimidating witnesses. When he was asked if he belonged to the Communist Party, he answered by declaring that J. Parnell Thomas was using a technique perfected in Hitler Germany to "create a scare." He charged that the Committee had deliberately set out to "smear the motion-picture industry." He claimed that some of the friendly witnesses were guilty of perjury. Finally, after several bitter exchanges with Thomas, he was ordered to step down. Lawson's last words were: "I have written Americanism for many years, and I shall continue to fight for the Bill of Rights, which you are trying to destroy." There were boos and applause as he was ushered from the stand; the chairman cautioned against demonstrations either for or against.

After Lawson was taken away, a Louis J. Russell, former FBI agent and investigator for the Committee, was put under oath and declared that in the course of his investigations for the Committee, he had been furnished with copies of certain Communist Party registration cards for the year 1944. One of them was made out to John Howard Lawson.

The chairman then announced that it was the unanimous opinion of the committee that John Howard Lawson, by refusing to answer the questions put to him, was in contempt of Congress.

One by one then, as the hearings went on, nine other "unfriendly" witnesses were called to the stand and, with more or less vehemence, repeated Lawson's performance. In each case they invoked the First (not the Fifth) Amendment to the Constitution, refused to answer questions about any political affiliations and expressed their belief that the Committee was exceeding its Constitutional powers. After each of the nine stepped down, Louis J. Russell was recalled to the stand and listed the number of another Communist membership card.* Like John Howard Lawson, each in turn was cited for contempt of Congress. (The contempt charge was upheld in the House by a vote of 346 to 17, 10 days later. The ten were subsequently jailed.) For reasons of his own, Parnell Thomas suspended the hearings after these ten were heard. The remaining nine who had announced they would be "unfriendly" witnesses were not even called.

The publicity surrounding the Hollywood Ten case was clearly not the kind Hollywood woos. It was generally agreed, if not in Hollywood then certainly in the financial circles which control the industry, that something had to be done. The industry acted promptly enough. On November 24, 1947, 50 members of the Motion Picture Association of America, the Association of Motion Picture Producers and the Society of Independent Motion Picture Producers, convened in Manhattan's Waldorf-Astoria. The gathering included such public figures as Paul V. McNutt and former Secretary of State James F. Byrnes, who served as industry counsel.

---

* Subsequently, the validity of these cards was questioned. Dalton Trumbo, for instance, wrote in "The Time of the Toad": "The Government in its trial of the twelve Communist leaders in New York, has developed the fact that the Communist Party of America was dissolved on May 22, 1944, and became the Communist Political Association. It continued to be the Communist Political Association until July 29, 1945, when it was reconstituted as the Communist Party. Yet the alleged cards introduced into evidence were all 'Communist Party' registration cards dated in November or December of 1944 to cover the year 1945. They were 'Party Cards' when no Party was in existence. 'Whether that change of name represented a technicality or an actuality is beside the point,' Mr. Ring Lardner, Jr. wrote in the New York *Herald Tribune*, 'obviously the Communists themselves must have taken it seriously enough to alter their official documents.' "

Both Trumbo and Lardner were mistaken. It is not true that the "alleged cards . . . were all 'Communist Party' registration cards." In the cases of Adrian Scott and Edward Dmytryk, for instance, "Communist Political Association" cards were introduced into the evidence. The cards Trumbo and Lardner apparently refer to were all clearly marked "1944 Card No............." They were not intended to "cover the year 1945," as Trumbo asserted.

The representatives were subsumed in the three established industry organizations, two of which were presided over by Eric Johnston. The Independent group was headed by Donald Nelson. But in the end it agreed to let Johnston act as spokesman for the entire assembly.

After two days of deliberation, Eric Johnston announced the decision the industry spokesmen had reached:

Members of the Association of Motion Picture Producers deplore the action of the ten Hollywood men who have been cited for contempt of the House of Representatives. We do not desire to pre-judge their legal rights, but their actions have been a disservice to their employers and have impaired their usefulness to the industry.

We will forthwith discharge or suspend without compensation those in our employ and we will not re-employ any of the ten until such time as he is acquitted or has purged himself of contempt and declares under oath that he is not a Communist.

On the broader issue of alleged subversive and disloyal elements in Hollywood, our members are likewise prepared to take positive action.

We will not knowingly employ a Communist or a member of any party or group which advocates the overthrow of the Government of the United States by force or by any illegal or unconstitutional methods.

In pursuing this policy, we are not going to be swayed by hysteria or intimidation from any source. We are frank to recognize that such a policy involves dangers and risks. There is the danger of hurting innocent people. There is the risk of creating an atmosphere of fear. Creative work at its best cannot be carried on in an atmosphere of fear. We will guard against this danger, this risk, this fear.

To this end we will invite the Hollywood talent guilds to work with us to eliminate any subversives; to protect the innocent; and to safeguard free speech and a free screen wherever threatened.

The absence of a national policy, established by Congress with respect to the employment of Communists in private industry, makes our task difficult. Ours is a nation of laws. We request Congress to enact legislation to assist American industry to rid itself of subversive, disloyal elements.

Nothing subversive or un-American has appeared on the screen. Nor can any number of Hollywood investigations obscure the patriotic services of the 30,000 Americans employed in Hollywood who have given our Government invaluable aid in war and peace.

The tone of the Waldorf Statement, as it came to be known, contrasted vividly with the defiant pronouncements that came out of Hollywood before the hearings, and with many of Johnston's own earlier statements. The switch did not pass unnoticed. The Los Angeles *Times,* for instance, commented:

A few weeks ago Mr. Johnston was chiding the Committee on Un-American Activities with smearing Hollywood. . . . Now, less than a month later, Mr. Johnston issues a statement in New York which will surprise the members of the Thomas Committee and quite a few Americans who are not in Congress. Of the ten witnesses who refused to avow or disavow communism, he says, "Their refusal to stand up and be counted resulted in confusion of the issues before the Committee." But it will seem to those who read Mr. Johnston's full-page newspaper advertisements and his statement to the committee that his own contribution to the confusion has been substantial. First the committee was wrong in questioning; then the witnesses were wrong in not answering the question.

Broadway columnist Ed Sullivan explained the apparent change of heart to readers of the New York *Daily News* on November 29: "Reason that Hollywood big shots rushed to New York and barred the 10 cited by Congress was forecast in my Nov. 1 column: 'Hollywood has been dealt a body blow that won't please Wall Street financiers, who have not less than $60,000,000 in picture companies.' Wall Street jiggled the strings, thas all."

In due time, the employed members of the Hollywood Ten were fired — Adrian Scott, producer; Edward Dmytryk, director; and writers Lester Cole, Ring Lardner, Jr., and Dalton Trumbo. Writers John Howard Lawson, Albert Maltz, Alvah Bessie, Samuel Ornitz, and writer-director Herbert Biberman became unemployable.

Such were the beginnings of blacklisting in the motion-picture industry. But years of Hollywood history led up to the events of October and November, 1947.

Communism in Hollywood

THE COMMUNIST PARTY of Hollywood was a very special unit. It attracted an élite membership. It was designed to do a job that it alone, among American Communist groups, was equipped to carry out. Most of its members were writers and office workers, primarily an intellectual and white-collar group. Only a few were recruited from the technical trades of the motion-picture industry.

The Party had a number of objectives in Hollywood.

It wanted the big names Hollywood had to offer, to lend glamor and acceptability to preaching of the party line. The endorsement of motion-picture celebrities sells soap, cigarettes and beer. It can as easily sell political ideas. Pat O'Brien, Rosalind Russell, Henry Fonda, Tallulah Bankhead, Joan Bennett and others have actively campaigned for Democratic candidates. Bing Crosby, Gary Cooper, Robert Montgomery, Adolphe Menjou and a host of fellow Republicans have supported GOP candidates. But few if any Hollywood celebrities ever came out publicly for Communist candidates; rather, the Party used them to promote its line through a proliferation of front groups with high-sounding names and ends.

The Communist Party sought a base in the California labor movement, specifically in the AFL craft unions that grew up around the movie studios.

The Communist Party needed funds. A thriving Hollywood unit made up of highly paid film workers offered great promise.

It served the Party's purposes to count among its followers those who could neutralize or eliminate anti-Communist or anti-Soviet content in American films. Active movie workers were in a position to do this.

Finally, the Party sought a reservoir of skilled "cultural technicians" who could be relied on to produce Party material. Even though such material was effectively outlawed from the commercial screen the "agit-prop" work of the Party required experienced craftsmen with solid reputations.

There were important differences between the Communist Party in Hollywood and elsewhere. These differences account for the fact that the Hollywood members were not so easily manipulated as devout and disciplined members in, say, New York. The turnover in Hollywood was great, for membership at any given time was largely dependent on how much appeal there was in the Party line of the moment. And the character of the membership at any given time determined to some extent the special objectives of the Hollywood group.

The élite nature of its membership was a source of both strength and weakness for the Party in Hollywood. The Party was strong because its members were uniquely capable of carrying out the work assigned to them. But there were weaknesses linked to these very capacities. Movie personalities were eminently suited to add prestige to front groups, for instance, but precisely because they were well-known and/or artistic personalities, they responded to forces other than Party directives. In a word, it was extremely difficult to bolshevize the members of the Hollywood Party. When, for example, the line shifted in 1939 from support of collective security and anti-Nazism to the more difficult neutralism demanded by the Hitler-Stalin Pact, membership dropped and the Party's influence was considerably weakened.

Writing in the *American Mercury* at the time, William Bledsoe, one-time editor of the *Screen Guild Magazine,* official organ of the Screen Writers Guild, reported that "nothing since the advent of the talkies struck Hollywood quite so hard as the news of the Soviet-

Nazi pacts. . . . Certain glamor boys and girls, famous writers and directors, were on their knees at the shrine of the crossed hammer-and-sickle when the bombshell fell. It hit them like a dropped option. They were still staggering when the Red invasion of Poland exploded around their ears, and the panic was completed by Russia's assault on Finland. Only in the breasts of the most devout can traces of the Stalinist faith still linger."

Hitler's attack on the Soviet Union in 1941, and American acceptance of the Soviet Union as an ally, gave the Party another golden opportunity. Patriotism became its most effective recruiting device. In this Browder period, when communism was preached as "twentieth-century Americanism," the Party in Hollywood waxed strong again. But when the Party was no longer identified with patriotic causes, its popularity diminished rapidly. In the crisis years of cold war after 1945, defections were again spectacularly high. The Party had simply not succeeded in converting patriotism into bolshevism. The isolation and personal immolation essential for a successful Party operation were just not to be found on any large scale in the brash, ego-centered, exhibitionistic film capital. Even the Communist Party was forced to take its pecularities into consideration.

But though it failed to harden its core, the Party had extraordinary success in softening the periphery. Some measure of that success was indicated in a complaint about the "new Hollywood" voiced by screenwriter Mary McCall, Jr. in the February, 1937, issue of the *Screen Guild Magazine:*

We're up to our necks in politics and morality now. Nobody goes to anybody's house any more to sit and talk and have fun. There's a master of ceremonies and a collection basket, because there are no gatherings now except for a Good Cause. We have almost no time to be actors and writers these days. We're committee members and collectors and organizers and audiences for orators. Either we're standing in the lobby of the Filmarte or the Grand International, keeping tab on the suspect eight hundred who go to see foreign films, or we're giving a cocktail party at which everyone pledges himself to do or not to do something.

Left-wing sentiment in Hollywood was of course enormously stimulated by the rise of Hitlerism. Leo Rosten, in his study of the film colony, *Hollywood: The Movie Colony, The Movie Makers,* recalls when proto-Nazi groups like the Hollywood Hussars and Light Horse Cavalry, which had "vigilante overtones featuring fine horses and bright uniforms," appeared in Hollywood itself. Liberal Hollywood was thoroughly aroused, and hundreds of well-meaning movie people wanted to "do something" about fascism. The Communists exploited the mood of the period and succeeded in winning the cooperation of many who would have steered clear of any cause they believed was truly revolutionary. But the true aims of the Party were successfully obscured at that time by its pro-New Deal, anti-fascist orientation.

Eugene Lyons, a veteran anti-Communist, wrote, in *The Red Decade,* of the "cinema rebels" who fell under Communist influence. "[They were] genuinely angry at Nazis and genuinely concerned for Spanish democracy, Spain's orphans, Chinese freedom and sharecroppers. They had not the remotest idea of what communism was in terms of economic structures or political superstates. For nearly all of them, it was an intoxicated state of mind, a glow of inner virtue, and a sort of comradeship in super-charity."

Nor did the careless labelling done by those on the right help matters any. There was a time, according to Rosten, when the charge of "communism" was hurled against anyone in Hollywood who held that Nazi Germany was a threat to America, that labor unions were legal organizations, or that civil liberties should be protected. So in most liberal circles warnings about Communist perfidy fell on deaf ears. Consequently, hundreds in Hollywood who would have been horrified at the thought of overthrowing the government by force or destroying the economic system which provided them with swimming pools and four-car garages, played along with the Communists.

The real Communists in the movie industry were few in number and almost all secret Party members. They were known to each other and to some of the people they influenced most but were rarely if ever publicly identified. The Hollywood group, several of its members later testified, was more secretive than the Party in New York.

There were sound reasons for the secrecy. The Hollywood group was special, to be compared with other special sections of the Party. If its prominent members were publicly identified, their effectiveness with liberal groups might have been cut down. To have come out openly and admitted membership in the Party might well have cost them their jobs — or at least have had serious effects on their box-office pull. From the point of view of their effectiveness as Party workers, it was important that they keep hidden. The unique value of Hollywood Communists depended on their ability to function as members of either front groups or mass organizations. And the cloak-and-dagger aspect of the Party appealed mightily of course to the romanticism that drove many into the Party in the first place.

Closely related to the secrecy of the Hollywood group was its organizational separation from other Party sections. Until late in its history the Party in Hollywood was under the direct control of the national office in New York. It was not attached, like other Communist units, to a state or regional organization. By and large, movie people were cut off from other Party members. Party officials and ordinary members were forbidden to make direct contact with the Hollywood group. Mervyn Rathbone, a former Party official, stated that the problems of Hollywood were only rarely discussed at State Central Committee meetings. If an official wanted to make contact with the movie group, he was required to go through the State secretary or national office. It was believed in

New York that the Party leadership in Los Angeles was not equipped to handle the Hollywood unit. As artists, and as Holly-woodians, the movie people required special treatment. Rathbone also stated that the national office did not want to open Hollywood for fear too much of its financial flow would be drained off into activities not controlled by the national organization. In any case, the Hollywood unit of the Party was one of the most exclusive clubs the Communists operated.

The Party in Hollywood made few demands on its members. Its activities generally consisted of lengthy discussions on the role of the "cultural worker." But even these discussions, according to screenwriter Roy Huggins, an ex-member, were extremely limited. "The Hollywood group was interested only in Hollywood and they never, as far as I know, had a discussion of world politics," he said. The movie Communists remained aloof from selling the *People's World,* marching in parades, making house calls on prospective members in the Boyle Heights area and the usual Party drudgery. Another former member of the radio unit, Roy Erwin, stated that they thought of themselves as the "commissioned officers" of the Revolution.

When they were lax in paying dues, as was frequently the case, no great pressure was put upon them. Edward Dmytryk — the director among the Hollywood Ten who broke with the Party* — told his *Saturday Evening Post* biographer that he never paid any dues, though he shelled out when the plate was passed at Party gatherings. Lee J. Cobb testified that during an eight-month period of Party membership he contributed no more than five or ten dol-

---

* Dmytryk summed up his own case in a *Saturday Evening Post* article: "I joined [the Communist Party] in the Spring of 1944 and dropped out the next. And I never completely broke with them until I was in jail. Though I was no longer a Party member, I stood with the Ten on my personal convictions about civil liberties and when we lost, I couldn't say anything until I served my time. I wouldn't have wanted it to appear that I was trying to escape any consequences of my original stand."

lars. Cobb was a highly paid actor at the time. Leopold Atlas, one-time treasurer of the Hollywood writers group, testified about the difficulties he faced in collecting dues from some of the group's wealthiest members. Only a few deeply committed members felt any obligation to go along with the Communist tithing system.

But the dues Hollywood Party members paid were not as important as the role they could play in softening up contributors to front operations. Eugene Lyons accepted as fairly accurate an estimate of $2 million milked from the film colony during its pre-war "Red" period. He reported in *The Red Decade* that the Anti-Nazi League, between May 14, 1936 and August 16, 1939, deposited $89,892.51 in a local bank. "Only one thing surprised the pioneering Communists prospecting in them thar Beverly Hills," wrote William Bledsoe, "the speed and size and ease of their strikes." The *Daily Worker* once reported that from five to eight thousand dollars were collected at every Spanish Loyalist meeting in Hollywood, and added — "Think of that, you New York provincials!" In its Annual Report for 1951, the House Committee on Un-American Activities stated that four Communist front operations in the State of California received approximately $1 million from Hollywood contributors. The money of course was paid out over a period of years.

Many, if not most, of the Hollywood Communists themselves were actually ignorant of the true nature of the Party. They were recruited on the basis of the Party's professed immediate objectives, which after 1934 did not include the revolutionary overthrow of the government. During the war years, when the Party reached its peak membership in Hollywood, members were told, if they enquired, that the Communist Party was not a revolutionary organization. David Lang, a screenwriter, testified he had been advised that if he heard otherwise, "it was strictly an attempt upon the party by the Trotskyite reactionaries . . ."

30

When the Party line changed at the end of World War II, some members got their first glimpse into the real character of the Party. Producer George Glass told of his reaction to a meeting called for a discussion of a Hollywood strike. The meeting, he said, was "a great eye-opener" for him after "the open candor of the Communist Political Association and its mild discussions on the type of philosophy outlined in Earl Browder's book *Teheran*." Glass "didn't like the feel" of the strike discussion because it "did not fit in with the peaceful keynote sounded at . . . that buffet supper."

Buffet suppers probably struck just the right note for the majority of Hollywood Communists. They were led to the Party from a variety of motives. Some were recruited during the 1936-39 period, the time of greatest growth, when the Party was identified as anti-Nazi, pro-Spanish Loyalist, pro-labor and anti-Jim Crow. The Party suffered in Hollywood, as elsewhere, during 1939-41, the years of the Hitler-Stalin pact. Several among those who had been closest to front activities contributed ambulances to Finland during this period. But Hitler's attack on Russia, and the overnight conversion of an "imperialist war" to a "people's struggle," set the stage for a remarkable renascence.

The Hollywood Communists plunged into the war effort with an intensity and devotion unmatched in the film colony. Their all-out support of the cause won a tremendous response from Hollywood liberals. All the anti-Hitler fervor of Hollywood was focussed on winning the war. The Communist Political Association (wartime name for the Party) became an attractive outlet for the liberals' stirring hopes for the postwar world. As an ally, the Soviet Union — whose resistance won general admiration — came to be endowed, even in conservative circles, with enormous virtues. Intellectually, socially and politically, it was highly acceptable to be pro-Soviet from 1941 to '45. For many, it seemed exciting, satisfying, challenging and even patriotic to work with the Communists. The movement appealed to the romantic and with its idealistic pretensions

31

succeeded in hushing the guilt feelings of some ferocious anti-fascists who found themselves fighting the war beside their swimming pools.

The Communist movement in Hollywood, during the war years, served as a great status-leveller, while at the same time it satisfied status drives. A $200-a-week writer, very low on the Hollywood scale, could mingle socially and politically in the Party with a $2,000-a-week writer, very high on the scale. The Party itself was a prestige group, whose members tried to take care of each other.

During the years since the first of the movie hearings, there has been a great deal of talk about the "blacklisting of anti-Communists" which the Party in Hollywood carried on when it was powerful enough to do so. It is often cited as a justification for the steps which the motion-picture industry ultimately took to "clean house," as Parnell Thomas asked it to do. The two operations are often equated, but there were distinct differences.

The "blacklisting of anti-Communists" was highly informal. It was a question of discrimination and mild treachery and was thoroughly despicable, but it did not involve the solid machinery, the institutionalization and formalization of the literal lists of "unemployables" that have come to be taken for granted in Hollywood. The present blacklisting operation is a stable agreement in the industry that certain persons whose names are listed in the House Committee's reports are unemployable; the Communists' "blacklist" was as elusive an undertaking as a rumor whispered over a luncheon table or a meaningful shrug in a conference room. The Communists' efforts to keep their opponents out of the industry were undoubtedly politically inspired, but they relied largely on *a*political gossip and innuendo ("So-and-so drinks too much, you know; he isn't very reliable," – or, "He'll never do justice to the part; he's just not the type," – or, "She's such a terrible reactionary and a troublemaker too, I don't know why you'd want to have her around"). The over-all evidence indicates that people were hurt

32

by this kind of sneak attack, though it is almost impossible to cite any clear-cut examples. An anti-Communist actor, say, might have known what was said about him behind closed doors; he might have noticed that his employment was falling off; but how could he ever prove that the reason he did not get a specific job was because of the gossip and scandal his political enemies spread about him — gossip, incidentally, that often had a grain of truth in it? The reason given would always be that he was not right for the part, that he was too tall, too short, too young or too old — never that he was too anti-Communist.

Other actors who actually were not right for the part, or who had lost their special appeal, often tended to salve their own feelings by claiming that they were discriminated against because of their patriotic outspokenness.

But for all the possibilities of mistaking individual cases, there seems little doubt that Communist Party members in Hollywood, during this period, tended to help their friends and punish their enemies. Writers exploited their close relationship to, and influence over, producers to discourage them from hiring anti-Communists. Secretaries who were Party members were counted on to pass along unflattering rumors about certain actors their bosses were in a position to hire. Rarely, except with other Party people, would there be an open discussion of politics as a factor in employment. It would have been too dangerous for Party members to expose themselves in such a fashion. Instead, they had to be content with spreading stories or passing judgments which seeped down through liberal circles to the men who actually did hiring and firing.

Where the enemy's talents were in sufficient demand, such rumors had little effect. A number of extremely outspoken anti-Communists — John Wayne, Gary Cooper and Leo McCarey, among others — were diligently sought after. Even the most politicized movie-makers were, and still are, interested primarily in making profits. If they had to make them with the help of "reactionaries," they could always still the voice of their "proletarian" consciences by making a suitable contribution to some left-wing cause.

The Communists in Hollywood were a tight, cohesive group bound together by a common belief, a common hatred of the ever-menacing "enemy" and a common smug feeling that they and they alone held the future by the tail. When someone joined their group — not unlike other groups — they did all they could to help his career along, not only because he was a "right guy" with the "right ideas" but because of the warm personal relations that grew out of mutual involvement in the cause.

Belonging to the Communist Party for some movie people meant, primarily, congenial, helpful and blessedly influential friends. For others, Communist activity satisfied, at least to some extent, their desperate striving to dignify the work they did with a sense of mission. Whatever doubts might have come in the night, a certain number of Hollywood writers, directors and producers were ultimately unwilling to accept the films they made as the purely commercial, money-making trivialities they too often were. There was comfort, then, in the Party's assurances that making commercial films served the interests of the meaningful "progressive" forces in American life.

Hollywood Communists were told by Party officials that the status they achieved in making featherweight movies, however worthless in itself, contributed mightily to the Cause in the long run. The maintenance of status, incidentally, justified large homes, swimming pools and staffs of obedient servants. It was necessary — so the rationalization went — to have these things if one wanted to hold his own in Hollywood. (After the war, a Communist leader suggested that the screenwriters in the movement drop films and take up the writing of proletarian novels, but few went along.)

The creation of new front groups or penetration of already existing organizations was probably the most successful activity of the

Hollywood Communist Party. These peripheral organizations were sharply distinguished from the Party itself. Their programs were limited and immediate. In every case they were nominally directed toward democratic (and often highly patriotic) goals; in some cases, they actually served these ends. Their membership included Communists, conscious fellow-travelers and non-Communist liberals. The last named group probably provided the bulk of membership. Most liberals of course remained steadfastly independent, but even those who resisted the blandishments of the Party could be counted on to propagate and finance the good causes, such as interracial justice, which the Party adopted.

Through these peripheral organizations, Communists were able to move into areas where the Party as such would have been outlawed. Party members and sympathizers sometimes achieved enviable positions of power and influence that could be traced back to the contacts made in the front groups. At the same time, the existence of a number of such groups meant that a solid body of public opinion could be mobilized when the Party set out to accomplish a goal. Finally, the groups themselves with their manifold interests provided congenial activity for Party members.

The Hollywood Anti-Nazi League, one of the earliest and most effective of these organizations, became the Hollywood League for Democratic Action after the Hitler-Stalin Pact. Still later it was rechristened the Hollywood Democratic Committee. The League was organized in June, 1936, with Donald Ogden Stewart as its chairman. Among its earliest sponsors was the Most Rev. John J. Cantwell, then Catholic Archbishop of Los Angeles. When the late Archbishop was invited to join in June, 1936, he accepted the invitation, writing, "I am very glad to be associated with the 'Hollywood League Against Nazism,' or with any organization opposing the wicked pretensions of Nazism." But three months later he withdrew. Archbishop Cantwell "wishes to have his name withdrawn from the list of sponsors . . . as he feels that the organization

35

is not what it seems to be and he has no desire to be connected with it," the Chancellor of the Los Angeles archdiocese informed the Executive Secretary of the League.

The Hollywood Anti-Nazi League was organized during the People's Front period, when the Party line was advocating collective security against fascism. The League's first public activity was a meeting addressed by "the Catholic Prince Hubertus and Princess Marie Loewenstein, German exiles, at the Wilshire Ebell Theatre." The presentation of the Prince and Princess paid off immediately. The League was instantly respectable. In some minds it actually became identified with the Prince and Princess. The Fredric Marches, for instance, were non-Communist liberals attracted to the League and active in its affairs. But Mr. March's account books identify contributions to the organization as having been given to "Prince Loewenstein's Anti-Nazi League." Mrs. March (actress Florence Eldridge) believed that the League was "originally started by Prince Hubertus von Loewenstein, then a refugee in California."

The Marches' understanding of the League was shared by other non-Communist liberals who participated in its anti-Nazi, anti-fascist (but not anti-Communist) activities. The League supported the Spanish Loyalists, sponsored a radio serial program written by Donald Ogden Stewart, "went on record as being in support of the anti-lynching bill," held a dinner-dance at the Ambassador to mark its first anniversary, with a "brilliant gathering of film celebrities" in attendance.

The League prospered. It campaigned against the visit of Vittorio Mussolini, son of the Duce, as "a friend of Hitler and an enemy of democracy." The son of the Duce was President of RAM, a short-lived movie-producing company. RAM took its name from its founders, Hal Roach, the veteran Hollywood producer, and young Mussolini. Roach told the press that Mussolini was coming to Hollywood to learn how to make movies. But the League's

36

weekly, *Hollywood Now,* soon warned him that Vittorio "in coming to Hollywood may see how effective protests — as well as motion pictures — are made." Later the League frankly mobilized its forces to blacklist Leni Riefenstahl, a celebrated German photographer and special friend of Hitler, in the Hollywood studios. In 1937 M-G-M signed up Louisa Ulrich, a German actress. Again the League protested loudly. Miss Ulrich, *Hollywood Now* revealed, "is a close friend of Propaganda Minister Joseph Goebbels."

The League pledged its support to a boycott of Japanese goods — "We're all wearing cotton stockings," *Hollywood Now* reported. It marked the fifth anniversary of Hitler's seizure of power by sponsoring a mass meeting addressed by Montana Congressman Jerry O'Connell, director John Ford and humorist Dorothy Parker. At this meeting, "concerted action by the democratic nations was agreed upon as the only effective measure against fascist aggression."

The League honored the distinguished German exile, Thomas Mann; held a meeting to warn of the fascist danger to Czechoslovakia; demanded collective security as "the basis of our foreign policy"; gave a "brilliant Hollywood première" to "Pins and Needles," the musical produced by the International Ladies Garment Workers; picketed a local German-American Bund convention "together with thousands of friends," including "the American Legion, Veterans of Foreign Wars, American League for Peace and Democracy, California Christian Church Council, AF of L, CIO and the Canadian War Veterans."

When Congressman Martin Dies accused the League of being a Communist front, he was attacked bitterly. The League's position was supported at a public meeting addressed by Melvyn Douglas, Judge Isaac Pacht, Dr. Bruno Frank, Congressman O'Connell and Jack Tenney. (Tenney later headed the California Un-American Activities Committee and became a symbol of "native fascism" to the liberal community in Hollywood.)

37

Membership in the Anti-Nazi League was eagerly sought. At its peak it numbered about 4000 members. The people who joined the group because of its immediate program of anti-fascism slowly absorbed the attitudes of its Party-controlled leadership. In time the League gathered enviable status and influence in the liberal community of Hollywood. Few put any stock in Dies' charges against the organization.

In December, 1938, the League "launched the Committee of 56, by initiating a meeting at the home of Edward G. Robinson, where outstanding motion-picture celebrities were invited to hear Clark M. Eichelberger, Director of the League of Nations Association and Director of the American Union for Concerted Peace Efforts." At the meeting, the celebrities sent "a declaration of democratic independence to the President and to Congress, requesting them to bring such economic pressure to bear against Germany as would force her to reconsider her aggressive attitude towards other nations."

Who could be against such a "declaration of democratic independence"? Nobody with decent liberal instincts and certainly none of the 56, who included such stellar names as Myrna Loy, Paul Muni, John Ford, Joan Crawford, Melvyn Douglas, Rosalind Russell, James Cagney, Gale Sondergaard, Aline MacMahon, Henry Fonda, Pat O'Brien, Jack Warner, Fay Bainter, Priscilla Lane, Dennis O'Keefe, Bette Davis, Groucho Marx, George Brent, Donald Crisp, Ben Hecht, Joan Bennett, Bruce Cabot, Elliott Nugent, Ann Sheridan, Dick Powell, Tony Martin, Alice Faye, Claude Rains, Miriam Hopkins, Spencer Tracy, Burgess Meredith, Jean Hersholt, Lucille Ball and Don Ameche. And undoubtedly hundreds of less "outstanding motion picture celebrities" would have been honored to attend the meeting at Mr. Robinson's home with its fabulous collection of modern art.

All during 1939, the League continued its spirited anti-Nazi, anti-fascist, anti-aggressor nation activity. But by the late fall of 1939, the entire character of the organization changed. The Communist Party line switched with the signing of the Hitler-Stalin pact and the Anti-Nazi League dutifully followed. Overnight it became the Hollywood League for Democratic Action; was no longer in favor of "concerted action" as "the only effective measure against fascist aggression." Its New Year's card for 1940 denounced "the war to lead America to war."

How was this abrupt change accomplished, and what effect did it have upon the liberal members of the League? Did the Communist members of the board propose that since Stalin had signed a pact with Hitler, the Soviet Union no longer identified its interests with the democratic bourgeois nations and therefore the Hollywood Anti-Nazi League should cease being anti-aggressor and become anti-imperialist war? Florence Eldridge March explained how the Communist leaders succeeded in converting the organization to an entirely different purpose. In a statement sent to the House Un-American Activities Committee, she wrote, concerning the Hollywood League for Democratic Action: "This was a change of name given to the Hollywood Anti-Nazi League. It was suggested to the board that to be *for something* (original italics) was more dynamic than to be *against* something (original italics)."

Dealing as they were with people who had an abundance of good will but were lamentably short on political sophistication, the Communist Party found it possible to manipulate such groups as the Hollywood Anti-Nazi League. Through it and groups like it, the orbit of the Party's influence grew larger and larger in Hollywood. The Hollywood Communists were very active in the Democratic Party, for instance. At one time, according to screenwriter Allen Rivkin, who has been long associated with the Democrats, John Howard Lawson was so active in party affairs he was offered a position on the executive committee of the Democratic Party in the area. Lawson refused, telling Rivkin that he could be more useful on the outside. Melvyn Douglas, too, had been active in

Democratic Party circles, but he resigned from the Motion Picture Democratic Committee when it overwhelmingly refused to consider a motion condemning the Soviet invasion of Finland.

But there was only a handful of Melvyn Douglases in the liberal community. There was never any organized, articulate and effective liberal or left-wing opposition to the Communists in Hollywood. They held the monopoly and got little or no competition from Socialists, Trotskyists, anarchists or any other leftist group. If, for instance, one were zealously in favor of an FEPC law, almost the only place to work was in a Communist Party front organization.

Because of their virtual monopoly on activist organizations, the attitude of the Communists towards their friends and enemies was suffused throughout liberal circles in Hollywood. "Trotskyite" became a hate word, endowed with loathing and horror. Enemies of the Party could be destroyed by the label. In Hollywood, philosopher John Dewey's investigation of the Moscow trials was publicly denounced in newspapers and by Party members and sympathizers. So, too, Dewey's Cultural Freedom group, which was fighting Communist influence among liberals, was the object of a bitter hate campaign. The only opposition the Communists got in Hollywood was identified by them as being anti-labor and racist-minded. Unfortunately, there was often truth, if not a great deal, in the charge. Some (certainly not most) of the anti-Communists in town belonged with the right-wing extremists.

Belonging to a Party-controlled group may have had a dash of danger, a touch of the romantic before 1941, but after that the Communist front had more in common with a Better Business Bureau than with any group dedicated to revolution. The most blatantly jingoistic organizations in the motion-picture industry were those in which the Party had influence. This later caused great confusion in Hollywood.

The Hollywood Writers Mobilization, for example, was founded during the war as a clearing house for scripts. Numerous ex-

Communists have testified that the organization, in which literally every radio and screen writer held at least nominal membership, was Communist-dominated. Yet an examination of its wartime record fails to disclose any subversive overtones. All the Mobilization did was coordinate and channel requests from governmental and private agencies. But it was precisely during this period that the Party line and the Government's line coincided most exactly — both were bent on beating Hitler. Thus, when an ex-Communist testifies publicly that the Hollywood Writers Mobilization was Party-dominated, dozens of non-Communists who belonged to the group are angered. The liberals' anger is not directed at themselves, since there was no possible way they could have known the extent of Party control over the Hollywood Writers Mobilization without having been a member of the Party. Instead, their anger is directed at the persons who have revealed the role the Party played in the organization and thereby embarrassed its former members. Only after the war, when many liberals had already left, was the character of the Hollywood Writers Mobilization revealed. After 1946, it was no different from any other front — espousing the cause of the "people's democracies," etc.

Did the Communist Party in Hollywood use the screen to propagandize? In the first of the Hollywood hearings, J. Parnell Thomas seemed convinced that it did. Some of the friendly witnesses apparently shared his conviction that it was "only logical" that "subversive and un-democratic forces should attempt to use this medium for un-democratic purposes." But the industry itself never accepted the charge. Eric Johnston, for instance, told the Committee that the producers were ready to run any movies which the Committee members might suspect: ". . . you can see for yourselves what's in them. The contents of the pictures constitute the only proof . . . it is the obligation of the committee to absolve the industry from the charges against it [that subversive and un-American material appeared on the screen]." The industry, however, was never formally absolved, though in subsequent hearings the whole question was muted. The concern Parnell Thomas felt in 1947 was so remote by the summer of 1955 that George E. Sokolsky, in a lapse of memory, could assert in his nationally syndicated column that Congressional investigators had never believed they would find Communist content in the films.

But though it is now generally accepted as true that there was no Communist propaganda in films, at one time the belief was widely held. Little or no persuasive evidence was ever submitted. It would seem that the Hollywood Communists — whatever their reasons might have been — had actually made only the feeblest attempts to peddle their Party line through American motion pictures. For one thing, they were almost certain to fail if they tried. Too many people are involved in the final preparations of a script. To get Communist propaganda to the screen would have taken the cooperation of almost the entire creative group concerned with a film. Again, many of the films written by Party members were simply not susceptible to overt preachment. The screen credits gained by the Hollywood Communists run the entire gamut — frothy musicals, westerns, comedies, serious dramas, soapy melodrama and tough-guy detective stories. More than one of their pictures ends as a complete vindication of capitalist and religious values.

Hollywood ex-Communists who became "friendly" witnesses told the House Committee that they were rarely if ever instructed to insert any particular content in the films they wrote. In response to a question as to whether he had ever been urged to slant his screenwriting, David Lang, a "fully cooperative" witness, stated: "No sir; I was never, because among other things I never worked on pictures that carried that particular type of situation, and I cannot say for sure that I know of any particular instance in which it was done." Bernard Schoenfeld, another writer, testified that the Party was unable to influence film content for two reasons: "One, the vast majority of screenwriters are highly individual and most of the ones I know, including myself, have always wanted to think for themselves. And the second reason is that the way the motion picture is organized, there would be too many factors which would not allow this material to be infiltrated into a movie."

During the war years, when the Communist Party and the United States Government had the same immediate interests, it was comparatively easy to serve both masters. In the earlier days, according to Richard Collins, another screenwriter who testified about his activities in the Party, Earl Browder had advised against putting more than a "drop" of Communist belief in a film. The "drop" often added up to an unobjectionable (and even laudable) treatment of minority racial groups. The Communists may have done more than their share to banish from the screen the stereotyped Negro, the dim-witted Italian and red-nosed stage Irishman. But uniquely Marxist values were rarely if ever inserted. A comedian member of the Party was once reprimanded for whistling a few bars of "The Internationale" in a movie scene where he was waiting for an elevator. In spite of the actor's joy that "even in Brazil they'll know where I stand!" he was rebuked by Party officials. It was dangerous, they argued, for a performer to expose himself that way. (In any case, the scene was left on the cutting-room floor.) The risk of exposure worked against the Party's encouraging outright propaganda in the films written by its members, even though they might feel heady enough to try it.

The Communists were content if their members succeeded in keeping anti-Soviet and anti-Communist material off the screen. William Alland, an ex-member, told the House Un-American Activities Committee: "I would say this, in my observation, that what they have been able to do is not so much to put Communist propaganda into films but . . . prevent to a great degree the expression of anti-Communist sentiment in films." But even this success was limited. Hollywood produced a number of anti-Communist movies

43

before the 1947 hearings: for example, "The Red Salute," "Ninotchka," "Comrade X" and "He Stayed for Breakfast." Oddly enough these films by and large were more successful at the box office than the rash of anti-Communist movies made after the Congressional hearings.

A recent study of the films made by the Hollywood Ten bears out the producers' insistence that "nothing subversive or 'un-American' has appeared on the screen."*

Perhaps there will never be an accurate assessment of the extent to which the Communist Party influenced cultural life in Hollywood. On the positive side, the Communists can be credited with much of the industry's long-delayed awareness of racial and minority problems. Hollywood traveled a long road from the days of "Birth of a Nation" to the days of "Pinky." So, too, as a result of Party influence, many Hollywood people became aware of social responsibilities that might otherwise have gone unnoticed forever. But the price paid for these values was high.

Character assassination and violent personal attacks — always the big guns in the American Communists' artillery — marked most political disagreements in Hollywood during its "Red" period. A political opponent was automatically characterized as a "reactionary" or "fascist." These became trigger words. The personal lives and habits of political opponents were fair game for lies and exaggerations. Tipplers became drunkards; flirts became bawds; the mildly prejudiced were turned into little Hitlers. Liberal thinking, in the paternalistic school the Communists operated, remained at an almost primitive level. No one thought it odd when Donald Ogden Stewart, Hy Kraft, Richard Collins, Jules Dassin and Ring Lardner, Jr. circulated a petition at M-G-M to halt production on a film with whose political content they disagreed. Hollywood was

---

* "Communism and the Movies: A Study of Film Content" by Dorothy B. Jones was made as a subsidiary project of this investigation. A resumé of Mrs. Jones' findings is included as an appendix to this report.

44

silent too when the Japanese-Americans were evacuated from the West Coast. With few exceptions, even the most conscientious liberals watched their fellow Americans being herded off to detainment camps. There was silence, too, when a group of Minnesota Trotskyites were tried and convicted under the same Smith Act which is so furiously denounced in the *Daily Worker* today.

Political activity in Hollywoood during the heyday of Communist influence was stringently limited and forced into rigid patterns. A wide and varied choice of organizations was offered but political action was shallow and sterile. Even to think about certain subjects was extremely unpopular and forbidden areas were broad indeed.

The cruelest blow, though, was the secrecy the Party maintained. Communist control of liberal organizations was covert and furtive. If a front group was accurately charged with being Party-dominated, the Communists themselves denounced the accuser as a "Redbaiter," and most of their liberal associates joined in the cry. People with every good intention in the world fell under the hidden Party influence and later paid heavily — in personal humiliations, public shame and loss of work — because they were "taken in." This accounts to a great extent for the bitterness many Hollywood liberals still nurture against individual members and former members of the Party.

Hollywood was long divided between an indeterminate "left" and "right," but the Communists on the left were generally accepted as fellow liberals. The secrecy of their operation came as a distinct shock when it was revealed. Feelings against them as individuals ran high. Many liberals still bitterly resent the fact that — as they see it — the Communists hopelessly confounded and compromised what had long seemed to be a clear struggle between liberal "decency" and the reaction and social blindness found on the right. More than one liberal, for that reason, feels a little pang of satisfaction when a Hollywood ex-Communist joins with the forces on the

45

right, which is still identified not so much in political as in moral terms. When it was pointed out recently that a certain ex-Communist had joined a far-right Hollywood group, one disillusioned liberal said, "That's where the sneaky so-and-so belongs!"

Labor in Hollywood

THE LONG BITTER STRUGGLE between the two political blocs in Hollywood is rooted deep in the history of the motion-picture trade unions. Roy M. Brewer, who for almost a decade was top labor man in Hollywood, arrived in the movie capital on March 12, 1945. A few months later he joined forces with the Motion Picture Alliance for the Preservation of American Ideals. Brewer was a leader of the MPA group when he left Hollywood to become an Allied Artists studio executive in New York early in 1955. During Brewer's years with the Alliance he and other leaders of the group were accepted as arbiters of who could and could not work in the studios. One writer described Brewer himself as "strawboss of the purge." A fairly high number of those purged insist that their difficulties arose not so much from Communist Party affiliations as from trade-union militancy — a militancy often directed in the past against Brewer's International Alliance of Theatrical Stage Employees and Motion-Picture Machine Operators of the United States (IATSE).

Through the years, Hollywood labor history has been marked by inter- and intra-union charges of "Communist!" on the one hand, and "racketeer!" on the other. Neither charge has been without meaning, for the unsavory fact is that dishonesty and graft on a spectacular scale have not been absent from the Hollywood labor scene, while some of those who fought against racketeer union leadership have been closer to the Communist Party than they have ever been ready to admit publicly.

The International Alliance of Theatrical Stage Employees has long dominated the motion-picture labor scene. The IA (as the union is popularly known) though always a child of the AFL, was, in a sense, one of the earliest industrial unions in the U. S. It was founded in 1893. Originally, its jurisdiction was restricted to stage hands. Membership was found largely in the big cities. But with the development of the traveling stock company and small-town vaudeville, the IA spread out. By 1908 motion pictures began to flicker in theatres across the country, and the IA received jurisdiction over movie projectionists, the first motion-picture workers to be organized. Having authority over the men who operate theater equipment later gave the IA a special bargaining strength in Hollywood. It could call on projectionists throughout the nation to back up its demands on the studios.

Even before the days of "The Great Train Robbery," the IA was involved in jurisdictional disputes with the craft unions. The line between a stage hand and a carpenter is narrow. So, too, in the early days of films, the IA clashed with the Electricians and the Machinists. For years these jurisdictional quarrels were a regular (and somewhat tedious) feature of AFL conventions.

The most troublesome conflict developed in the late Twenties. Talking pictures had arrived and both the IA and the Electricians claimed jurisdiction over a new group of Hollywood craftsmen, the sound technicians. The IA had organized a local of 600 sound technicians by 1933, while the International Brotherhood of Electrical Workers had only 60. Under the terms of a Studio Basic Agreement, neither union could request recognition from the studios until the jurisdictional dispute between them was settled. The IA, however, succeeded in signing contracts with a number of independent studio heads who had not endorsed the Basic Agreement. When Columbia Pictures refused to sign a contract, the IA called a strike at the studios.

The craft unions, especially the Electrical Workers and the Car-

48

penters, had no hesitations about supplying replacements for the striking workers. In a short time practically the entire Hollywood IA went back to work carrying cards in other unions.

The IA suffered a severe setback but by 1935 had regained its strength. Paramount Pictures was making a film that year which required shots of various airports across the country. The cameraman assigned to shoot the film, a member of the IA, was told that he had to join the Electrical Workers. The theatrical union would not agree to this. In the ensuing dispute, the IA, under the leadership of a new president, George E. Browne, used its deadliest weapon: it appealed to its theater-projectionist members and succeeded in closing down all the movie houses in the nation-wide Paramount chain. Paramount, caught between the Electricians' jurisdictional demand for studio cameramen and the economic pressure exerted by the closing of its theaters, gave in to the IA. The IA's price for the settlement of the strike was high — a closed-shop agreement for all its former members in the entire industry. As a result of the agreement, IA membership increased to 12,000 in 1936. It more than regained the strength lost in the strike of 1933. The former members who had abandoned the IA to join the craft unions during the '33 strike turned tail again. Now they left the craft unions and returned to the IA.

George Browne, who had become president in 1934, was chiefly responsible for the success of the strike. His prestige shot up accordingly. He had brought his union back to its previous strength, had obtained the first agreement in the motion-picture industry and was gradually increasing the IA's jurisdiction. But racketeering elements were gaining power in some of the IA locals. Browne himself appointed Willie Bioff, a professional hoodlum imported from Chicago, as his personal representative in Hollywood. Bioff simply transferred the locale but not the character of his racketeering operations to the West Coast.

49

During the period he was Browne's representative in Hollywood, between 1936 and '40, Bioff negotiated several wage increases for IA members but held off from negotiating others and thereby picked up a number of $100,000 bribes for himself from the movie studios. By using the threat of strikes and reducing trade-union demands, Bioff extorted enormous sums of money in Hollywood.

While Bioff's shady operations were in full swing — operations carried on, it was discovered later, with the approval of Browne as well as the collusion of studio heads — the craft unions were still working to gain back their jurisdictional losses. During this same period, the lusty young CIO made plans to move in on Hollywood. And still another group, this one within IATSE itself — called the "IA Progressives" — was determined to break Bioff's and Browne's hold on the Hollywood locals.

The AFL craft unions not affiliated with the IA but jealous of its jurisdiction set up the Federated Motion-Picture Crafts (FMPC). Out of this loose federation emerged an ex-prize fighter named Herbert Sorrell, who for ten years was the dominant figure in the anti-IA struggle within the AFL. The CIO anti-IA operation was headed by Jeff Kibre, who later became head of the Fisherman's Union, expelled from the CIO as being Communist-dominated. Kibre was responsible to Harry Bridges, then CIO chief on the West Coast, whose maritime union was ultimately expelled under the same charge.

The craft unions (under Sorrell's leadership), acting through the FMPC, called a strike in the studios in April 1937, demanding recognition and a wage increase. Browne and Bioff did what the craft unions had done to *their* strike in '34 — they broke the solidarity of the strike front. Within a few weeks, studio laborers left Sorrell's union, which was striking for $.75 an hour, joined a local of the IA which had just been set up, and were granted $.82½ an hour by the studios. They were followed by the make-up artists, who left Sorrell, joined Browne and Bioff, and went back to work.

The FMPC strike might have been counted a lost cause, except that Sorrell's federation landed a 15% increase and an arbitration clause. Probably more significant though was the fact that Sorrell had succeeded in negotiating the first contract between the studios and a *local* union. This contract set the precedent for the entire operation of the Conference of Studio Unions (CSU) which was organized a few years later. Many people in the film capital at the time thought that the best solution to Hollywood's labor problems would be the establishment of an industry-wide bargaining agent, fashioned after the great industrial unions which were then getting under way in Detroit and Chicago. They looked trustingly to Sorrell for leadership.

After the unsuccessful strike, all three anti-IA forces, the AFL's Sorrell, the CIO's Kibre and the disgruntled "IA Progressives," combined their strength to establish the United Studio Technicians Guild. The Guild was granted a CIO charter and the National Labor Relations Board ordered an election in 1939. Studio workers were asked to choose between the IA and the new CIO union. The IA, still under the leadership of Browne and Bioff, won the election by a two-to-one vote, to the keen disappointment of many pro-labor people in Hollywood who were disgusted with the IA. Before the election was held, Bioff had attacked the new union as being Communist in origin and development. Many felt that this kind of "red-baiting" (as it was called in those distant days) turned the tide in the racketeers' favor. But doubtless the election returns were also influenced by the fact that at the time of the election the IA was in negotiation with the producers for a much-heralded 20% wage increase. Immediately after the election the IA settled for 10%.

Carey McWilliams, then a Los Angeles labor lawyer, now editor of *The Nation,* brought about the first investigation of Browne's and Bioff's activities in Hollywood. The investigation, conducted by a California Assembly Committee, was inconclusive but marked

51

the beginning of the end for the two racketeers. At the hearings, studio workers testified that their union cards had been taken away from them because they refused to pay a two percent assessment for a fake union fund that Bioff simply pocketed. Herb Sorrell told of how Bioff and some of the studios had tried to buy off his Painters rather than offer a wage increase they had legitimately won. Bioff airily brushed all this aside. He was only trying to fight the Communists, he said, and the Communists of course would do anything or say anything to "get" him.

After the hearings, Bioff continued as Browne's representative in Hollywood, but the case was not dropped. Others began to look into Bioff's history, notably columnist Westbrook Pegler. Pegler revealed, among other things, that Bioff had once been convicted of pandering and had been given (though he never served) a six-month jail sentence by a Chicago court.

In 1941 Browne and Bioff were indicted and convicted for conspiracy and extortion. When Bioff left Hollywood to serve his sentence in 1940, he announced that he had been "framed" by Communists and "moneyed interests." Richard Walsh, who had been vice-president under the convicted Browne, became president of the IA.

Throughout all this, the role of the studios was far from that of innocent bystander caught between the struggles of competing unions. As employers, the studio chiefs were very much involved in behind-the-scenes manipulations, playing off one group against the other. When bribes were paid to Willie Bioff, it was the studio bosses who paid them. Some of them said later that they were in mortal fear of what might have been done to them had they called on the law. But in other sworn statements (given in trial depositions and affidavits) they acknowledged that by agreeing to the Browne-Bioff "arrangements" about wage-cuts and increases, the movie companies had saved approximately $15 million. After the "arrangements" had been thoroughly exposed, a Chicago tax court stated that "the payers knowingly and willingly paid over the funds and in a sense lent encouragement and participated with full knowledge of the facts in the activities of Browne and Bioff."

Through the years of Hollywood's turbulent labor troubles, it must be said, the studio-union relationship was uncommonly corrupt and venal. In every jurisdictional fight, either the IA or the craft unions opposing it broke the strike by making private deals with the producers. Until quite recently the studios maintained a policy of handling labor relations on a personal "deal" level. The cozy tête-a-tête between movie czar and labor leader replaced the formidable conference table in Hollywood. Such a tradition set the stage perfectly for a man like Willie Bioff, who, for a price, could be talked into reducing trade-union demands.

The revelations that came out in Bioff's trial, of course, reinforced the Hollywood liberal's image of the IA as a racket-ridden, corrupt, criminal organization. During the 1945-46 strike called by the anti-IA Conference of Studio Unions, the IA could muster very little community support. When it charged the CSU with being Communist-dominated, Hollywood liberals recalled that Bioff, the gangster, had made the same charge in 1939 against the United Studio Technicians Guild. Because it was Bioff, the gangster, who had made the charge originally, the accusation was largely discredited. Few even bothered to enquire into its truth or falsity. Charges of "Communist" were never popular in liberal-minded Hollywood and especially so when the accuser turned out to be a criminal.

The Conference of Studio Unions first appeared on the Hollywood scene in 1941. Its origins are shrouded in obscurity, but it is clear that Herb Sorrell was the dominant figure. The first members of the Conference were Screen Cartoonists, Screen Office Employees Guild, Film Technicians Local 683 of the IA, Local 1185 of the Machinists and Sorrell's own Local 644 of the Motion Picture Painters. Several officers of these unions were subsequently named before Congressional committees as members of the Communist Party.

The original unions in the CSU were not large. They were peripheral to the industry and hung on the fringes of the IA's jurisdiction. Actually the IA had taken little interest in these groups and it was only through Sorrell's efforts, in the period from 1939 to 1941, that they gained any strength at all. Sorrell at that time was the business agent for the Moving Picture Painters.

Sorrell set the tone for the Conference of Studio Unions. An ambitious, aggressive, cocksure labor leader, he was ever more interested in bread-and-butter issues than in the political positions adopted by his union. Whatever his relations to the Communist Party (and they have long been the subject of debate), Sorrell resolutely rejected the ideological straitjacket. The Communists for their part treated him with uncommon care. When Sorrell disagreed with a Party decision, several ex-Communists have testified, the Party tried to adjust itself to his position. Sorrell was clearly not amenable to discipline but did not hesitate to accept Communist support when it was offered.

From the very beginning the CSU set out to unite all the non-IA locals in Hollywood; at the same time it was busy organizing new trade-union groups. One of the problems it faced was the impossibility of organizing the studios within the craft internationals. Though the Conference could organize screen publicists in one group, office employees in another and cartoonists in still another, it could not relinquish jurisdiction of these separate units in favor of the international unions without sacrificing its own indentity. To get around the difficulty, all the groups received charters from Sorrell's own Painters Union. Thus it was that so many Hollywood stenographers, set designers and other unlikely specialists paid their union dues to the International Brotherhood of Painters of

54

America. (After all, it was sometimes said facetiously, everyone in the movie business is involved in painting dramatic pictures.)

At no time in its history, prior to the 1945 strike, did the Conference of Studio Unions diverge from the Communist Party line. In August, 1942, it endorsed the Second Front resolution. It took a lively interest in the Harry Bridges case. It supported the National Lawyers Guild, the People's Educational Center, International Labor Defense, the Hollywood Democratic Committee, the Joint Anti-Fascist Refugee Committee, the League of American Writers, etc. The Conference participated in an attempt to stop production on a film glorifying Eddie Rickenbacker (the flyer's name had long been mud in labor circles), but after Rickenbacker praised the Soviet Army the protests ceased. When President Truman proposed that Congress consider a bill to draft workers (a proposal supported by the Communist Party, despite AFL and CIO opposition) the CSU was on Truman's side.

The CSU's stated purpose was: "(a) to unite the motion picture unions for the protection of the autonomy of each and (b) to advance through joint consultation and action the economic welfare of the motion-picture unions and their members." Its constitution provided that in the event any member of the Conference went out on strike, or took any economic action, all the member unions of the Conference were bound to respect its picket line. The CSU, therefore, had a bloc of unions behind it to back up its demands. There is no doubt that many workers not in a position to bargain for themselves individually, as the talent groups were, or to bargain through collective strength, were greatly assisted by its efforts. The fact that CSU may have been Communist-created or Communist-manipulated cannot detract from this particular merit. The liberal group in Hollywood, with reason enough, felt that in the emergence of the CSU, the labor movement in the film industry had taken a long step forward. Sorrell became a kind of folk-hero to those who regarded the IA as a corrupt, reactionary force.

While the back-lot unions were fighting the studios and each other in the Twenties and Thirties, attempts were made to organize Hollywood talent guilds. The two most important groups among the talent people of course are actors and writers. Actors are concerned, as other people are, about wages and the hours and conditions of work. Writers have special problems. Because they are often selling not so much their time as their ideas, movie writers are required to behave like businessmen as well as employees. The wage minimums set by the writers' union directly affect only a small percentage of its members. But, indirectly, the minimums affect a much larger group. They serve as a kind of measuring rod. A few years ago a $500-a-week writer was getting twice the minimum. Today, with the minimum at $350-a-week, a writer of the same calibre can call for $700. Probably the most important function of the writers' union is its control over screen credits. Writers live on their credits. Without recognition, the writer's individual contribution to a film is largely lost. For bargaining purposes if nothing else, a writer needs reputation and reputation is built on credits. Today, if a dispute arises between a writer and his studio, or between writers themselves, the Screen Writers Guild is the final arbiter of credits.*

Film actors began to organize in the Twenties. Their early union activities were sporadic and generally unsuccessful. But a group of actors finally succeeded with the Screen Actors Guild in July, 1933.

---

* After RKO refused to give screenwriter Paul Jarrico screen credit for "The Las Vegas Story," the Writers Guild sued Hughes for breach of contract. Hughes won the case, basing his refusal to credit Jarrico on the "morals clause" in Jarrico's contract. In subsequent Guild agreements with the studios a clause was added providing that if a writer make a false statement he has not been a member of the Communist Party, or refuses upon the request of a producer to make a statement as to such membership, or refuses to testify as to such membership before a Congressional investigating committee, the producer is relieved of obligations under the collective-bargaining agreement to grant the writer screen credit. This step represented a radical departure. Previously the Writers Guild had insisted that screen credit should be awarded solely on the basis of work done.

The new Guild affiliated with the American Federation of Labor and began to participate in California AFL Council activities, though the studios did not recognize it as an official bargaining agency for four more years.

The Screen Writers Guild (now Writers Guild, West) grew out of a series of meetings of Hollywood scenarists. It was decided at these meetings to organize one hundred writers, at initiation fees of $100 each, who would pledge among themselves to accept strike discipline. From the first meetings there was a split between a political left and right in the group, but John Howard Lawson — leader of the Hollywood Ten some 14 years later — was elected first president by acclamation, on April 6, 1933. It was seven years before the Guild got its first contract. In the meantime a bitter internal struggle within the group might have served as a portent of things to come.

In April, 1936, John Howard Lawson appeared in Washington before a House Patents Committee which was studying author copyrights. He declared that the studio executives were ultimately responsible for smutty motion pictures because they snubbed qualified dramatists. Lawson asked for legislation strengthening authors' rights to decide how their writings were to be used in Hollywood. "In Hollywood," he said, ". . . we find that the writer has none of the protection, none of the dignity he has attained in other fields. One finds cases in Hollywood of very well-known writers, writers of standing, who are treated practically as office boys."

Lawson's testimony caused an uproar in Hollywood. Not only studio executives but members of his own Guild were aroused. Among the most severe critics were screenwriters Rupert Hughes and James K. McGuiness. Both men testified eleven years later that Lawson tried to make the Writers Guild "an instrument of Communist power." Two other dissenting guildsmen, Horace Jackson and John Lee Mahin, issued a letter protesting Lawson's remarks in Washington. They insisted it was "important to show

57

loyalty to the industry, to adjust our own grievances, and to protect ourselves against accusations of being dirty little boys writing dirty words to order."

Lawson's first attempt to consolidate the bargaining position of the writers' group was to join with the Authors League in an effort to prohibit individual writers from signing contracts without reference to Guild demands. Rupert Hughes, Howard Emmett Rogers and James K. McGuiness were again aroused. (The constitution proposed for the Authors League of America and the Screen Writers Guild, Hughes told the House Committee on un-American Activities years later, "provided for disciplinary measures to be applied by the Board of Directors of the Guild to writers guilty of conduct prejudicial to the good order of the Guild — without specifying what that conduct was. . . . A man could be destroyed economically under that authority!")

Hughes and McGuiness led a revolt in the Screen Writers Guild. They withdrew, formed another group called the Screen Playwrights, and almost immediately reached an agreement with the studios. "Of late," Hughes told the New York *World-Telegram* (May 11, 1936), "a certain school of writers is not only trying to align the writing craft with the labor unions, but to amalgamate all writers into one grand national union. . . I now felt it time to join the traitors against this unforeseen soviet and we secessionists are forming a new association devoted to correction of abuses and the betterment of the craft in cooperation with producers as sincerely interested in the prosperity in the picture industry as are we writers . . . While there are many of my friends among the crusaders for the closed shop in the grand union I beg to be delivered from my friends. I have no desire to be ruled by rival writers who are always competitors."

The studios echoed Hughes: "Not by the widest stretch of the imagination," said a joint producers statement, "can a writer . . . place his interest and problems on a plane with a man who joins a union not only to protect his job, but to establish standards of wages, working conditions and hours of labor."

Gene Fowler, writing in the *Hollywood Reporter,* said, with maybe a touch of prophecy, that labor union strategy on the part of writers was "off key"; he predicted that it would "bring down the papier mâché walls of this rookery like the collapse of an opera hat . . . the threat of strikes and public battle will inspire a Congressional interference that will throw everyone to the ravens."

The Screen Playwrights revolt put the Screen Writers Guild out of the running for a year. But during those twelve months John Howard Lawson and a small group met in secret and made plans to revive the Guild. When the National Labor Relations Board machinery was set up, Lawson and his supporters came out in the open again and called a mass meeting of all Hollywood writers. An NLRB election was held. By this time it seemed clear to many in Hollywood that Browne and Bioff were trying to extend their domain to the talent groups. At a meeting of the Writers Guild on June 27, 1937, Dudley Nichols described the "dangers of IATSE threats which would affect all writers should they remain divided and not united in one solid body." At the same meeting Dorothy Parker read a *Motion Picture Herald* report of the IATSE convention in Cleveland. The report quoted George Browne's statement that IATSE planned to "embrace the entire industry."

The Screen Writers Guild won the NLRB election over the Screen Playwrights by a whopping vote. But it was not until 1940 that the Playwrights' contract was voided and the new Guild contract was signed. Four years later Rupert Hughes, McGuiness, Rogers and others who had revolted against Lawson's trade-union concept of the Writers Guild helped organize the Motion Picture Alliance for the Preservation of American Ideals. From the very beginning the Alliance had a reputation as a labor-baiting force in Hollywood life. There was bad blood between it and the leadership of the Screen Writers Guild.

The Hollywood Strikes

THE 1945 AND '46 STRIKES called by the Conference of Studio Unions were among the most involved and complex in the history of American labor. What appeared on the surface to be a continuation of inter-union jurisdictional disputes was, in fact, a major conflict of warring social forces.

Between 1941 and '45 there had been numerous jurisdictional disputes between the IA and the CSU craft unions. A number of groups had a stake in the CSU. The AFL craft unions saw it as a rival to *their* ancient rival, the IA. The Communists saw it as a base for Party operations in Hollywood. The studios saw it as an IA rival which could sap IA strength. And Herb Sorrell, its fiery leader, may have seen it as a vehicle for his own ambitions.

The controversy originally concerned 77 set decorators who had been the subject of dispute for several years. Originally they had formed their own organization, the Society of Motion Picture Interior Decorators. The Society had negotiated a contract in 1937 and renewed it in 1942, although they had never been certified by the NLRB. In 1939 the IA chartered its Local 44 for jurisdiction over set decorators and asked the producers to negotiate an agreement. The producers refused, arguing they already had an agreement with the Society and would not recognize the IA set decorators until they were certified by the NLRB.

In 1943, the set decorators' Society joined the Painters and became part of the CSU. Sorrell tried to negotiate for them in 1944. The producers refused again, demanding now that the

Painters get an NLRB certification. The IA intervened in these proceedings and showed that ten percent of the decorators were members of its Local 44. The Painters withdrew their requests for certification and the producers did not ask for an election, as they could have. The thing dragged on until October, 1944 when Sorrell demanded immediate recognition for his group of set decorators. Sorrell called a strike when the demand was turned down.

The War Labor Board appointed an arbitrator who ruled that the producers should deal with the Painters until an NLRB election was held. At the end of February, 1945 the producers asked for an election between the rival groups. A preliminary hearing began on March 7, 1945. Five days later the Painters struck. The strike was immediately supported by the AFL craft unions in the CSU. But four of the CSU unions returned to work immediately. They had to go through a picket line to do so. According to Sorrell, these four unions (the Screen Publicists, Office Employees, Cartoonists and Story Analysts) "were influenced by the Communists." Sorrell stated that "when the strike started in March, 1945 the Communists bitterly opposed the action since it did not conform to their slogan of no-strike-during-wartime. A few Communists started a back-to-work movement which nearly wrecked the strike . . ."

The Communists were embarrassed when the strike was called. For some time they had been losing patience with Sorrell, who was giving increasing evidence that he was not in their pocket. They opposed the strike because of their all-out support of the war. Yet they were loath to cut off the support they were getting within the CSU. Inside the party, a controversy raged on the question of the strike. The *People's World,* Party paper on the West Coast, ran an editorial about Sorrell called "A Good Guy Gone Wrong" and urged a back-to-work movement, although it blamed the producers for the strike.

In the unions where they had influence, the Communists took

61

the same line. The executive board of the Screen Writers Guild placed an ad in *Variety* calling upon the strikers to return to work. A Guild membership meeting, held the same day the ad appeared, was enlivened by an argument between Dudley Nichols and Frank Partos on one side, and John Howard Lawson and William Pomerance on the other. Partos and Nichols objected to the ad's being run without the approval of a membership meeting. They stated their belief that the Guild membership had no desire to take sides on the strike. From this time on, Lawson's faction in the Screen Writers Guild met with increasing opposition.

It was not until after the publication of the Duclos letter* in May, 1945 that the Communist attitude toward the strike changed. As the Communist line became more and more militant, the Party rallied more and more support for the strike. Pomerance, who had supported the back-to-work movement, now spoke of "new developments" in the strike and asked the Screen Writers Guild to re-evaluate its neutral position and endorse the strike. The four unions which had returned to work went back on strike. The Party now marshalled its forces to support Sorrell and CSU.

The key figure in the IA operation was newcomer Roy Martin Brewer. Brewer arrived in Hollywood the very day the strike broke out. He had only recently resigned from a job in Washington with the War Labor Board. Before that he had been an IA execu-

---

* The letter was written by Jacques Duclos, with Maurice Thorez the most powerful leader of the French Communist Party, in May, 1945. It was sharply critical of the *Teheran* line of Earl Browder, general secretary of the American Communist Political Association. Browder, throughout the war period, held that a peaceful evolution of socialism was possible, and this theory had provided the basis for the wartime cooperation of the American Communists with the Washington Administration and even with big business. As a result of the letter Browder was expelled from the Communist Political Association. The Communist Party was reconstituted a few months later and took a militantly hostile attitude toward President Truman and "Wall Street." It was at this time that the American Communists gave up their support of the no-strike pledge and took an aggressive position within the American labor movement.

tive and as head of the Nebraska Federation of Labor the youngest president of a state AFL organization. He had come west at the request of IA president Richard Walsh, who had cast about for a tough, trained unioneer to direct IA strike strategy in Hollywood. The Nebraskan had a reputation as a labor trouble shooter. Brewer packed his bags for a two-week stay on the Coast, but, he says, he found the situation within the IA "very bad" — Sorrell was "making hay" by exploiting the Browne-Bioff scandal. Brewer decided to stay in Hollywood.

Brewer claims he first became aware of the Communist problem in the CSU when, at a Central Labor Council Meeting, Norval Crutcher, of the IA local in CSU, voted against him, while Tommy Ranford, a Painters business agent, voted for him. This surprising reversal of the usual AFL practice, he says, alerted him.

In the first weeks of the strike the IA's public attitude implied that here was simply another jurisdictional dispute. But on March 28, 1945, 16 days after Brewer arrived in California, the IA began issuing daily bulletins to its members and the strikers which vigorously attacked the CSU and the "progressive" IA groups supporting the strike. At first only an occasional reference was made to Communist Party-CSU connivance. The bulletins were long, single-spaced mimeographed analyses of the situation. But all this changed on April 24, 1945. On that day, the first of a series of attractive leaflets was issued, sharply directing attention to the Communist question. Titled "This is For You, Mr. Striker!" the handbills asked a question a day, gave the IA answer and listed the number of days the strike had gone on, the man-hours and wages lost.

The second leaflet set the tone for the series. The question was: "Is This a Union Labor Strike?" The IA answer was "No!" The leaflet went on to explain that the strike "must be a result of a long-range program instituted many years ago by a certain political party for one reason: To Take Over and Control Organized

Labor in the Motion Picture Industry." The strike was described as a "political strike." Sorrell was charged with being "sympathetic and definitely interested in the communistic idea."

For weeks the leaflet barrage kept up. Even though the Communist Party was not supporting the strike at the time, Sorrell's and the CSU's past associations with the Party were unearthed. Leaflets attacked the CSU for its endorsement of the "National Service Act when it was opposed by the AFL . . . the CSU protested the deportation of Bridges in open challenge to the AFL . . . the CSU furiously opposed the AFL position on participation in the so-called London World Labor Conference." Sorrell was attacked not only for his "communistic associations" but for his denunciations of President Roosevelt as a "warmonger" in 1940, his support of the Yanks-are-not-coming campaign and associations with other Communist causes. Day after day the leaflets hammered away: "Ask Mr. Sorrell why he changed his mind on June 22, 1941?" — the date of the Nazi attack on Russia.

Meanwhile, the studios were operating with IA replacements who crossed the CSU picket lines every day. In the old manner, Brewer learned to deal with the producers on a personal basis. When an NLRB election was held in May, every ballot cast was challenged either by the studios, the IA, the CSU or the NLRB. It was impossible to reach a decision. Picketing of the studios grew to mass proportions. When the Communist Party entered the strike, Sorrell somewhat charily accepted it as an ally.

On October 5, 1945, tear gas and fire hoses were used to break up a mass picket line at Warner Brothers. Jack Warner and his staff stood on the roof of their studio through the very worst of the battle, while relays of strikers and police, some with their heads cracked open, were treated in the infirmary below. National attention was now drawn to the labor showdown. There were demands on all sides that the strike be settled.

The NLRB ruled on October 12 that the set decorators wanted

affiliations with the Painters. But the strike continued until the end of October. At that time, the AFL executive council ordered (1) an immediate end to the strike, (2) local negotiations for 30 days on jurisdictional questions, (3) return of all strikers to their jobs and (4) final disposition, by a three-man committee of the AFL executive council, of any question not solved during the 30-day arbitration.

So ended the first CSU strike.

But it was not the end of the antagonisms generated by the strike. Some CSU members refused to return to work at the side of men who had replaced them during the bitter days. Only one small jurisdictional controversy was solved by the local negotiations. The remaining disputes between the IA and the Painters, Electricians, Plumbers, Building Service Employees, Machinists and Carpenters were referred to the arbitration committee.

The strike became a vital issue in the movie community and in the talent guilds. In the Screen Writers, Emmet Lavery, then president, supported by a number of others, had successfully resisted the attempts of certain members of his Board of Directors to involve the union in the strike. But the Board vote had been close. On two occasions Lavery himself stepped down to break a seven-to-seven tie. At membership meetings the all-out Sorrell supporters were more decisively beaten. Oliver Garrett denounced a resolution that the Guild support the strike. He traced the resolution to the Communist Party line and received general endorsement.

Throughout the strike the Screen Actors Guild, like the Writers, remained neutral. The actors had supported the right of a performer not to cross a picket line "where any possible threat of violence exists," but on the jurisdictional question it maintained an attitude of "impartiality and neutrality." (Communist influence in the Actors Guild had been kept to a minimum. During the war the Actors, under the leadership of Robert Montgomery, had attempted to make an anti-Communist resolution part of the policy of a proposed inter-talent union council. The council had split on the issue but the resolution was solidly adopted by the Screen Actors themselves.)

The 1945 strike settlement actually settled nothing. The three-man committee of the AFL executive council handed down a decision which satisfied no one, and the warring groups prepared for their next battle. Under the terms of the settlement, the IA lost jurisdiction over set decorators, but the Carpenters lost jurisdiction over set erection. Some 350 jobs were transferred from the Carpenters to the IA.

Brewer was beginning to gain strength both organizationally and politically. Organizationally, he consolidated his gains by developing relationships with other AFL unions and establishing friendly contacts with the movie producers. Politically, he committed himself to a hard-boiled anti-communism and looked around for allies. The Motion Picture Alliance for the Preservation of American Ideals was ready-made for the battle Brewer saw ahead. There were a few labor people in the Alliance, but the MPA was generally regarded as anti-labor and Brewer endangered his reputation as a union leader when he joined.

Elsewhere Brewer found little support. Some help came from the building trades within the AFL. Only a small group of anti-Communists within the CIO supported his attacks on Sorrell, Brewer says. For the most part the labor and liberal communities in Hollywood were outspokenly anti-Brewer, though he was openly a supporter of many New Deal causes. In these circles Sorrell and his CSU were largely viewed as healthy, honest, progressive forces. Inevitably Brewer bore some of the old stigma attached to the IA.

Even the group carrying on the fight for neutrality in the Screen Writers had little use for Brewer. For one thing they didn't like his choice of allies. The Motion Picture Alliance was thoroughly

66

despised because of the reactionary attitudes of so many stalwarts within the organization. California's Senator Jack Tenney, another Brewer supporter, was heartily disliked for his blunderbuss attacks on many groups supported by liberals.

Within CSU, too, things were sticky. Brewer boxed Sorrell into a corner in May, 1946. One of the CSU affiliates was the Machinists Union, which was no longer in the AFL. Brewer and a Teamsters Union representative got an AFL charter for studio machinists. Then Brewer asked the Central Labor Council to take action against the unaffiliated machinists. The Council went along with Brewer by informing the producers that it refused to "accept, work with, or handle any products going to or coming from machinists employed by the studios who are not members in good standing in the American Federation of Labor." Thereupon the producers discharged all machinists who refused to join the AFL union. The CSU then refused to handle work done by any but Machinist Union members. Another strike was called. It was quickly settled by the NLRB, but Sorrell lost some of his strength by even agreeing to such intervention.

Sorrell promptly called for another strike, demanding a 25% wage increase and certain other concessions. Again, this strike was settled almost immediately when the producers granted the increase to both CSU and IA members.

Sorrell was continually pushed into corners. Brewer was working with the producers now, trying to convince them that it was to their interest to deal with him rather than with Sorrell. He was lining up support within the AFL. He had become active in community work and Democratic Party politics. He was gaining influence and prestige in the MPA; the anti-Communists were full of admiration for his success in whittling away at Sorrell's prestige.

Charges of being a Communist were preferred against Sorrell within the Los Angeles Central Labor Council. In July, 1946 the

67

CSU leader was put on trial. The prosecution was conducted by one Ed Gibbons, who had helped Brewer in the preparation of the anti-Communist leaflets used in the 1945 strike. (Subsequently Brewer broke off relations with Gibbons. Gibbons became the co-owner of *Alert,* a "nationalist" paper published in Los Angeles and proudly listed in the *First National Directory of Rightist Groups, Publications and Some Individuals in the United States.*)

At the trial all Sorrell's past connections with the Communist Party were brought up. The CSU lawyers were attacked as being close to the Party. Sorrell's alleged Party membership card, which was in the possession of the California Tenney Committee, was discussed.

Sorrell stated his philosophy at the end of the first trial session. In the course of a long speech defending his activities he said:

> Now understand, if I was a Communist I wouldn't be up here saying I wasn't, because a lot of the things the Communists do I think is pretty good. I think when I get through here I will prove to you that I think along the lines of the Communists in many respects. I think also that I will prove to you that the Communists think I am a phony. I think that I will prove to you that I couldn't be a Communist and be in the position I am. I think that further I will prove to you that no matter what happens to me it doesn't make any difference in my young life.

While Sorrell's trial was droning on to an indecisive end in the dingy downtown quarters of the AFL, another struggle was being waged in Beverly Hills and Hollywood. In labor and liberal groups there was a growing awareness that something was amiss. People were becoming uneasy about the political positions being taken by former friends and associates. Most liberals were still unwilling to wage an all-out war against the Communists. "Red-baiter" was still a dirty name to be avoided. But the new "hard" Party line was beginning to show, now that the war was over.

Typical of the incidents disturbing Hollywood liberals was the editing of *The Screenwriter,* organ of the Writers Guild. Dalton

68

Trumbo was its first editor and Gordon Kahn served as Managing Editor. Richard Macaulay, an active and vocal anti-Communist, had submitted an article to the magazine which attacked an article written by Alvah Bessie. The editorial board simply refused to print Macaulay's rebuttal. Editor Trumbo wrote Macaulay of the decision, stating among other things: "It is difficult to support your belief in 'the inalienable right of man's mind to be exposed to any thought whatever, however intolerable that thought might be to anyone else.' Frequently such a right encroaches upon the right of others to their lives. It was this 'inalienable right' in Fascist countries which directly resulted in the slaughter of five million Jews."

Ronald Reagan, then president of the Screen Actors Guild, though never remotely attracted to the Party himself, was a favorite of the Hollywood Communists immediately after he returned from active service in the war. Reagan at the time was active in a number of liberal organizations and causes which the Party was supporting. He had also started to make speeches on the German question. He says that he was wooed by certain people he later discovered were Communists. "I was their boy!" he recalled bitterly not long ago. But after the movie star was invited to join the executive committee of HICCASP,* where he immediately joined forces with an anti-Communist group centering around Olivia de Haviland, Dore Schary, Johnny Green and a few others, his popularity in Communist circles rapidly diminished. This group within HICCASP tried to get the organization to go on record condemning communism, but without success.

Some of the old front groups were showing signs of stress and strain as the Cold War got under way. The reconstituted Communist Party was not so genteel as the Communist Political Association had been. "Twentieth Century Americanism" now made harsher

---

* Hollywood Independent Citizens Committee of the Arts, Sciences and Professions, a section of the Progressive Citizens of America.

demands. The Party itself showed signs of wear and tear. Members started to drift away. Even such a stalwart as screenwriter Richard Collins was nursing doubts. The debate over Browder's expulsion was taking its toll.

Then came the 1946 CSU strike.

This strike on the surface was also over a jurisdictional question. The AFL executive council, under pressure of "Big Bill" Hutcheson, president of the Carpenters union, had ordered a "clarification" of the December, 1945 decision on IA and Carpenters jurisdiction. A West Coast AFL organizer had reported that the IA was violating the 1945 decision and that a strike was impending. The "clarification" was supposed to clear the air.

The "clarification" clarified nothing. The Carpenters understood it to mean that they had regained jurisdiction over the set-erection jobs which had been taken away from them. But the "clarification" also stated that the unions had to "strictly adhere" to the previous decision. The Carpenters, backed up by the CSU, demanded that the producers carry out the "clarification." The IA held that the "clarification" did not take the disputed jobs away from it. But even if it did, the union declared, it would take whatever steps were necessary to prevent this from happening. The producers protested that the AFL had no authority to modify its first decision.

The producers discussed the situation. They took the IA's threat to mean that a general motion-picture strike would be called if the Carpenters' demands were met. According to the minutes of the producers' meeting (revealed at a Congressional hearing a year later), Roy Brewer attended most of the producers' meetings.

Brewer assured the producers that the IA would not honor the picket lines of any other unions and would supply replacements for any strikers. Further assurance came in a letter from Brewer's chief, IA president Walsh, to all the IA locals in Hollywood. With

70

this to go on, the producers began to discharge all carpenters and other CSU members who had refused to work on sets erected by IA members. By September 26, virtually all movie set construction was stopped by CSU action. The studios discharged all CSU members and requested the IA to furnish replacements. The CSU, claiming that it had been locked out, expanded the area of its demands. It asked for wage increases and arbitration of jurisdictional disputes in addition to immediate application of the August "clarification." The producers ignored CSU's requests and the battle was joined.

Now the sides were clearly drawn. The producers, IA and Teamsters were lined up against the CSU and craft unions; the latter side was vigorously supported by the Communists. The Screen Actors and Screen Writers maintained their neutrality, with the issue serving as a focal point for a bitter struggle between pro- and anti-Communists in the two groups. The AFL executive council, beset by pressures from the Carpenters on one side and the IA and Teamsters on the other, did nothing.

The conflict grew sharper. Mass picketing and mass arrests took place every day. IA workers went through CSU picket lines in busses driven by members of the Teamsters union. Violence broke out regularly. Feelings ran high.

The Screen Actors Guild tried to mediate but with practically no success. A delegation of actors and CSU representatives, including Sorrell, went to the 1946 AFL convention in Chicago in an attempt to settle the jurisdictional dispute. But the AFL Council would take no clear position. The actors and Sorrell returned to Hollywood dejected.

While they were in Chicago, the Actors Guild representatives discussed the roles of Sorrell and of the Communists with Hutcheson. Hutcheson told the Actors Guild people that the Carpenters were "using" Sorrell and the Communist Party to break the IA and had every intention of dumping them afterwards.

71

The SAG delegation returned home, saddened, discouraged and somewhat wiser in the ways of AFL politics, but still found the heart to continue mediation attempts. On October 25, 1946, a multi-party telephone conference was arranged between two of the three AFL arbitrators, Actors Guild officers, and CSU representatives. The CSU and actors' groups had returned to Hollywood with conflicting versions of what the AFL officials had said in Chicago. The phone conference was supposed to clear up the confusion.

Actor Edward Arnold began the attempt to clarify the "clarification." "This," he said of the telephone conference, "is something that is going down in the annals of labor history." (If the conference does get in the history books, it may be as an example of utter confusion.) The arbitrators steadfastly refused to take any position whatsoever. All parties, they agreed blandly, were right in their claims. (During the conference the arbitrators declared that the controversial "clarification" was not the one they had written — the "clarification" *they* had written had never been received in Hollywood. But the next morning when they sent a telegram to the unions with the correct "clarification," it turned out to be an exact copy of the "clarification" they denied ever having written!)

Finally, at the end of the telephone conference, the two arbitrators took a position which amounted to support of the IA's contentions. One of the arbitrators offered some gentle advice which summed up the general innocuous tone of the mediation attempts: "If you people in the studio who know what this thing is all about would get together and settle your troubles," he offered, "and don't say anything to anybody outside the studios, you will get along."

The Catholic Archbishop of Los Angeles assigned two priests — Father John Devlin, film industry representative for the Archbishop, and Father Thomas Coogan, a professor of Labor Relations — to study the studio strike situation. The priests recommended, among other things, that a permanent arbitration machinery, headed by an impartial chairman who was not from the ranks of labor or from the industry, be agreed upon to settle future jurisdictional differences. But the suggestion was never taken up. The priests, incidentally, decried the "most negative" attitude the producers had taken on the strike and stated, in their report to the Archbishop:

Nor can we becloud the air with cries of Communism, radicalism. It is true that Communists have tried hard to infiltrate into the ranks of the CSU. But the strike is not Communist-inspired nor Communist-directed. It is also unfortunate that the CSU has turned again and again to left-wing sympathizers' support. But to desire the extermination of a union because of an accusation of Communism is not in keeping with the facts nor with the spirit of labor ethics.

Later the Screen Actors made still another attempt to settle the dispute when they arranged to get Joseph Keenan of the national AFL staff to serve as a mediator. Keenan's attempts at mediation were unsuccessful, the Actors Guild officials hold, because the CSU lawyers constantly raised new issues or backed away from the consequences of already settled questions. In any case, the actions of the CSU attorneys convinced the actors' group that the CSU was not seriously interested in settling the strike.

The strike also became a critical issue in the Screen Writers. Some members wanted the Guild to donate $10,000 to the one IA local which was supporting the CSU. The motion was defeated.

The CSU strike petered away when CSU members began to return to work with IA union cards. It ended in a welter of law suits, conspiracy arrests, a Congressional investigation, numerous AFL directives which were not applied and smaller and smaller picket lines. Finally, in 1949, the IA won a decisive NLRB election. The jurisdictional strike was at an end. Roy Brewer and the IA were in a position of great economic — and, as it turned out, political — strength.

"Clearance" in Hollywood

When Chairman J. Parnell Thomas abruptly closed the Hollywood hearings on October 30, 1947, he emphasized that his Committee would resume its investigation as soon as possible. Thomas advised the motion-picture industry to "set about immediately to clean its own house and not wait for public opinion to force it to do so." But the industry's attempts to "clean house" were neither prompt nor sweeping enough for some long-time critics of Hollywood's political life. As months and even years passed without spectacular shakeups in the studios, the conviction grew in these circles that the public needed prodding if it was ever going to force the industry to do anything. In the Hearst papers, and in an expanding list of anti-Communist newsletters, fact-sheets, etc., there were recurrent demands that Hollywood do more to implement its own Waldorf policy. Drew Pearson, for one, criticized the new chairman of the House Committee on Un-American Activities for not taking up where Parnell Thomas had left off.

It was generally known that even the decision to banish the Ten from the studios had been accepted with reluctance by certain important movie executives. Darryl Zanuck had told the press the decision was reached after a day and a half of argument — a disagreement reflected in the producers' own frank acknowledgement that there were "dangers and risks" lurking in the new policy. Dore Schary once admitted publicly that he did not hold with the majority opinion about what to do with the Ten. But it was Schary who was chosen to proclaim the new policy at a stormy meeting of the

Screen Writers Guild, where he announced that henceforth the industry would no longer hire a Communist or anyone suspected of being a Communist. A few weeks after the Waldorf meeting, Lillian Ross, Hollywood correspondent for *The New Yorker,* quoted Schary as saying that he had been faced with the alternative of either supporting the stand taken by his company or quitting his job. "I don't believe you should quit under fire," Schary told her. "Anyway I like making pictures. I want to stay in the industry. I like it." Miss Ross added that many of his colleagues were critical of Schary, "yet they understand why he has done what he's done."

In reversing his stand, Schary was observing the Hollywood tradition that loyalty to the industry comes first. As loyalty is the cardinal virtue, so disloyalty is the capital sin. And it seemed to many in Hollywood at the time that those members of the Motion Picture Alliance for the Preservation of American Ideals who had cooperated with Parnell Thomas were guilty of disloyalty. No one in Hollywood was prepared to deny that there were Communists in the industry, but it was the moviemakers' honest belief that "nothing subversive or un-American has appeared on the screen." In going along with the underlying theme of the Thomas probe, certain of the friendly witnesses had outraged the patriotic feelings of the executives. If "subversive" and "un-American" material *had* appeared on the screen — which the executives vehemently denied — then the clear implication was that the executives, at the very least, had been remiss in fulfilling their duties. After the 1947 hearings, consequently, the two most unpopular groups in Hollywood were the Ten, who had embarrassed the industry by their behavior in Washington, and the friendly witnesses from the Motion Picture Alliance who testified about Communist "infiltration" and encouraged J. Parnell Thomas in his belief that the films had been used to convey Red propaganda.

In all probability, there was some carryover of this ill-feeling toward the friendly witnesses in hiring practices. Although nothing so clear-cut as the blacklist applied against the Hollywood Ten resulted, the records show the employment for some of the friendly witnesses fell off immediately after they testified.

The case of screenwriter Morrie Ryskind — who told the Committee "the only trouble is that the producers won't listen to me . . ." — is often cited. From 1941 to '46, Ryskind gained writing credits for such high-budgeted films as "Claudia," "Where Do We Go From Here?" and "Penny Serenade." Since his 1947 testimony, he has not had a single credit. One prominent executive, when asked recently whether he would hire Ryskind, replied: "Yes, but not at the price he wants. Ryskind hasn't submitted a script nor come up with a new idea in years. He's just not worth the kind of money he demands." Another said lamely: "No, I wouldn't hire him. But it's not because of his politics. It's just that he's too hard to get along with." (Though Ryskind is often cited by others as an example of an anti-Communist who sacrificed his career, he does not make the charge himself.)

Another example of a screenwriter who has not had a single credit since his 1947 testimony as a friendly witness is Richard Macaulay. From 1941 to '47, Macaulay had credits for nine films. He never worked on major pictures but from his credits it can be assumed that prior to 1947 he was a competent writer of B pictures. Why he should have lost his competence at exactly the same time he testified remains an unanswered question.

It is also claimed that Adolphe Menjou suffered loss of employment because of his testimony and identification with the Motion Picture Alliance. It is true that Menjou, long a Hollywood fixture, did not appear in films as frequently after his testimony, but in his case it is considerably more difficult to draw a cause-and-effect conclusion. Menjou was at a turning point in his career in 1947. He was no longer young. He could no longer pass as the dapper, debonair man of the world — the "type" he created — and there may have been fewer parts suited to him.

No simple set of facts can be accepted as a final answer to the charge that anti-Communists were discriminated against for co-operating with the Thomas Committee. If Menjou, for instance, was blacklisted in some front offices (as has often been claimed), what about Gary Cooper and Robert Taylor, who testified at the same hearing?

In any case, it seems clear that if such friendly witnesses were discriminated against, it was not on the basis of an industry-wide policy such as that set forth in the Waldorf Statement. There was an abundance of ill-feeling against these witnesses. The antipathy, though, was not based on the fact that they were anti-Communists so much as on the general belief in the Hollywood community that by cooperating so eagerly with the investigators they had betrayed the entire industry.

As a result of the Waldorf policy, ten men were fired immediately. That left the nine "unfriendlies" who, for some unstated reason, Parnell Thomas never got around to calling. Those among the nine who continued to work at the major studios after they returned to Hollywood had been required to sign a statement that they were not members of the Communist Party. Others felt the effects of the Waldorf policy immediately.

Actor Larry Parks, first of the "unfriendlies" to switch his position, testified before the House Committee on Un-American Activities in April, 1951. Parks said he believed his career had been "ruined." Screenwriter Waldo Salt was told when he returned from Washington after the 1947 hearings that his contract with RKO would not be renewed. Salt's agent was shown a letter written by an RKO executive which said, "Fire Scott, Dmytryk and Salt," Salt recalls, though he remembers that Dore Schary assured him he was not being fired for political reasons. After he was banished from RKO, Salt found work with the independent producers until he was re-subpoenaed in 1951. Then he refused to cooperate with the Committee and joined the ranks of those completely blacklisted. Gordon Kahn, another "unfriendly" screenwriter, found it hard to get work after 1947. Richard Collins, who later broke completely with the Communist Party and provided the Committee with the names of 23 movie people he said he knew as members, was confined to work on the fringes of the industry during this period.

The threat of being blacklisted was not limited to the remaining "unfriendlies." As soon as the 1947 hearings were over, the demoralized Committee for the First Amendment began to disintegrate. Some of its members were simply weary and disillusioned. They felt they had been "used" during the hearings, both by the House Committee and the partisans of the Hollywood Ten. Others saw which way the political wind was blowing and decided to go along with it. One of the Committee's founders recently told a visitor: "People got scared. The pressure groups, especially the Motion Picture Alliance, frightened the hell out of everybody." Another member of the Committee, who was not so prominent in its organization and still works in the industry, confirmed the remark: "I would not be surprised if all the members of the Committee were warned to get out of it, either by their studios, their agents or families. The entertainment industry is the only one I know where livelihood depends on the attitude of the public toward a person's name." A third explanation was summed up this way: "I came to understand that it is not right or fair for an actor who has enormous influence because of his popularity to campaign actively and take a political position. He takes unfair advantage. He is entitled to a vote or an opinion, but his influence is all out of proportion to his knowledge."

Besides the dozens who had exposed themselves to the shadow of blacklist by signing Committee for the First Amendment advertisements, another long list of names appeared in the trade press only a few days after the 1947 hearings closed. This was a list of 208 actors who, under the auspices of the Actor's Division of the

Progressive Citizens of America, bought an ad in *Daily Variety* which declared:

The Thomas-Rankin Committee must go! We the undersigned members of the acting profession acclaim Larry Parks, one of the "unfriendly 19." We acclaim those actors who appeared in Washington to protest the star-chamber proceedings . . . those others who broadcast their indignation on the air and in the press . . . and those who remained to fight here. We are proud that they are upholding the finest traditions of our profession and our country.

Still a third long list of names appeared two years later as signatures on an *amicus curiae* brief submitted to the Supreme Court on behalf of the Hollywood Ten. (The Ten had taken their contempt-of-Congress case through the courts in the hope of winning a reversal.) Until the Supreme Court refused to review the case, few in Hollywood believed that the ten men would actually go to jail. When they were imprisoned, a cloud of apprehension settled over the film colony. By this time hundreds of prominent Hollywood personalities were on record against the proceedings that had brought about the sentence. As early as 1948 some of them began to feel the effects of the new policy.

Among those who had participated in every major public protest against the hearings was Anne Revere, a character actress who had won an Academy Award for her performance in "National Velvet" and had been nominated for roles in "Gentlemen's Agreement" and "Song of Bernadette." Between 1940 and '50, Miss Revere appeared in 40 motion pictures and her career ascended steadily until the end of 1947. That year she worked 40 weeks. In 1949, when her name appeared on the *amicus curiae* brief, she worked eight days, and in 1950, when her name appeared in *Red Channels,* she worked only three weeks. That year her agent went directly to the major Hollywood producers to find out if she was being blacklisted. The agent reported back to her that Dore Schary of M-G-M said he would hire her if he had a suitable part but Y. Frank

Freeman of Paramount and a Warner Brothers executive both said bluntly that their studios wanted no part of her. When the Hollywood hearings were resumed in 1951, Anne Revere was one of the first subpoenaed. She invoked the First and Fifth Amendments and has not worked in films since.

Gale Sondergaard, wife of Herbert Biberman of the Hollywood Ten, found that she was suddenly "unemployable" after her husband refused to testify, though she had previously made about 45 pictures, had won an Oscar for her performance in "Anthony Adverse" and had been nominated for another after she appeared in "Anna and the King of Siam." Following the 1947 hearings, Miss Sondergaard made only one film, produced by Mervyn LeRoy. LeRoy told her that he had been questioned by dozens of people who asked him wonderingly if he did not know who she was.

But if some of the lights in Hollywood were dimming, others brightened steadily. For years the militant anti-Communists in the film colony had complained bitterly that no one listened to them. Now their day had come. Roy Brewer, who had exacted unconditional surrender in the long labor war, was bringing new prestige to the Motion Picture Alliance for the Preservation of American Ideals. He had set up and was chairman of the AFL Film Council. He was establishing the Motion Picture Industry Council. His strength seemed to grow daily.

The Hollywood AFL Film Council was Brewer's version of Herb Sorrell's defunct Conference of Studio Unions. The Council was established early in 1948 to "promote closer unity and cooperation by and between affiliates of the AFL and the motion-picture industry, and to promote harmonious industrial relations with the employers in the motion-picture industry." Through the new organization, Brewer set out to coordinate collective bargaining in Hollywood, promote legislation favorable to the industry and in general carry out the functions of a trade-union council. Non-AFL unions were excluded from membership, as was any organization or person "who participates in proceedings of any meeting or in any organization or in any activity connected with, or sympathetic to, Communism or Fascism, or related to, or dominated by, or under the control of any foreign organizations, group or government, generally recognized as being hostile to the AFL movement, or advocating the violent overthrow of the U.S., or who supports or holds membership in any such organizations or group."

The Council, early in its history, made a film about the National Farm Labor Union strike at the vast Di Giorgio holdings near Bakersfield, California. Senator Jack B. Tenney, who had described the strike leaders as Communists, strongly disapproved of the film and of the support Brewer gave the strikers. The two men never saw eye to eye again, though until that time, Brewer later stated, he had regarded Tenney as a "helpful ally." By breaking with Brewer, Tenney cut himself off from the influence he might have had in Hollywood in the crucial days ahead. (Tenney has since associated himself with a number of West Coast hate-groups and has thereby become wholly anathema to Brewer.)

Brewer's AFL Film Council became an important cog in the Los Angeles labor movement. By bringing all the CSU and unaffiliated unions under the IA's jurisdiction, Brewer built his union's strength in the studios. As the unions joined the IA, they joined the Council and became involved in the general life of the community. The AFL representative on the Los Angeles Community Chest, for instance, was a Brewer appointee. Collective bargaining was professionalized through the Council (an economist was appointed to assist in preparing negotiating briefs), and whenever possible union negotiations with the studios were conducted on an industry-wide basis.

The Council also provided Brewer with a personal forum. He used it to broadcast his views on the Communist problem in Hollywood. By this time he had become convinced, Brewer says, that

Hollywood had to drive the Communists out of the industry. "Communists want to use the movies to soften the minds of the world," he told a reporter. "They shouldn't work in Hollywood because we shouldn't make it possible for them to subvert the free world. I wouldn't be opposed to their working in an industry where they wouldn't hurt anybody, but I'm absolutely opposed to their working in the movies."

Brewer did not confine his anti-communism to the AFL craft unions. He says that when the Hollywood Independent Citizens Committee of the Arts, Sciences and Professions moved against him in the 1946 strike, he found it necessary to "hit back in the cultural field." So he began to line up allies in the talent guilds. Some guildsmen who had once been outspoken critics of the IA moved reluctantly into Brewer's camp. This was especially true in the Screen Actors Guild, many of whose members were still bitter about Communist tactics during the CSU strike. The national leadership of the AFL provided Brewer with strong support. Victor Riesel, syndicated labor columnist, wrote pieces about Roy Brewer's anti-Communist fight in Hollywood. George Sokolsky lauded him in another nationally read column. Brewer's influence was felt in the Democratic Party in California.

He was also a key figure in setting up the Motion Picture Industry Council (MPIC). This Council was composed of representatives of all the Hollywood unions, guilds and industry organizations. It provided the IA chief with another forum. In its early days the MPIC had little prestige. It attempted to bring the Communist problem to the attention of the producers but met with small success until the 1951 hearings. But within MPIC, Brewer gained new adherents, among them many liberals who were beginning to believe what he said about the Communists. The militant anti-liberals within the Motion Picture Alliance for the Preservation of American Ideals took almost everything he said with the utmost seriousness. He became chairman of the board of the Alliance. It was something of a novelty of course to find a labor figure leading the Alliance. After Brewer took over, some once prominent members dropped out, including Ayn Rand and Lela E. Rogers, who had given some of the most sensational testimony during the 1947 hearings.

As a result of his position in the Alliance, Brewer was developing contacts with the American Legion and the House Committee on Un-American Activities. The Legion showed a growing interest in Hollywood, and Washington investigators were on the West Coast at the time, quietly assembling material which would be useful when the Committee again turned its attention to the film colony.

During this period Brewer began a singularly important personal association — he met Edward Dmytryk of the Hollywood Ten group. After the 1947 hearings, Dmytryk had gone to England, returned home, served a six-month jail sentence for contempt of Congress and before he left prison issued a statement attacking the Communist Party. He came back to Hollywood but found no work. Dmytryk asked a friend, an independent producer, to arrange a meeting of "the toughest anti-Communists in town." Brewer attended the meeting and heard Dmytryk explain his reasons for joining the Party and later breaking with it. During a discussion period Brewer asked questions and was impressed with Dmytryk's answers. As a result of hearing Dmytryk, he came to the conclusion, as he himself put it not long ago, that "the people who had broken with the Party had to be helped, both because it was the right thing to do and because it hurt the Communist Party."

Through Dmytryk, Brewer met screenwriter Richard Collins, another of the original 19. Collins, since the 1947 hearings, had moved further and further from the Communist Party. In March, 1950, he went to the FBI, admitted his past Party membership and offered the Bureau full cooperation. In Communist circles it was generally understood that Collins had drifted from the Party, but no one knew he had talked to the FBI. Collins put Brewer in touch with other ex-Communists who were finding it impossible to get employment in the major studios.

Dmytryk, with Brewer's assistance, was the first of the ex-Communists to go back to work. In May, 1951, the *Saturday Evening Post* published a sympathetic article about the director's experiences which made his name acceptable at the box office. Others then turned to Brewer for help, and a "rehabilitation" procedure was developed that became more or less standardized.

By this time Brewer had added to his personal staff an ex-Communist named Howard Costigan. When a former member of the Party came to Brewer for help, Brewer usually turned him over to Costigan. The first thing Costigan insisted on was that the ex-Communist go to the FBI with all the information he had. Then the ex-Communist was put in touch with the House Committee and some kind of public repentance was worked out. The ex-Communist was expected to testify (which meant naming names in public session), denounce the Party at union meetings and, if he was prominent enough, make some kind of statement for the press, write an article for a magazine, or in some other way publicly express his new feelings about the Party. Some converts refused to be "rehabilitated" on these terms. They objected especially to the requirement that they name others.

The theory behind the public repentence, according to Costigan, was simply this: Since these people had used their position to aid the Communist Party, they were under special obligation now to help publicly destroy it. In some cases both Brewer and Costigan felt that the penitents still did not understand the nature of their sin, and it was Costigan's special duty then to convince them that whatever their *subjective* motives had been for joining the Party, *objectively* they had served an evil cause. Costigan spent hours expanding on this theme. Occasionally, especially with the more important ex-Communists, Brewer took over.

Brewer put the weight of the Motion Picture Alliance behind his "rehabilitation" program. When the Alliance was willing to go out on a limb for one of the blacklisted, studio executives were inclined to take notice, since MPA's support of X could be cited if and when complaints came in because X was working again. Individual members of the Alliance, like actor Ward Bond and screenwriter Borden Chase, went out of their way to find jobs for the ex-Communists who cooperated with Brewer's program. However, a faction within the Alliance held that "once a Communist, always a Communist," and disapproved of the whole program.

Costigan's and Brewer's contact with so many ex-Communists not only gave them access to names not yet publicly revealed but an intimate knowledge of the Party's operations in Hollywood. And when graduates of the "rehabilitation" course appeared before the House Committee, they testified with a degree of "cooperation" unknown during the first Hollywood probe. After they testified, most of them went back to work.

Another "rehabilitation" program got under way when, in 1950, Sterling Hayden, a prominent star, called on his lawyer, Martin Gang, of the firm of Gang, Kopp & Tyre. Hayden had a problem. It was a new kind of problem for Gang, a prosperous theatrical lawyer. After Hayden left, the lawyer called in his secretary and dictated a letter to J. Edgar Hoover:

This office has a client who has discussed with us a problem which I believe can only be answered through your organization.

In June of 1946 this young man, in a moment of emotional disturbance, became a bona fide member of the Communist Party in the State of California. In November of 1946 he decided that he had made a mistake and terminated his membership and his association with the Communist Party. Ever since November of 1946 this client has had no connection whatsoever with the Communist Party or with any organization affiliated with it.

The gentleman in question is an American-born citizen with a distinguished war record. He enlisted in the Marine Corps as a private and received his termination as a captain. Because of his distinguished services he received the Silver Star medal with citation from the Commanding General, Mediterranean Theater of Operations, United States Army. The citation recognized his gallantry in action in the Mediterranean Theater of Operations with the United States Marine Corps Reserve.

Our client is not engaged in any activity where security is involved. However, since the commencement of the operation in Korea, he has felt that the time may come, in the near future, when his services might be of aid to the United States. He is concerned with the fact that his brief membership in the Communist Party, as aforesaid, may operate to prevent the use of his services.

In addition to the foregoing, he is married and has young children. If his services are not needed by the United States, conditions may develop so as to require an answer in connection with ordinary employment to the query: "Are you now or have you ever been a Communist?"

Our client can, of course, answer honestly and frankly that he is not now a member of the Communist Party. He could not answer the rest of the compound question without (a) either lying, or (b) if he told the truth he would probably find himself unable to earn a living.

While it must be admitted that a mistake was made in 1946, it does appear that justice requires some method by which one mistake does not operate (a) to prevent the United States from making use of the services of our client, (b) to prevent our client from earning a living.

He is perfectly willing to submit to any interrogation or examination by the Federal Bureau of Investigation so that that organization may be convinced of his sincerity and of the truth of all the statements related herein.

The purpose of this, of course, is to permit our client, if the compound question is asked him, to say in answer to the question, "Please inquire of the Federal Bureau of Investigation." The Federal Bureau of Investigation could then notify the prospective employer that there was no reason for not employing our client.

We would appreciate hearing from you at your earliest convenience.

Two weeks later, Hoover answered:

Your letter of July 31, 1950, has been received and I want to thank you for making these facts available to me. I have given your letter careful consideration and I am fully cognizant of the problem which confronts you and your client.

I regret to inform you, however, that it has been a long-standing policy of this Bureau not to grant a clearance to any person and I am, therefore, unable to assist you in the manner which you suggest.

May I suggest, however, that inasmuch as this Bureau has primary investigative jurisdiction of matters concerning the internal security of our country, it is considered advisable that your client furnish our Los Angeles office with details concerning his membership in the Communist Party together with the nature of the party activities during that period. . . .

Hayden went to the Los Angeles FBI in the fall of 1950 and made a complete statement of his activities in the Communist Party. In March, 1951, he was subpoenaed by the House Committee on Un-American Activities and named a number of others he had known as Communists.

Gang's further involvement rested on a series of coincidences. Subpoenas had also been served on Abe Burrows, the Broadway-Hollywood musical writer, Meta Reis Rosenberg, a former screen editor, and Richard Collins. Like Hayden, each of these three asked Gang to represent them. Burrows had previously been a client; Mrs. Rosenberg's husband was one of Gang's clients; and Collins' wife was related to one of the partners in Gang's firm. Prior to the 1951 hearings Gang made a number of trips to Washington to ascertain what attitude the Committee would take toward Hayden and his other clients.

Gang says that he did not agree with the Committee's insistence on "public exposure" but was satisfied that the Committee staff were "decent people" and advised his clients to testify fully. Following the appearance of these first clients, he began to represent others before the Committee. In time, studio workers who had to appear before the Committee began coming to him for advice. Somewhat to his own surprise, Gang says, he became a pioneer lawyer in the Age of Investigations. Since 1951 he has represented or advised close to 50 people called by the House Committee, 20 of whom were from the motion-picture industry. Some had been regular clients, while others were referred to him by studios, theatrical agents and other lawyers.

In addition to the clients he represented before the House Committee, Gang also advocated the cause of 25 others who had never been Communists but found they were being blacklisted in the studios. Gang pleaded their case with the studio executives, with Roy Brewer, and with others who had to be satisfied that these people, despite their "front" records, were trustworthy. "They had no way to put themselves on record, like those who *had* been Communists and were able to testify before the Committee," Gang recently told a reporter. "They were in a tough spot. The Committee would not hear them because they had nothing to tell so they couldn't clear themselves. Somebody had to go to bat for them and I did."*

Gang became known in Hollywood as a "clearance lawyer." It was no secret that he was on intimate terms with the staff of the House Committee. Committee members were grateful to him because he had persuaded two of the first key witnesses to testify (Meta Reis Rosenberg's and Richard Collins' knowledge of the Party's activities was extensive) and advised all his clients to cooperate fully. Word got around that the Committee tended to make the ordeal somewhat easier for Gang's clients, and he was frequently sought out.

The attorney recalls only two potential clients who refused to accept his advice to testify. One was a movie director who wanted

* Hollywood has long been flooded with stories that Martin Gang "sells clearances" and has grown rich on the profits. The stories are untrue. Gang, whose fees as one of the top theatrical lawyers in the business are normally high, does not claim to have worked for nothing. But he estimates that in terms of his time he has lost about $50,000 as a result of activities as a "clearance" lawyer, since many of his clients were unable to pay his regular fees.

to cooperate with the Committee but was dissuaded by his wife. The other, a screenwriter, kept a memorandum of what happened in Gang's office. This is what he wrote:

"My agent informed me that inquiry here and there at different studios had convinced her that I was not employable in the industry. Her advice to me was to find some way to clear myself. She told me that this could be done with the help of attorney Martin Gang. My reply was that inasmuch as I was opposed to any kind of political screening in order to secure work, and inasmuch as such screening was forbidden by law,* I did not want to engage in any kind of subterfuge which would only result in one individual's escaping the blacklist while the blacklist itself and the principle involved would not be touched. But on my agent's repeated urging that I might at least investigate what plan Martin Gang had, I accepted.

"On Wednesday, October 17, 1951, accompanied by my wife so that I might later be in a position to discuss with her whatever suggestions or terms Martin Gang might propose, I went to Mr. Gang's office. . . .

"Mr. Gang began by rejecting the use of the word 'blacklist.' Again and again he stopped me during our conversation to make me use another word. There was no blacklist, he asserted repeatedly. The studios had no blacklist, but certain organizations did have lists of names and had announced that they would picket any theatre showing pictures on which any of these names appeared. Since such picketing would result in loss of income as a result of

---

* There is a California Act setting forth that "no employer shall coerce or influence or attempt to coerce or influence his employees through or by means of threat of discharge or loss of employment to adopt or follow or refrain from adopting or following any particular course or line of political action or political activity." The California Supreme Court, however, has decided that this statute does not prohibit an employer's discharging persons whose loyalty to the nation has not been established to the satisfaction of the employer, because disloyalty or "subversive" activity is not a protected "political activity."

diminished attendance, the banks had come to the decision not to lend money for the production of any pictures which used people whose names were on any of these lists. Since studios could not produce pictures without financing from banks, they were therefore unable to employ anyone on these lists.

"Mr. Gang's connection with this situation was not very clearly stated. He explained his interest in my difficulty as due to a desire to 'help.' He said he was privately rich and therefore the matter of fee would be a secondary consideration. He even declared that he was opposed to methods employed by the Committee on Un-American Activities, expressing himself particularly severely against the Committee's use of the expression 'hiding behind the Fifth Amendment,' as if the Constitution had not been designed precisely for the protection of every citizen's right.

"But Mr. Gang felt that one could not oppose the 'unemployable' lists by any direct method. War was coming on and to oppose the Committee and these lists could only lead to the concentration camp. He assured me that this was where I was headed if I didn't clear myself. Moreover any hope I might have of writing for other media was vain, for these organizations and their lists were going to move into all fields, radio, television, book and magazine publication and so forth.

"Apparently, according to Mr. Gang, there was no blacklist, and yet it was possible to get off this list. How did one clear oneself? Mr. Gang told me that I must prepare myself for questioning, and I must do so with great thoroughness. I must make a full list of all my activities, all my associations, all my writings, all my articles, speeches, meetings, lectures, contributions, subscriptions, to any and all movements no matter how slightly radical or innocent I might think them to be, and for this purpose I had better go through all my files, all my correspondence, all my checkbooks. How far back? As far as I could possibly go, was Mr. Gang's answer.

90

"I called to Mr. Gang's attention that all names I might bring into this questioning would be immediately subject to blacklisting in their turn, and that I might thus involve a lot of names of absolutely innocent secretaries, friends, employees, also persons long since departed from any association with any so-called subversive activities, and that furthermore since no man's memory is perfect, particularly mine, I might subject families and children to financial difficulties and indeed real hardship, and that I could not saddle my soul with such offenses, and that since people who might be accused through me were not genuinely accused of any crime for which they would have a right to defend themselves in a court, with all the rights that our law gives to the accused, but would be immediately presumed guilty, that such action on my part would be tantamount to violating the Ninth Commandment against bearing false witness, and that I could not as a religious person see myself doing anything of this kind.

"It seemed to me, I told Mr. Gang, that those who accused me of subversive activities ought to avail themselves of the law of the land and bring me to court charged with specific wrong-doing and bring forward their evidence. Indeed, I challenged anyone to accuse me of any kind of treasonous activity, or the violation of any law. Mr. Gang said this was not the point. And he went through the same old argument: there were lists, and the studios needed financing and these organizations declared they would picket certain theatres and therefore the banks couldn't lend money and I was therefore 'unemployable.'

"I said to Mr. Gang that as far as my own activities were concerned, I would be glad to tell anyone about them, for I had nothing to hide, but that I could not show my files and give him names, unless ordered to do so by a regularly constituted court. Mr. Gang's argument was that I could not avoid mentioning names. When the raisin cake is opened, said he, the raisins are there."

The Mass Hearings

HOLLYWOOD REACTED to news of the impending investigation in 1951 with something like panic. A *Life* reporter wired her editor at the time that the movie people put her in mind of "a group of marooned sailors on a flat desert island watching the approach of a tidal wave." The industry was not sure it could take another investigation, which would inevitably bring on more "revelations" and bad publicity and might mean picket lines around the nation's movie houses. To add to this anxiety, business was spectacularly bad. In 1946 domestic film rental stood at a dizzy $400 million; weekly movie attendance climbed to an all-time record of 80 million. But by 1951 television was a going thing and movie attendance was in the lower depths of a decline that finally, about February 1953, levelled off at 46 million.

In the lush days of World War II movie companies had expanded enormously, buying up vast studio facilities and adding to their rosters of high-priced talent. All the major studios had stockpiled costly films. Things looked black indeed. Although the slump lasted for seven years, its most severe effects were felt in the period between Congressional probes. These were years marked by big lay-offs and frequent theater closings. The movie companies were finding it difficult to get bank credit and dreaded the consequences of political controversy. What banker in his right mind would put up the money for a picture that might be picketed because one of its stars had the habit of signing petitions? Trouble had piled up on trouble for the moviemakers. When the government won an anti-trust action and theater chains were separated from their distributor-producer owners, the industry — as *Fortune* magazine put it — "began to feel like a man with a loud humming sound in his head."

In March, 1951, just before the hearings began, *Variety* reported that in New York, Joyce O'Hara, acting president of the Motion Picture Association, had met with studio advertising and publicity heads and announced that movie people who did not firmly deny communistic ties would find it "difficult" to get work in the studios after the hearings closed. The Association had no intention of repeating the mistakes that had made Hollywood look foolish in 1947.

The House Committee on Un-American Activities was different too. In December, 1949, J. Parnell Thomas was convicted of payroll padding and was later reunited with members of the Hollywood Ten in prison. If the film industry managed to salvage any consolation from that, it was short-lived. For this time the Committee returned to the subject of Communism-in-Hollywood under new auspices (Georgia's John S. Wood had succeeded Thomas as chairman) and vastly changed circumstances.

In 1947 the wartime friendship between the U.S. and Russia was still a fresh memory. By 1951 U.S. soldiers were at war in Korea with the forces of two Communist powers and the Cold War with Russia was at its height. With the Hiss-Chambers, Klaus Fuchs and Judith Coplon cases behind it, the nation was becoming ever more security-conscious and, in the opinion of many, was afflicted with a bad case of political jitters. A Senator named McCarthy was becoming a front-page fixture. And, above all, the House Committee itself had a spanking new policy implemented by the Committee's new research director, an ex-FBI man named Raphael I. Nixon. Nixon, comparing the 1947 with the later hearings not long ago, commended Parnell Thomas' work but said it was unfortunate that in 1947 the Committee had focussed its attack on movie content, "the weakest argument."

93

Parnell Thomas' pursuit of Communist propaganda in films admittedly had led the Committee up a blind alley.* In Nixon's opinion, the 1947 Committee could have centered a more pertinent and fruitful enquiry on the "prestige, position and money" the Communist Party picked up in Hollywood. And that is what the Committee went looking for in 1951.

Hollywood was chosen for a "broad base investigation," Nixon explained to a reporter, because of the volume of cooperation the Committee got there. But a critical Democratic Congressman whose district borders on the movie capital once suggested another reason. "The yearning for publicity on the part of some members of the Committee," he said, "could only be satisfied by the famous names a movie hearing would produce." Nixon recognizes that such charges were made against the Committee but argues that it was the newspapers rather than the Committee itself which put the emphasis on big names. "We couldn't overlook our responsibilities just because prominent people were involved."

By 1951, a number of prominent persons were begging the Committee for a chance to testify and the Committee had to disappoint some of them. There were, first of all, the ex-Communists, who by now looked upon the hearings as the only public forum open to them. If they wanted to prove to the world that they had broken with the Party, they had to testify. And until they did prove this, they were unemployable in the studios. The Committee welcomed them. But another class — persons who had never belonged to the Communist Party but suffered from unfavorable rumors — were also eager to go on record as anti-Communist. Many wanted to be heard but, according to Nixon, Edward G. Robinson, Jose Ferrer

---

* At the close of the 1947 hearings, J. Parnell Thomas announced that "at the present time the committee has a special staff making an extensive study of Communist propaganda in various motion pictures." The study was abandoned. Thomas also announced that at the next hearing the Committee would have "a number of witnesses who will deal with propaganda in the films and techniques employed." These witnesses never materialized.

and the late John Garfield were the only three called where the Committee had no proof of Party membership, past or present. Robinson requested a hearing. Garfield and Ferrer were subpoenaed because they had been "the subject of considerable interest on the part of private organizations."

At first the Committee wanted Garfield and Ferrer to testify in private session. "But," Nixon said, "we were catching it all over — from George Sokolsky, Victor Riesel and even from Ed Sullivan. No one came right out in print and said so, but there were intimations of payoffs. Mr. Moulder [Congressman from Missouri] was subjected to criticism for stating that he thought Garfield was all right." Nixon also recalls that at the time some inexperienced anti-Communist groups were given to making loose, unsubstantiated charges, and the Committee drew fire for not acting on the "leads" these groups provided. From the other extremity, the Committee was attacked for "establishing blacklists."

Whether or not the Committee was interested in "establishing blacklists," it is now beyond question that many who testified (or who refused to testify) found themselves "unemployable" after they appeared as uncooperative witnesses before the Committee. During the scattered movie hearings of 1951, 90 Hollywood figures, almost all well-established in their careers, appeared on the witness stand. They took a variety of positions. Ferrer and Garfield swore that they had never been Party members; their names did not appear in the Committee's long lists of unfriendly witnesses published later. Thirty others, like novelist Budd Schulberg and Sterling Hayden, said they had been Party members and named people they knew as Communists. Their names appeared in the Committee's 1952 Annual Report as "Individuals who, through the knowledge gained through their own past membership in the Communist Party, have been of invaluable assistance to the Committee and the American people in supplying facts relating to Communist efforts and success in infiltrating the motion-picture industry."

One of these witnesses, screenwriter Martin Berkeley, named 162 persons he swore he knew as members of the Communist Party. His list included Dorothy Parker, who had spent some time in Hollywood as a screenwriter, Donald Ogden Stewart, Dashiell Hammett, Lillian Hellman, Edward Chodorov, writer-producer, and Michael Gordon, now a Broadway producer. Berkeley had originally been named before the Committee by Richard Collins. Berkeley later testified that after he learned Collins mentioned him, he sent a "very silly" telegram to the Committee. "I charged Mr. Collins with perjury and said I'd never been a member of the Communist Party, which was not true. I was not at that time a member and have not been for many years. [Berkeley left the Party in 1943.] Why I sent the telegram — I did it in a moment of panic and was a damn fool." But before Berkeley realized his "foolishness" and admitted there was truth to Collins' charge, several friends had begun to organize a defense fund for him. This campaign was under way when Berkeley sheepishly admitted that Collins had told the truth.*

Berkeley joined the Motion Picture Alliance for the Preservation of American Ideals after his sensational testimony and became a leading figure in the organization. An MPA spokesman said not long ago that the group relied more on Martin Berkeley than on any of its other members to identify Communists and "Communist sympathizers" in the movie industry.

During the hearings that followed the 1951 sessions, other co-operative witnesses who provided names for the House Committee included actor Lee J. Cobb, director Elia Kazan and playwright Clifford Odets.

---

* In later years Berkeley was cited by columnist George Sokolsky as a prime example of an anti-Communist who suffered unemployment for cooperating with the Committee. Many in Hollywood, however, believe that by his erratic behavior Berkeley had made himself unpopular and it was this rather than his anti-communism *per se* which caused his difficulties.

A list of 324 names was made available to the public by the House Committee in its 1952 and '53 Annual Reports. Names of those cited as Communists by cooperative witnesses were listed alphabetically. Everyone cited was blacklisted in the studios. But methods varied from studio to studio and from person to person, perhaps to avoid the "illegal conspiracy" which Paul V. McNutt warned against in 1947.

If the named people were under contract when they were identified or called to testify, their contracts were cancelled, bought up, or simply not renewed. If they were free-lance workers, usually their agents told them they could no longer find work for them, and they stopped receiving "calls." Most were urged by their agents or studio executives to "clear" themselves of the charges made against them, either by testifying fully before the Committee or putting themselves in the hands of Roy Brewer or Martin Gang.

Larry Parks was the first Hollywood witness who decided to admit he had been a Communist. Parks was under the impression that it would be possible for him to testify without being required to name others he had known as Communists. While he was on the stand, Committee Counsel Frank Tavenner read off a list of names and asked the actor to tell what he knew about them. Parks hesitated. Then Congressman Charles Potter of Michigan and Committee Chairman Wood took turns with Tavenner in explaining to Parks why he had to involve others.

Congressman Wood told Parks ". . . I for one am rather curious to understand just what the reasons are in your mind for declining to answer the question." Potter added, "Now, I assume you share the belief that we share that an active member of the Communist Party believes in principles that we don't believe in, in overthrowing our Government by force and violence. Now, you say you would readily give information concerning a man you have knowledge has committed murder. Wouldn't you also give information to the proper authorities of a man you knew or a woman you knew or believed to be working to overthrow our Government by force and violence?" The actor pointed out that it was not yet illegal to be a Communist, but Potter answered: "So when we are drafting men to fight Communist aggression, you feel that it is not your duty as an American citizen to give the committee the benefit of what knowledge you might have . . ." Parks replied: "Well, yes; I wanted to do that. I think that there is a difference, Congressman, in my opinion. There is a difference between people who would harm our country and people who in my opinion are like myself, who, as I feel, did nothing wrong at the time . . ."

Congressman Francis E. Walter of Pennsylvania (later chairman of the Committee) came to the actor's rescue: "How can it be material to the purpose of this inquiry," he asked, "to have the names of people when we already know them? Aren't we actually, by insisting that this man testify as to names, overlooking the fact that we want to know what the organization did, what it hoped to accomplish, how it actually had or attempted to influence the thinking of the American people through the arts? So why is it so essential that we know the names of all the people when we have a witness who may make a contribution to what we are trying to learn?"

Tavenner answered Walter: "Although there is information relating to some of these individuals as to whom I had expected to interrogate this witness, some of them have evaded service of process, so that we cannot bring them here. That is one point. Another is that this committee ought to be entitled to receive proof of information which it has in its files as a result of its previous investigation relating to a matter of this kind. There would be no way to really investigate Communist infiltration into labor without asking who are Communists in labor. And the same thing is true here in Hollywood. Those are the reasons I think it is material."

Larry Parks made a last desperate plea: "Don't present me with

98

the choice of either being in contempt of this committee and going to jail or forcing me to really crawl through the mud to be an informer, for what purpose? I don't think this is a choice at all. I don't think this is really sportsmanlike. I don't think this is American justice. . . . I think it will impair the usefulness of this Committee to a great extent, because it will make it almost impossible for a person to come to you, as I have done, and open himself to you and tell you the truth. So I beg of you not to force me to do this."

Tavenner's reply is often cited as proof that the Committee was "compiling a blacklist."*

"Mr. Parks," he said, "there was a statement you made this morning in the course of your testimony which interested me a great deal. This is what you said: 'This is a great industry . . . It has a very important job to do, to entertain people; in certain respects to call attention to certain evils, but mainly to entertain.' Now, do you believe that persons who are in a position to call attention to certain evils ought to be persons who are dedicated to the principles of democracy as we understand them in this country? . . . What is your opinion as to whether or not members of the Communist Party should be in positions of power and influence in the

---

* In its 1953 Annual Report, the Committee noted that, as a result of its work, and the greater "cooperation" received from the motion-picture industry, "it can be stated on considerable authority that perhaps no major industry in the world today employs fewer members of the Communist Party than does the motion-picture industry." It went on then to acknowledge that ". . . particularly those individuals who have been identified under oath before the committee as one-time members of the Communist Party and who, in turn, invoked the fifth amendment in refusing to testify, have charged that the committee is compiling a 'black list.'"

"The absurdity of this charge is obvious when it is considered that these individuals, of their own accord and volition, joined the Communist conspiracy, and that it is on their own personal determination that they have refused to affirm or deny sworn testimony placing them in the Communist Party."

The Committee seemed to be describing how and why a "black list" was compiled, rather than how "absurd" it was to say that such a list did result from its hearings.

various unions which control the writing of scripts, the actors, and various other things which we have mentioned during the course of this hearing? . . ." Parks answered by agreeing with Tavenner that such people should not be "in any position of power" in the industry. Tavenner went further: "Or to influence the course which [the industry] takes?" Parks agreed again. "Then," Tavenner said, "we will ask your cooperation before this hearing is over in helping us to ascertain those who are or have been members of the Communist Party, *for that particular purpose* which we have mentioned." (Emphasis added.) Larry Parks, in executive testimony, later offered the Committee the names it sought.

Reticence similar to Parks' was expressed by playwright Lillian Hellman. After she received her subpoena, she wrote to the Committee:

DEAR MR. WOOD:

As you know, I am under subpoena to appear before your committee on May 21, 1952.

I am most willing to answer all questions about myself. I have nothing to hide from your committee and there is nothing in my life of which I am ashamed. I have been advised by counsel that under the fifth amendment I have a constitutional privilege to decline to answer any questions about my political opinions, activities, and associations, on the grounds of self-incrimination. I do not wish to claim this privilege. I am ready and willing to testify before the representatives of our Government as to my own opinions and my own actions, regardless of any risks or consequences to myself.

But I am advised by counsel that if I answer the committee's questions about myself, I must also answer questions about other people and that if I refuse to do so, I can be cited for contempt. My counsel tells me that if I answer questions about myself, I will have waived my rights under the fifth amendment and could be forced legally to answer questions about others. This is very difficult for a layman to understand: But there is one principle that I do understand: I am not willing, now or in the future, to bring bad trouble to people who, in my past association with them, were completely innocent of any talk or any action that was disloyal or subversive. I do not like subversion or dis-

100

loyalty in any form and if I had ever seen any I would have considered it my duty to have reported it to the proper authorities. But to hurt innocent people whom I knew many years ago in order to save myself is, to me, inhuman and indecent, and dishonorable. I cannot and will not cut my conscience to fit this year's fashions, even though I long ago came to the conclusion that I was not a political person and could have no comfortable place in any political group.

I was raised in an old-fashioned American tradition and there were certain homely things that were taught to me: To try to tell the truth, not to bear false witness, not to harm my neighbor, to be loyal to my country, and so on. In general, I respected these ideals of Christian honor and did as well with them as I knew how. It is my belief that you will agree with these simple rules of human decency and will not expect me to violate the good American tradition from which they spring. I would, therefore, like to come before you and speak of myself.

I am prepared to waive the privilege against self-incrimination and to tell you everything you wish to know about my views or actions if your committee will agree to refrain from asking me to name other people. If the committee is unwilling to give me this assurance, I will be forced to plead the privilege of the fifth amendment at the hearing.

In his reply, the Chairman advised Miss Hellman that "the Committee cannot permit witnesses to set forth the terms under which they will testify."

In her testimony later, Miss Hellman invoked the Fifth Amendment.

In 1951 and '52, the Committee issued subpoenas in batches of 15 or 20 to actors, writers, story editors, screen analysts, producers and directors. The economic pressure to become a cooperative witness was not only implicit in the spreading blacklist, it was underscored by the apparent collaboration between studio executives and House investigators. Subpoenas were delivered in dressing rooms and in the legal offices of studios, though home addresses were known to the investigators who served the subpoenas. Many at first did not admit that they had received subpoenas. Later, as the numbers grew, the subpoenaed grouped together, raised money

101

for lawyers' fees and formed classes for legal consultation. A sense of shock was experienced by many when they were subpoenaed. One person described it this way:

Even though you know what takes place in that committee, you are so accustomed to respecting government in all its forms that your fear is enormous. Intellectually, you understand what's happening, but you can't control the fear. An insidious form of self-guilt sets in. You accept the views of the committee in spite of yourself. It's quite bewildering. Afterwards, you find yourself guarded and evasive whatever you do, wherever you go.

By the time the 1951-52 hearings were well under way, the Smith Act had been held valid by the Supreme Court.* Some of those subpoenaed in the spring of 1951 did not know whether they would be jailed or not. They knew that if they failed to cooperate with the Committee there was absolute certainty that they would be blacklisted. The only real question, then, was what defense they might use to avoid imprisonment. The Ten had been jailed after depending fruitlessly on the First Amendment, and no other de-

---

* Smith Act (Alien Registration Act of 1940) provides the following:
Sec. 2. (a) It shall be unlawful for any person —

1. to knowingly or willfully advocate, abet, advise, or teach the duty, necessity, desirability, or propriety of overthrowing or destroying any government in the United States by force or violence, . . .

2. with the intent to cause the overthrow or destruction of any government in the United States, to print, publish, edit, issue, circulate, sell, distribute, or publicly display any written or printed matter advocating, advising, or teaching the duty, necessity, desirability, or propriety of overthrowing or destroying any government in the United States by force or violence;

3. to organize or help to organize any society, group, or assembly of persons who teach, advocate, or encourage the overthrow or destruction of any government in the United States by force or violence; or to be or become a member of, or affiliate with, any such society, group, or assembly of persons, knowing the purposes thereof.
Sec. 3. It shall be unlawful for any person to attempt to commit, or to conspire to commit, any of the acts prohibited by the provisions of this title.

All prosecutions under the Act have been on the basis of Section Three (conspiracy to advocate). After the release of the first group convicted under the Smith Act during the Foley Square Trial, the Government announced its intention to charge them with Section Two, part 3.

fense from a contempt charge for declining to answer questions before a Congressional committee had been definitely established. The Fifth Amendment, with its clause protecting a witness against self-incrimination, appeared to many to be their only safe course.

This, however, carried with it a serious disadvantage. In 1950, the Supreme Court had decided in *Rogers* v. *U.S.* that a witness could not refuse to answer a question about the Party under the Fifth Amendment, once he had admitted Party membership. Since the Committee made it clear during the Larry Parks hearing that after a man had admitted Party membership he was expected to name others he had known as Communists, witnesses who would not name others but wanted to stay out of jail had the choice of either denying Party membership and running the risk of perjury indictments, or of refusing to answer the question at all.*

This meant that they also had to remain silent about accusations of disloyalty, espionage and conspiracy which they were anxious to deny. Two witnesses named as one-time members of the Party, for example, insist they can prove they were serving overseas in the Armed Services when, according to the testimony of the House Committee hearings, they were supposed to be attending Communist Party meetings in Hollywood.

To prepare witnesses and to keep them from answering questions that might cause them to lose their immunity privilege under the Fifth Amendment, teams of lawyers rehearsed their Hollywood clients by simulating the examinations they would be put to on the witness stand. Variations of the Fifth Amendment position were developed. For instance, Carl Foreman, who was the writer and associate producer of "High Noon," invoked what later became known as the "diminished Fifth." He denied that he was a Party member at the time he was testifying but would not answer the

---

* It is beyond the competence and legal knowledge of the author of this report to venture an opinion on whether they were justified, according to this reasoning, to resort to the Fifth Amendment.

question as to whether he had been a Party member at some previous date. Another variation was employed by producer Robert Rossen ("All the King's Men," "Body and Soul," "The Brave Bulls"). The first time he testified, Rossen invoked what came to be known as the "augmented Fifth." He said that he was not a member of the Communist Party, that he was "not sympathetic with it or its aims," but declined to say whether he had ever been a Party member in the past. Eventually, though, those who invoked variations on the Fifth Amendment position found themselves as thoroughly unemployable in Hollywood as those who simply "took the Fifth," as the position came to be described.

Tension gradually increased in Hollywood. Once it was clear that the hearings were not to be stopped before the Committee had unearthed every available witness who could provide it with names, pressure to give cooperative testimony was exerted on all sides. Families were divided. Some of the "unfriendly" witnesses moved to new neighborhoods to avoid the ostracism they felt certain they would meet once their testimony was publicized.

Among the prominent Hollywood figures subpoenaed by the Committee was Sidney Buchman, a Columbia producer. Buchman had been an executive assistant to Harry Cohn, in charge of production at Columbia. He wrote the screen plays for "Mr. Smith Goes to Washington" and "Here Comes Mr. Jordan," produced "The Jolson Story" and wrote and produced "Jolson Sings Again." As a Columbia executive Buchman had worked on films featuring many of Hollywood's top stars. When he testified before the Committee on September 25, 1951, he took a position many unfriendly witnesses say they too might have taken had they believed the penalties would be as light as those later inflicted on Buchman.

Buchman testified that he had been a Communist but refused to name anyone he had known in the Party. He did exactly the thing which, according to precedent, should have meant a contempt citation. Observers were puzzled, until it was noted that Congressman Donald Jackson, California Republican, had left the hearing room in the course of Buchman's testimony but before the producer had refused to answer questions. This left the Committee without a quorum and, consequently, unable to issue a contempt citation against Buchman for his refusal to give full testimony. Buchman's lawyer noted the lack of a quorum at the conclusion of the testimony.

Public curiosity about Buchman's good fortune was expressed in various sections of the press. The Committee served Buchman with another subpoena, but this time he did not appear at the appointed time and was cited for contempt of Congress. On March 17, 1952, Buchman was indicted on two counts of contempt — for having failed to appear on January 25 and again on January 28. One count was later thrown out because Buchman had been cited twice on the basis of a single summons.

On March 25 District Judge T. Blake Kennedy in Washington, D. C. fixed the bond at $1,000 after the movie producer had been arraigned and pleaded not guilty. On May 9 a motion to dismiss the indictment was filed, argued and denied. Ten months later, jurors were sworn and the trial started March 9, 1953. On March 10 a judgment of acquittal was entered on the first count. On March 12 the jury delivered a verdict of guilty. The jury was polled and Buchman was permitted to remain on bond pending sentence. On March 16, 1953, Judge Kennedy sentenced Buchman to pay a fine of $150. The court suspended imposition of a prison sentence, and the defendant was placed on probation for a period of one year.

Edward Bennett Williams, Buchman's lawyer, says that Congressman Jackson left the hearing room at the fortuitous time because he had to drive Senator Potter of Michigan, a guest in his home, to the airport. Williams claims that the reason Buchman got off with such a light sentence was that the jury had been deadlocked, so the judge delivered what is known as an Allen charge:

the judge was required to inform the minority in the jury to re-member that the majority was acting according to its best lights and then to turn to the majority and repeat the same admonition in favor of the minority. However, says Williams, Judge Kennedy, for some unaccountable reason, became confused and delivered both charges to the minority members of the jury. After the judge realized this, he felt constrained to prevent any further complica-tions in the case and decided to let Buchman off with a light sentence.

Buchman no longer works in the motion-picture industry and is engaged in other business in New York City.

The first witness from Hollywood to invoke the Fifth Amend-ment was an actor named Howard Da Silva, who is as well-known on Broadway as in Hollywood. Da Silva had appeared in the origi-nal cast of "Oklahoma!," in "Waiting for Lefty," "Golden Boy," "A Doll's House" and "Abe Lincoln in Illinois." For years he had moved back and forth between the Hollywood studios and the New York stage. In 1939 he went to Hollywood for the film ver-sion of "Abe Lincoln in Illinois." From then until March, 1951, when he appeared before the House Committee, he played in about 40 films, working at all the major studios and serving under con-tracts for periods at Warner Brothers and Paramount. He appeared in "The Lost Weekend," "The Great Gatsby," and "Keeper of the Flame," among others. His income showed a continuous increase from 1939 to 1951.

During his 1947 testimony, Robert Taylor said he did not know whether Da Silva was a Communist but that he "always has some-thing to say at the wrong time" at meetings of the Screen Actors Guild. After that, Da Silva had trouble. Between 1947 and '51, he changed agents four times in an attempt to improve his lot. Again and again, his agents reported that film executives said, "We can't hire him — he's too hot." Da Silva managed to make some films after 1947 and even completed a co-starring role after he was subpoenaed. But on March 21, 1951, he appeared before the House Committee and said, "I object to being called to testify against myself in this hearing. I object because the First and Fifth Amendment and all of the Bill of Rights protect me from any inquisitorial procedure and I may not be compelled to cooperate with this Committee in producing evidence designed to incriminate me and to drive me from my profession as an actor."

After that Da Silva found no more work in Hollywood. He returned to New York and found roles in a few radio shows, but he was removed from this medium too, almost immediately. His agent told him that the William Morris agency, which packaged a show he had been on, had received six letters from American Legion posts objecting to Da Silva's appearance.

Da Silva tried to return to Broadway, but again he ran into serious trouble. Two potential "angels" raised objections when he read for roles and once a producer told him pointblank: "We can't use you because the theater will be picketed. It is a case of blacklist but I can't help it."

Witnesses who invoked the Fifth Amendment were banished from the studios in a variety of ways. Most studio executives, remembering Paul V. McNutt's warning about the illegality of an industry-wide "conspiracy," took pains to conceal the reasons for firings. Howard Hughes, then chief at RKO, furnished an exception. Paul Jarrico, a screenwriter, was working at the Hughes studio at the time he invoked the Fifth Amendment before the House Committee on April 13, 1951. Jarrico recently described his subsequent experiences in Hollywood this way:

"In my case the evidence that I was blacklisted was simple and unmistakable. On March 23, 1951, I was subpoenaed to appear before the House Committee on Un-American Activities. The serving of the subpoena was publicized by the Los Angeles press, most of the newspapers quoting me accurately as saying I was not certain yet what my position before the Committee would be, but 'if I have to choose between crawling in the mud with Larry Parks or going to jail like my courageous friends of the Hollywood Ten, I shall certainly choose the latter.'

"I was fired from my employment as a screenwriter at RKO that very day, forbidden to come onto the studio lot even to pick up my personal belongings. I appeared before the Committee on April 13, 1951, and was a most unfriendly witness. I not only exercised my privilege under the Fifth Amendment, I assailed the Committee for trying to subvert the American Constitution.

"I was subsequently informed by my agents, the Jaffe Agency, that there were no further possibilities of my employment in the motion-picture industry, and on June 20, 1951, at their request, I released them from the obligation of representing me. Though I had worked as a screenwriter more or less steadily for almost 14 years prior to the date on which I was subpoenaed, I have not been employed by any Hollywood studio since.

"In the Spring of 1952, I became involved in a highly publicized legal controversy with Howard Hughes. As head of RKO, he had arbitrarily removed my name from a film called 'The Las Vegas Story,' which had been my last writing assignment at RKO. I had been awarded a screen credit on this film by the Screen Writers Guild, which, under its collective-bargaining agreement, had exclusive authority to determine writing credits.

"Hughes sued me for declaratory relief, asserting that I had violated the morals clause by my stand before the Committee. I filed a cross complaint, asking for damages. The Screen Writers Guild sued Hughes independently for breaching the collective security agreement. Hughes won, both as against the Guild and me. Successive appeals of the Guild were defeated and the Guild finally accepted a compromise in which it gave up its hard-won authority to determine credits solely on the basis of literary contribution. My appeals were also denied.

108

"In the course of these suits and in the public statements surrounding them, Hughes made it very clear that he maintained and intended to maintain a political blacklist. *The New York Times* reported on April 7, 1952, that RKO 'will operate on a curtailed production basis for an indefinite period . . . in a drastic move for time to strengthen a political "screening" program to prevent employment of persons suspected of being Communists or having Communist sympathies.' The *Times* quoted Hughes further as asserting that 'every one' of eleven stories, selected as the best for filming out of 150 read by the studio over a period of six months, had to be discarded because 'information concerning one or more persons involved in the past writing of the script or original story showed that those writers were suspected of Communist ideas or sympathies.' Added Hughes: 'All studios have at their disposal information concerning the people who have been connected with one or more of the well-known Communist front organizations.' "

At a meeting of the Motion Picture Alliance on May 15, 1952, according to the Los Angeles *Daily News,* Roy Brewer declared that not one of the witnesses who "hid behind the Fifth Amendment" in the previous year and a half of hearings had subsequently been offered employment in the film industry. Later, it became apparent in Hollywood that workers who were named as Communists but had neither been called to testify nor come forth to answer the charges made against them, were also blacklisted. Brewer confirmed this, too, in another public statement. In answer to a charge in *Frontier* magazine that he was "strawboss of the purge," Brewer replied that the only blacklist he knew of was the list "established by the House Committee on Un-American Activities containing names of persons who have not repudiated that [Communist] association by comparable testimony."

Though 324 people had been named between 1951 and 1954, when Hollywood's "mass hearings" ended, they were not all motion-picture workers. Some had left town years before they were named, others were wives of studio employees, others were trade-union or Communist Party functionaries who had never held jobs in the industry. But, when these people are eliminated from the list of those named, 212 remain who were active motion-picture workers, many of whom had never made their living in any other industry. These 212 do not work in the industry today, though there is a small *sub-rosa* effort on the part of a few producers to buy the services of some of them (at cut-rate prices!) and present their work to the public under some other name.

The blacklisting proceeded through 1951, '52 and '53. Those dropped by the studios were not limited to persons who could influence film content, or who would receive screen credit for their work. The industry had accepted the Committee's new emphasis on "prestige, position and money."

For example, there is the case of composer Sol Kaplan, who had scored more than 30 pictures in Hollywood between 1940 and 1953. Kaplan received a subpoena while he was working on a 20th Century-Fox sound stage. He had never been publicly identified as a Communist. John Garfield, who denied before the Committee that he had ever been a Communist, said in the course of his testimony that Kaplan was a friend of his. Though Kaplan had been under contract to 20th Century-Fox for one year, he was fired when this happened. Later he was reinstated on a week-to-week "probation" basis after he protested that many top studio executives (including the man who was firing him) were also friends of Garfield. Kaplan was subpoenaed in April, 1953. Shortly before he was scheduled to testify, a Fox business executive in charge of the music department told him that his job, despite economy firings, was safe. During his testimony, on April 8, 1953, Kaplan challenged the Committee to produce his accusers and invoked almost the entire Bill of Rights when he refused to cooperate.

After the hearing, he returned to work at 20th Century-Fox.

The musician says that his colleagues looked surprised when they saw him in the studio. Nothing happened the first day, but on the second he was told to call one of Fox's top producers. The producer, who was a friend of Kaplan, told him that Darryl Zanuck, production chief of the studio, did not want to fire him. Congressman Clyde Doyle, Democratic member of the Committee, the producer said, did not believe that Kaplan was a Communist. If Kaplan would appear privately before Doyle — which could be "arranged" — he might be able to keep his job at Fox. The producer added that "no one would even know you spoke to Doyle." Kaplan said that he would not consider taking such a position because he did not believe in "deals" where important principles were concerned. Fifteen minutes later he received a telephone call from the same executive who had assured him that his job would be safe in case of economy firings. A new order had made Kaplan's dismissal necessary, the executive told him. When Kaplan pressed him, the studio executive finally admitted that the musician was being fired for political reasons.

If the unfriendly witnesses before the Committee suffered social ostracism and loss of employment, the cooperative witnesses also paid a price. Not only Communists but many non-Communists looked upon them as "informers" (or, as they were described in the official Communist press, as "stool pigeons"). Everyone in the movie colony had seen the British officer contemptuously push the money across the table with his swagger stick in John Ford's classic "The Informer." Everyone remembered how Victor McLaglen, as the Irish Judas, had picked it up. Also, many Hollywood liberals were bitter about the uses to which, in earlier days, the Communists had diverted their innocent good will to Party causes. Now, when they saw some of these same people playing the "informer" role, they found even more reason to turn on them. The remaining Communists did all they could to encourage the feeling.

111

For those who supplied the Committee with the names it wanted, social life became extremely difficult. Richard Collins, for instance, remembers going to a Screen Writers Guild meeting after he testified where only a half dozen persons were willing to speak to him. Meta Reis Rosenberg recalls being denounced as a "stool pigeon" by someone who shouted from the balcony of a La Cienega Boulevard art gallery. Many of the "friendly" witnesses tell stories of how they were insulted and avoided. The wife of one witness says that the only people who offered any sympathy or financial help during this period were members of the Motion Picture Alliance for the Preservation of American Ideals. "When we needed friends as we never needed them before, Ward Bond telephoned and asked how we were doing," she recalls gratefully. Rebuffed as they were by liberal Hollywood, a number of the cooperative witnesses completed the full circuit from the Communist Party to the right-wing Motion Picture Alliance for the Preservation of American Ideals where they were welcomed.

Social ostracism was not the only price paid by the ex-Communists who gave the Committee "names" during the mass hearings. Some, especially the earliest witnesses, found they were on an informal "blacklist." Only after influential figures in the MPA, powerful individuals like Roy Brewer, and members of the House Committee began to exert pressure on the studios, were the cooperative witnesses reemployed. In the beginning the studio heads were not sure that ex-Communists would find any more favor with the patriotic pressure groups than unfriendly witnesses.

But as the parade of ex-Communists to the witness stand lengthened, it became less difficult for them to find work, though in some circles it was felt that people who played the "informer" were beyond the pale. Even today there are some in the industry who, though they have no sympathy with Communism, feel so strongly about this that they are extremely reluctant to hire any ex-Communists and are adamant about not hiring specific ones.

Martin Gang, according to the blacklisted screenwriter who called on him, spoke of the danger of nation-wide picketing by private organizations. That same month, October, 1951, movie picketing began in Los Angeles by a group called the Wage Earners Committee. The Wage Earners Committee, according to its Executive Director, "had the humblest sort of origin." "In typical American fashion," a waiter, a telephone switchman, a small restaurant owner, and a retired salesman formed the organization. The Committee — which was later found by the National Labor Relations Board to have accepted financial assistance from an employer who "intended to establish and set up Wage Earners as an instrumentality to offset legitimate collective bargaining" — immediately declared its belief in the "inalienable rights of the individual, as opposed to regimentation, communization, or dictatorship in any form." Politically, it was opposed to "every candidate controlled by the Labor Boss" and pledged itself to give its support to "the honest candidates the Labor Boss is attempting to purge."

The Wage Earners began their attack by picketing a film written by one of those named as a Communist before the House Committee. They carried signs which read: "This picture written by a Communist. Do not patronize." Later the group focussed its attack on the film version of "Death of a Salesman." It picketed a theater where the picture was showing and handed out circulars attacking Arthur Miller, author of the play, Fredric March, the star, and the producer, Stanley Kramer. Picketing of other films followed.

Then the full force of the Wage Earners was turned against Dore Schary, production chief at M-G-M. Pickets carried signs reading: "Communists are killing Americans in Korea. Fellow travelers support Communists. Yellow travelers support fellow travelers. Don't be a yellow traveler." Another sign read: "Please do not patronize. This is an MGM picture. Dore Schary 'Boss' of MGM. See House un-American Activities Report . . . See Calif. Tenney Committee Reports . . ." Page numbers were listed.

Meanwhile, a publication of the group, the *National Wage Earner,* listed 92 current films "which employ commies and fellow travelers and contain subversive subject matter designed to defame America throughout the world." The Executive Director of the Committee, R. A. McConnon, announced, in a mimeographed letter demanding retraction of statements published about his organization in *Daily Variety,* that the Wage Earners were dedicated to providing "revelations of the identities and operations" of "subversive propagandists" in the motion-picture industry. The group would stop picketing, he declared, "if the Industry would make an honest, and resultantly effective policing of the medium. And this must include the immediate cessation of all pictures in which Americans are pictured as being intolerant and prejudiced against any so-called minority groups." Representatives of the Wage Earners offered to consult with the studios about the content of motion pictures and the loyalty of artists considered for employment.

In the circulars distributed by members of the Wage Earners Committee, producer Kramer was characterized as being "notorious for his red-slanted, red-starred films." The "true facts" about Kramer, the WEC held, were that he "taught at the Los Angeles Communist training school in 1947" and had employed a certain number of performers with "Communist-front" records. (Kramer's "teaching" actually consisted of a single guest lecture given at the People's Educational Center where he spoke on a technical aspect of motion-picture making.) The Wage Earners belabored Fredric March with charges that had been made against him by the New York *Counterattack* — but ignored the fact that the actor later received a retraction and reached an out-of-court settlement with that publication.

Among the page references in the Tenney Committee reports cited against Dore Schary was a reprint of an article from the *Hollywood Reporter* describing the meeting of the Screen Writers Guild at which Schary announced the Waldorf policy. At the meeting, the trade paper reported, one of the Hollywood Ten had called Schary a "thief." The other references were to Schary's participation in several organizations designated by Senator Tenney as "Communist-dominated." There was no indication in any of the references cited that the film executive was personally "subversive" or "disloyal." The case against him, whatever there was of it, was based solely on "association."

Schary and Kramer both filed suit against the Wage Earners Committee, on grounds of libel and, in Schary's case, of willful interference with contractual relations. Picketing by the Wage Earners was then stopped by court order.

In Washington, D. C., members of the Catholic War Veterans picketed Judy Holliday's "Born Yesterday." Later, in New York, the Catholic veterans picketed her second picture, "The Marrying Kind," and distributed leaflets describing her as "the darling of the *Daily Worker*." Miss Holliday, along with Garson Kanin, author of "Born Yesterday," was listed in *Red Channels*. Her studio, Columbia Pictures, was alarmed by the picketing incidents. She had won an Academy Award for her first starring role and promised to be an extremely valuable and lucrative "property."

Columbia Vice President B. B. Kahane told a reporter not long ago that after the picketing started, he questioned the star and was completely satisfied that her loyalty was beyond challenge. Columbia was satisfied, but that was not enough to call off the picket lines. The film company enlisted the services of Ken Bierly, a former editor of *Counterattack* turned public-relations consultant. Bierly's first job for Columbia was to "clear up the confusion about Judy Holliday." Soon after Bierly took over, the picket lines disappeared. Later, he told Merle Miller, author of *The Judges and the Judged*: "You might put it that I had something to do with getting the facts, the true facts to the right people."

It was not only a question of getting the "true facts" to the "right" people but also of getting them to a large number of Americans who had been led to believe that Judy Holliday was a suspicious if not subversive person. A public-relations campaign was necessary if Columbia was to realize its investment in the star. Miss Holliday's future was turned over to a group of skilled publicists. Gradually the rumors about her were silenced.

On March 26, 1952, Judy Holliday went to Washington, D. C., the "Born Yesterday" locale, and testified before the Senate Internal Security subcommittee. She admitted that she had been "duped" into supporting Communist-front organizations but convinced the subcommittee she had always been anti-Communist. Senator Watkins asked her: "You watch it now; do you not?" Miss Holliday in accents reminiscent of Billie Dawn replied: "Ho, *do* I watch it now!"

Other veterans groups threatened to take an active interest in Hollywood's employment practices. A California unit of Amvets asked studio heads to define their position regarding the hiring of persons suspected of disloyalty. But no further action was reported after a number of persons in the same organization denounced the move as a publicity scheme.

In November, 1951, a Hollywood post of the American Legion sponsored a resolution to provide for the picketing of theaters showing pictures which carried the name or credit of "unfriendly" witnesses. The resolution was not adopted. Later, the same post sponsored resolutions before local and regional organizations of the Legion to establish a committee of the California Department which would act as liaison with representatives of the film industry. The committee would be organized "for the purpose of conferring concerning any person now employed or contracted with, or hereafter to be employed or contracted with by such studio who is a Communist, or whose acts, ideas or ideals are inimical to the welfare of the United States, and, in the event a result deemed satisfactory to the committee is not obtained, to take such other and further steps or action as the committee may deem fit and proper,

116

including lawful demonstrations at such times and places as it may deem necessary to carry into effect the purposes of this resolution." But these resolutions also failed to pass.

With all this adverse activity and with the threat of more to come, the Hollywood producers were feeling harassed and put upon. Their brave resolutions after the Waldorf Conference that the industry would not be "swayed by hysteria or intimidation from any sources" seemed less persuasive by the hour. The "mass hearings" of 1951 put Hollywood on the defensive, and the producers were feeling pressures from all sides.

The American Legion

IN MAY, 1953, the *American Legion Magazine* stated that in the year then past, the Legion had been "linked more closely with events in the Hollywood motion picture industry than in any previous period." The claim was something of an understatement. The Legion had not merely been "linked" with events in Hollywood — in many respects it had become their prime mover.

Robert B. Pitkin, Associate Editor of the Legion magazine, reported that the hearings in Hollywood "shook the American film industry." Nearly 300 past and present studio employees were identified as having at one time or another belonged to the Communist Party. But, Pitkin pointed out, an even greater blow to the film industry was a "secondary effect" the hearings had — the American Legion interested itself in Hollywood to an unprecedented degree.

The Legion had long been concerned about communism in Hollywood. Officials of the organization had discussed the problem with Roy Brewer and leaders of the Motion Picture Alliance. Then, in the late spring of 1951, Donald R. Wilson, a prominent Legionnaire from West Virginia, visited the movie capital to attend a convention of the California Department. Wilson, who was fairly certain at the time that he would soon be elected National Commander, proposed that representatives of the Legion hold an informal meeting with leaders of the movie industry, either in Miami at the time of the national convention or during the year-end holiday season, when Wilson planned to be on the West Coast again for

118

the Rose Bowl game. By the time Wilson made this suggestion individual posts of the Legion had already engaged in sporadic picketing of movie theaters.

October rolled around, but the movie executives sent no message to the Legion convention. Wilson (who *was* elected National Commander during the convention) and other Legion leaders were annoyed by the industry's seeming indifference, and before the final session the convention "instructed" the editor of the *American Legion Magazine* "to publish all information on Communist associations of all people still employed in the entertainment industry." It was the first time the Legion convention had given the editor such specific instructions. Later the *American Legion Magazine* explained why the step was taken: The Legion veterans have long been dedicated to fighting communism by means of "public exposure." When the convention ordered the article on Hollywood it was acting within this general aim by "giving the widest possible distribution to (a) information identifying the American Communists, and (b) information which seems strongly to relate people and activities to Communist influence."

To fulfill its mandate, the *American Legion Magazine* published an article in December, 1951, entitled "Did the Movies Really Clean House?". The article — as the Legion magazine later described it — provided a "long listing of associations with Communist movements of people still active in films; of the studios where they worked, and of their current productions." The Legion editor assigned J. B. Matthews to write the article. Matthews' article threw Hollywood into near panic.

Joseph Brown Matthews was probably better prepared to produce such an article than any other American journalist. Matthews first came to attention of the general public in 1938 when he appeared before the Dies Committee as a witness. Before Matthews' testimony, the Committee was fairly obscure and found it difficult

119

to gain suitable appropriations. Matthews' testimony, though, made news across the country and the Chairman found his work had become somewhat easier.

As Howard Rushmore, one of Matthews' ardent admirers, explained it in an *American Mercury* article: "In those days, Congress was not particularly concerned over the Communist menace. The Dies Committee had not been granted a permanent status and was operating on a small appropriation. And Martin Dies, Joe Starnes, and other Committee members certainly were not experts on the subject. Matthews, who had been recommended by George Sokolsky as an excellent authority, testified for ten hours in executive session at the United States Court House. *That lengthy record formed the backbone of the Committee's tactics and strategy to come . . .*" (Original italics.)

Matthews testified volubly about Communist "infiltration" from first-hand experience. In all, he named a total of 94 "left-wing" groups with which he had been associated over a period of seven years. He stated, for instance, that the American League for Peace and Democracy, then a thriving organization, was linked directly with Moscow. He named more than a dozen other organizations with which he had been associated between 1932 and 1935 as "Communist fronts." Soon after Matthews testified, Congress upped the Dies Committee's $25,000 appropriations to $100,000. A few weeks later Matthews himself was appointed chief research director for the Committee.

As research director, according to Rushmore, Matthews was the "brain truster back of the Committee's relentless exposures," doing more work than all the regular Committee members put together. He began his research from scratch by building a file on a few copies of the *Daily Worker*. Within three years the Matthews' file became "the most complete collection of Communist publications and documents yet assembled . . . Thousands of names were cross-indexed." On the basis of this research Matthews prepared hundreds of re-

120

ports, "examined 400 witnesses in public sessions, 600 more in private meetings."

This was only the beginning. Matthews' "crowning work," in Rushmore's opinion, was the preparation (with the assistance of Benjamin Mandel) of the monumental "Appendix IX."* "The six volumes of this report contain the names of thousands of persons

---

* " 'Appendix Nine' was published in seven volumes numbering just under 2,000 pages. It was prepared in the closing days of 1944 by the so-called Costello subcommittee of the Dies Committee, presumably to preserve the files of the latter committee, which were thought to be threatened with destruction. Seven thousand sets were published at a cost of $20,000, and were delivered to the committee. When the publication came to the attention of the full committee early in 1945, it was ordered restricted and the existing copies destroyed. However, a number of sets had already been sold by the Government Printing Office to private subscribers. Others had been distributed by the committee to government Service Commission, the FBI, the State Department, Army and Navy Intelligence, and the Legislative Reference Service of the Library of Congress. The volumes carry the title, *Communist Front Organizations with Special Reference to the National Citizens Political Action Committee.* There is no introduction to the volumes, and they carry no explanatory statement concerning their purpose or use. The first six volumes are divided into 245 sections, in which alleged Communist front organizations (or groups of organizations) are examined. In each of these sections the organization is described in a series of introductory paragraphs which are followed by a series of 'exhibits' consisting of miscellaneous documents taken from the Dies Committee files. Benjamin Mandel told the author that these exhibits are 'a fair cross-section of our files today.' (The Dies Committee files were not destroyed but were turned over to the permanent committee in 1945.)

"The seventh volume in the set is an index which contains some 22,000 names, chiefly of individuals. An examination of this list immediately reveals that many of the persons named are neither Communists nor fellow travelers. Mandel admitted to the author that this was so and said he regretted that the volumes did not carry an explanatory note warning users that the presence of a name in the index did not necessarily mean that the person was a subversive. He also stated that many of the persons suspected in 1944 of being fellow travelers may have subseqeuntly proved their loyalty. In any case, the continuing use of these volumes by intelligence officers or by private individuals can only lead to dangerous and irresponsible results. It is quite clear that attacks by private persons and organizations upon specific individuals are the result of access which these organizations have had to 'Appendix Nine.'

"When the author attempted to query Representatives Wood and Nixon about the continuing use made of 'Appendix Nine' each man professed complete ignorance about the publication and its contents. Interviews with Mandel and Wood, Jan. 31, 1950. Interview with Nixon, Feb. 2, 1950." (Robert K. Carr, *The House Committee on Un-American Activities, 1945-1950,* Cornell University Press, 1952, pp. 338-9.)

who sponsored Communist fronts from 1930 to 1944, and the master index is still used by government agencies and private investigating groups all over the country."

After his hitch with the Dies Committee, which ended when Dies left Congress in 1944, Matthews continued the career of a full-time anti-Communist. Today, he is affectionately described by publications like the *American Mercury* and the *American Legion Magazine* as "Mr. Anti-Communist" himself. Matthews was 44 when he began working with the Dies Committee. Before that he had applied himself with comparable intensity to a wide range of commitments. As a young man he served as a Methodist missionary; later he was a teacher. At one time he was a pacifist who put special emphasis on interracialism. He was for a time a Socialist and theoretical Marxist. Later he crusaded against organized labor and vigorously championed the free-enterprise system.

In 1938, he wrote an autobiography (dedicated to Martin Dies and the members of his Committee) in which he apologized for his changing youthful passions to reform the world. Commenting on this when the book came out, his friend George Sokolsky noted that Matthews in his younger days "was apparently in a hurry — but the world was not. He had that to learn, and I think he has learned it."

Since he discovered that the world is in no hurry to be changed, Matthews has done his most significant work as a behind-the-scenes power. Only occasionally has he attracted public attention — as when he served as chief investigator in 1948 during the Illinois State investigation of the University of Chicago. Though he usually avoids the limelight he made first-page news in June, 1953 when Senator McCarthy named him as executive director of his Senate investigating subcommittee. Only a short time before his appointment was announced, "Mr. Anti-Communist" had written an article in the *American Mercury* claiming that through the years the Communist Party had enlisted the support of at least 7,000 Protestant

122

clergymen as "party members, fellow-travelers, espionage agents, party-line adherents and unwitting dupes." There were so many angry protests when McCarthy announced he had signed up the author of that article the Senator was forced to accept Matthews' resignation 18 days after he appointed him.

Later McCarthy presented Matthews with a desk set inscribed: "To J. B. Matthews, a star-spangled American, from one of his pupils and admirers." McCarthy and some 300 self-styled "Red-beaters" paid homage to Matthews at a testimonial dinner held in New York in February, 1953. At the dinner Matthews received citations from the American Legion, the Catholic War Veterans, the Jewish League Against Communism, and the New York Committee against Communism.

When word leaked out in Hollywood that the *American Legion Magazine* was going to publish Matthews' article, leaders of the industry attempted to set up an immediate meeting with Legion representatives to forestall publication. But the magazine had gone to press before such a meeting could be held. When the article did appear, the Legion magazine later admitted, "on at least half the major studio lots, resentment toward the Legion boiled over." In the article Matthews hinted broadly that the motion-picture industry had not gone nearly far enough in "cleaning house." He indicated that the Legion would not be satisfied until certain other studio employees were eliminated. The movie executives had nightmarish visions of nation-wide American Legion picket lines when they read the concluding sentence of the article: "Only an aroused public opinion is likely to exert the necessary pressure to cleanse Hollywood of all Communist influence." (The attack had shifted from actual Communists to "Communist influences." The circles in which Matthews moved had, of course, never been overly discriminating about what constituted a "Communist influence." Some in the group, for example, were given to describing responsible newspapers as "uptown editions of the *Daily Worker*" and branding Americans for Democratic Action as carriers of the Communist contagion.)

Seventeen of the 66 movie personalties Matthews named were listed *solely* as having signed an *amicus curiae* brief for the Hollywood Ten. Others were named solely as signers of the *Variety* advertisement which attacked the House Committee investigation in 1947. Others were merely described as having been "affiliated" with numerous Communist fronts, as having a long record of "supporting" Communist fronts, or as having a record of pro-Communist "connections." But the specific "affiliations," the nature of the "support" and the degree of the "connections" were left unstated.

The long-delayed American Legion-film industry meeting took place in Washington on March 31, 1952. The Legion magazine reported later that the meeting was arranged only after the "top executives of the major film companies [the New York officers] . . . stepped in and took the play away from the studio lots," where bitter criticism of the Legion was rife. The financial backers of the motion-picture industry were understandably concerned: individual Legion posts had already begun to picket theaters on the basis of Matthews' charges. Perhaps even more disturbing was the fact that among the Legion's members were men who could simply refuse to book certain films into the theaters they owned.

Representing the American Legion at the Washington meeting were Commander Donald R. Wilson and one aide, former National Commander James F. O'Neil, director of Legion publications. Eight major movie studios (Columbia, M-G-M, Paramount, Republic, RKO, 20th Century-Fox, Universal and Warner Brothers) sent highly placed delegates, and Eric Johnston was on hand to represent the entire industry.

At the conference, the Legion spokesmen explained that they were not unsympathetic to the plight the film industry found itself in, but nonetheless the Legion had to continue its "public information" anti-Communist program — the Legion would not "call off its dogs" just to be a pal, as its official magazine later reported. The organization was willing to cooperate in any "earnest" attempts the industry might take to clear up the situation, but the emphasis was on "earnest." If the Legion had been mistaken about the information it published it would welcome any corrections the studios might make.

Spyros Skouras, head of 20th Century Fox, said his studio would be interested in knowing what possible charges the Legion might make in the future. Skouras told the Legion representatives that he had consulted with columnist George Sokolsky and as a result was collecting all allegations against his employees and inviting them to arm him with "written, signed, explanations or denials" to prove their innocence. Nate Spingold, of Columbia Pictures, announced that his studio had been embarked on a similar program for almost a year. The RKO representatives reported that they already had information on employees who might find themselves in difficulties.

Commander Wilson then suggested that the movie people compare notes with the Legion "in the hope of confining the Legion's criticism to personnel whose studios could find no factual defense for them." Every studio representative present welcomed the suggestion, and the motion-picture executives requested that the Legion give them whatever information it had, large or small, which tended to link any of their employees with communism. The Legion officers agreed to supply the data — on condition, according to the Legion's account of the meeting, that the information would be seen only by top studio personnel and the individuals involved.

A few days later the American Legion sent a formal letter to the eight major studios naming some 300 persons. The Legion later cheerfully admitted that the list was compiled from "scattered public sources" . . . "We respectfully request that you check this material for any factual errors and make such reports to us as you deem proper," the Legion instructed studio executives.

The list, according to the Legion, was almost immediately misused by certain studio executives. The Legion blamed a vice-president of M-G-M for getting the impression abroad in Hollywood that the organization has issued a secret blacklist to the motion-picture producers. After an interview in the vice-president's office, an M-G-M writer who was completely innocent of any meaningful association with communism came out believing that the Legion had demanded he be liquidated from the industry, on the basis of unevaluated information the Legion had supplied. The M-G-M writer protested loudly. And – according to the Legion's own account – "Commander Wilson, irked at an apparent misuse of the information, was tempted to call off any further attempts to cooperate with the motion-picture industry." But M-G-M made prompt apologies and assigned a more discreet executive to the job. The Legion's officials were somewhat mollified, though later there were complaints that the false notion of the list was circulated all over the country.

Soon after the list appeared in Hollywood, Legion headquarters was swamped with requests for political "clearances" from nervous Hollywood actors and writers. The national officers claim that the Legion was completely opposed to "clearing" movie personnel or determining who should or should not be hired in the studios and said so at a second meeting with the producers. Letters sent to the Legion's headquarters in Washington asking for "clearance" were simply left unanswered. Other movie workers, citing their anti-Communist credentials, asked the Legion to demand that they be hired. But these requests were also ignored.

However, several Hollywood performers on the list who were cleared after months of unemployability claim that a visit to a local Legion official was part of their clearance procedure.

Everyone at work in the studios who was on the American Legion

126

list was called in and asked to disavow or "explain" the Legion's citations. Those who failed to answer the question of Communist Party membership were fired immediately. Those who denied Party membership but refused to disavow past activities cited by the Legion were hounded by studio officials until they did. If they refused, they were simply not rehired at that studio. Others who were not employed by any studio at the time the Legion list first appeared discovered that they had become unacceptable at the casting offices. In some cases this knowledge was gained only after months of mysterious and nerve-racking unemployment.

"At first I didn't realize what it was," one performer explained not long ago. "Actors often go long periods without getting a call. I began after awhile, though, to think I was simply washed up. I was full of doubts about myself and demoralized when my agent finally told me what the real trouble was. Of course it seemed outrageous to have been quietly buried that way. But still, I was greatly relieved to hear the news — it was not that I had lost either my looks or my ability, as I half-believed!" The performer made the rounds seeking "clearance" and was eventually put back to work. The Legion's listing in the case of this particular artist was based on two trivial "associations" — participation in the Committee for the First Amendment activities and an appearance at a Russian relief benefit during the war.

Those who agreed to "explain" the associations against them by the Legion were required by the studios to "write the letter," as it became known in Hollywood at the time. The need for some kind of court to sit in judgment on these letters was clear from the beginning. "Experts" were required. To fulfill this extra-legal judiciary function, the most widely acceptable "expert" of them all was asked to participate.

This most acceptable of experts was George E. Sokolsky, the veteran Hearst columnist, who suggested the program in the first place, after conversations with Spyros Skouras and other top movie men "back East." Sokolsky had written columns about Hollywood, and, though he confesses readily that he does not see many films, his interest in the political life of the film colony was well known.

In the 1954-55 edition of *Who's Who in America,* George E. Sokolsky listed himself as columnist, author, lecturer and industrial consultant. No doubt his work in all these capacities contributed to the effectiveness of the role he played in making judgments as to who of the Hollywood penitents were worthy of immediate absolution and who should be referred to the "experts" on the West Coast for further consideration. But probably more pertinent, though unlisted in *Who's Who,* is the image of Sokolsky as a kind of gray eminence, a behind-the-scenes operator bestowing on individuals and causes at will the benefits of his accumulated wisdom, ingenuity and undoubted influence. These benefits appear to be bestowed sometimes to serve specific political purposes, sometimes for capricious or romantic reasons — but more often Sokolsky seems to combine both.

Sokolsky is generally recognized as one who transcends factional differences within the anti-Communist movement that directs its energies toward the entertainment media. He is a court of last appeals, an almost universally accepted father-figure. One public-relations man, widely experienced in the field of "clearance," said of him not long ago: "He's impartial, generous, extremely practical, as objective as anyone writing, kind, with no meanness in him." That represents a widely held view of the columnist. Other "clearance" experts have at different times felt that he was not being as shrewd as he might be in his judgments and was giving his blessing to people who did not deserve it. There have been schoolboy grumblings about "Sok" among the lesser "clearance" men. But his authority is rarely questioned.

He has been variously described as the Pope of the Right Wing presiding over a loyal College of Cardinals and as Chairman of the

128

Blacklisting Board of Directors. Certainly, in the Supreme Court that has grown up since blacklisting in the entertainment world began, he has served as Chief Justice. Run-of-the-mill cases can be handled in the lower courts, and in the normal course of events Sokolsky is not called upon. But when leaders of the movie industry looked around for a man to sit in judgment on the American Legion "letters," the columnist was readily suggested.

Sokolsky met all the requirements. He was eminently acceptable to the American Legion and other groups whose views Hollywood was learning to respect. He qualified as a "sophisticated anti-Communist" in the circles where no greater encomium than that can be given to anyone. He was generally reputed to be a reasonable man. He writes a widely syndicated column that is read and admired by the kind of people who are likely to start picketing movies. He was aggressively "conservative" in his political opinions, yet his intellectual attainments were equal to those of the totally unacceptable "egg-head liberals": no critic of the program could convincingly charge Sokolsky with being a yahoo or a bigot. Best of all, Sokolsky had at his command the results of his friend J. B. Matthews' long research endeavors into the field of "Communist infiltration." Not long ago the columnist told a harrassed radio-television sponsor that since the "file" at his disposal contained several million items it is only a matter of a telephone call and a 20-minute wait before anyone in show business can be thoroughly "checked."

Sokolsky once stated that he would have no objections to a Communist's being employed in the motion-picture industry if it were not for the fact that such a Communist would be likely to give significant financial support to the Party. (The producers would see to it that a movie Communist did not use the screen to propagandize.) His main political interest in the films, he said, is in getting Hollywood people out of the Communist orbit and back again into normal American life. He is opposed to making that

129

transition so difficult it is practically impossible. On this score, Sokolsky grows impatient at times with the extremists in his own political camp. During one of his visits to Hollywood, for instance, he appeared at a Motion Picture Alliance meeting and publicly chastised anti-Communists who were so rigid and unforgiving that they were hurting the cause.

The columnist insists that he was not responsible for any individual's being blacklisted in the Hollywood studios. He *did* assist in putting people back to work who without his approval might have found themselves "unemployable." Of course those who did not pass the tests Sokolsky applied were in greater difficulty than before their "letter" reached his desk. But, according to the American Legion itself, less than 30 persons out of all those listed failed to provide "satisfactory" explanations.

Sokolsky, unlike some lesser "clearance" men, was not interested in dealing out punishment and thoroughly disapproves of anyone's accepting money for what he regards as essentially "rehabilitation" work.*

When he was satisfied that there was no danger of a performer's or a director's falling under Communist influence, he was willing to pass an "explanation" for past indiscretions, even though he and the writer of the explanatory letter might take quite different sides on legitimate political issues.

Sokolsky, who is not at all the unfeeling man his column sometimes suggests, did not relish the thought of consigning any artist to the limbo of "unemployability." In a speech given in 1940 he ex-

---

* When, not long ago, another newspaperman in the East accepted a generous check from a radio-television sponsor as a "token of appreciation" for helping out in a "clearance" case, Sokolsky was deeply disappointed. He told the sponsor in no uncertain terms that he thought his colleague was out of line in accepting such a "token." His disappointment must have been compounded when he learned that the colleague claimed he broke down the four-figure "token" into smaller "tokens" and sent them around to other "clearance" men, in order to create good will for the company!

pressed a cultural attitude that has influenced his decisions as Chief Justice. "We have to find sanctuary here for great performers," he wrote in that pre-war column. "We have to find sanctuary here for people who just think, and who dare to think independently and freely. . . . We have to be big and broad about that. . . . We have to be so big and broad that when this holocaust is over we can give back to each country that which is priceless because it cannot be replaced if lost. The human mind, and the human spirit, and the human appreciation of things that are fine and beautiful."

Another hint of that side of Sokolsky was expressed in a column he wrote on September 24, 1953. In what seemed like a remarkable recognition of the misery the "house-cleaning" program caused in Hollywood, he praised Roy Brewer's "rehabilitation" program: ". . . men and women, whose careers appear to have been wrecked, are now working. . . . Great talents have been redeemed from fears attending their errors for a clear road to useful work."

But whatever his reservations about "wrecking careers," Sokolsky, "in the absence of a national policy" — as the Waldorf statement put it — agreed to take on the burdens of a private citizen judging the political trustworthiness of other private citizens.

After listees turned in their "explanations" to the Hollywood front offices, the letters were forwarded to American Legion headquarters. Some "explanations" were patently satisfactory; others were sent on to the columnist and it was his grim duty then to separate the liberal lambs from the Communist wolves. Where there were lingering doubts, cases were referred to Brewer and Ward Bond in Hollywood.

A "letter" written by Z.Z., a top-flight Hollywood star, was typical of many. Z.Z. directed his letter to James F. O'Neil at Legion headquarters in Washington and sent copies of it to all the studios distributing either his own pictures or those made by the company he owns.

DEAR MR. O'NEIL:

My name is [deleted]. I am one of the owners of [name of company]. I am also an actor in the motion-picture industry. It has come to my attention that a list attached to a letter from an official of the American Legion includes my name. I am informed that my name was included in that list because of certain activities with which I concerned myself some years ago. I have examined the items in question and I am writing to you to explain the use of my name. I also give you my permission and authority to show this letter to any person to whom you may wish. First, let me tell you what you wish to know. I am not a Communist. I have never been a Communist. I have never been a member of the Communist Party or of the Communist Political Association. To the best of my knowledge and belief I have never knowingly belonged to any organization which was a Communist front.

1. In 1947 together with hundreds of the foremost citizens of Southern California, both in and out of the motion-picture industry, I permitted the use of my name in connection with what was known as the Committee for the First Amendment. Even with the benefit of hindsight I cannot believe any fair-minded person would consider the use of my name in connection with that committee as the use of my name for a Communist front. To my personal knowledge, this Committee for the First Amendment never was a Communist front, nor was it ever used for any Communist purposes even though certain of its opinions may at that time have paralleled the opinions of the Communist Party. As far as I am concerned, I permitted the use of my name in connection with the Committee for the First Amendment for only the most patriotic of motives.

2. My name was used in connection with the brief *amicus curiae* filed on behalf of Lawson and Trumbo seeking a hearing by the Supreme Court. The list of people who permitted their names to be used in this connection is almost as illustrious as the list of names used in the formation of the Committee for the First Amendment. I permitted the use of my name because I felt that the Constitutional issues presented were of such importance that a decision by the Supreme Court would be helpful. Permitting the use of my name had nothing whatever to do with the individual beliefs of Trumbo or Lawson. I am sure that if anybody reads the brief *amicus curiae* the reader will see that the signers merely requested that the Supreme Court grant a hearing. To my

132

knowledge no signer of that petition in any way condoned the actions of Trumbo or Lawson or indicated any sympathy with the political beliefs of the men.

3. My name appears in an advertisement published by the *Hollywood Reporter* on October 28, 1947 headed "Hollywood Fights Back." I permitted the use of my name because this was an ad sponsored by the Committee for the First Amendment, of which I was a member. My recollection is that this advertisement clearly sets forth the honest beliefs of all people who permitted the use of their names by the Committee and in the ad. I call to your attention the manner in which the Committee on Un-American Activities has conducted its hearings since January of 1951 in order to point out the difference between properly conducted hearings and the way in which the hearings were conducted in 1947.

4. I am also informed that I was listed as a sponsor of a dinner benefit rally for the Hollywood Ten supposedly held March 5, 1948 at the Beverly-Wilshire Hotel in Beverly Hills. I was not a sponsor, nor did I attend that dinner or that rally. I did not give any money to the Hollywood Ten. I have read the item in the 1948 Report of the Committee on Un-American Activities in California issued by the Senate Fact Finding Committee of that state and find on page 241 my name listed with many others as a sponsor for that dinner. I have been unable to find any document upon which the Senate Fact Finding Committee based that statement. The record itself does not show the form in which my name was used and there is nothing in the Senate Report which causes me to change the statement which I have heretofore made with reference to the use of my name in this connection.

The actor's "explanation" was acceptable.

This performer was not alone. A number of top stars were named on the list the Legion sent to the studios. Of these a few were getting special attention from the *Firing Line, Facts for Fighting Communism,* a publication of the Legion's National Americanism Commission. The newsletter brought their damning "associations" to the attention of Legion leaders all over the nation. The studio executives, with heavy investments at stake, were particularly anxious for these stars to "explain" themselves. In the vast number of cases, the studio chiefs were convinced, the "associations" were meaningless; at the worst they represented bad judgment. Clearing them up was simply a matter of recalling past circumstances and expressing regret. The letters designed to do this were carefully worked out. In some cases "explanations" teetered on the abject.

This is the way *Firing Line* reported on one Hollywood star who had a big-budget picture ready for release:

"The following material has been compiled by the research staff in response to numerous requests for information on motion-picture actor [his name]. [This actor] plays the part of . . . in a movie to be released shortly . . ." A list of "Communist associations" was cited.

The actor directed his "explanations" to the head of his studio. *Firing Line* had cited him as a speaker at a rally of 1500 teenagers under the auspices of American Youth for Democracy. The AYD, the newsletter pointed out, was cited as a subversive Communist front by Attorney General Clark. In his letter to the studio head the actor explained that in the spring of 1946 he was in Chicago and was asked to address some high-school students. He was told that there had been some race rioting in the city around that time. In making the speech, he said, he felt he was doing his duty as a citizen. If the AYD perverted this action of his for its own propaganda ends, he wrote, it was a typical Communist maneuver and was abhorrent to him. In answer to another Legion charge, he admitted he had been an officer of the Hollywood Independent Citizens Committee of the Arts, Sciences and Professions; but he joined the organization because he wanted to work for President Roosevelt's re-election. He stated he was alerted when the organization became unnecessarily involved in studio strike matters. After the war he joined others in the group who were resisting the Communist Party line; but by the end of 1946 it was clear that the Communists were dominating HICCASP policy and he resigned.

The actor "explained" his interest in the Committee for the First Amendment by saying it was now obvious to him he had been drawn into a Communist-front activity, based on an appeal that at the time seemed to involve a decent American principle.

Six months later an executive of the studio releasing this actor's picture wrote to James F. O'Neil at American Legion headquarters:

> As you know, it is our very firm opinion, based on our knowledge of [the actor] and his activities, that he is a fine and upstanding American. I have gathered from our talks that there was no reservation in your mind regarding the patriotism and Americanism of [the actor]. It is our belief and our hope that, similarly, there should be none as far as the American Legion as a whole is concerned. . . .

The Legion accepted the star's "explanations." His picture was released and shown without crippling incidents.

Not all studio workers got through the investigation as successfully as most of the big stars in trouble.

In a letter to a friend, H. W., a screenwriter, described an interview he had with a studio executive who tried to get him to disavow the activities cited against him. The letter read as follows:

> Mr. *M.* (the studio executive) tells me the studio pictures are being picketed. Cannot afford it. Trying to clear everyone. Will I write Mr. *P.* (studio president) a letter? *M.* tells me what they want in the letter. Particularly names, names, names. Why such and such happened, when I got out, who got me in, etc., etc. And he said, even if I did write this letter and was cleared, this is no guarantee, he realizes, that the next day they may not say they don't like my tie or my hat. I ask what Mr. *P.* will do with the letter. He tells me that when some of these organizations come in protesting against a picture, Mr. *P.* will show my letter. Or he may give it out for publication. I will have no control whatsoever over the letter. Then he begins to read my dossier. . . .
>
> I walked politely out, saying I was going to think. I told my agent that I would not write the letter. He said it was fine with him. But they will settle my contract immediately. Just can't keep me. Everyone

else, I gather, has conformed. So we no longer have any problems here of who to invite with who and so forth. Just the problem of selling the house and breaking off our lives here.

After the first interview, the screenwriter wrote the following letter to the studio executive:

DEAR MR. *M.*:

First let me thank you for your tactful handling of a situation which must have been just as unpleasant for you as it was for me.

For some time I had been expecting a request to write a letter such as you outlined to me in our meeting. Long ago I had made up my mind that I could not dignify the real source of this request by writing. But because of your courtesy and consideration, I gave the matter further thought. However, I cannot alter my decision.

I feel that if I wrote such a letter I would be violating every principle of democracy and freedom in which I believe.

My patriotism, my love and loyalty for my country and for the principles for which it stands and for the form of government which I cherish has never been questioned and cannot now be questioned. I will match my feelings and my actions in this respect against anyone, particularly my accusers.

I am not a Communist. I have never been a Communist and never could be. I have never wavered in my devotion and loyalty to the United States.

I hope you understand why I must refuse your request. Why I must adhere to my principles. After all, I must live with myself for many years to come.

A second conversation took place at which the studio executive demanded again that the screenwriter disavow his political past. The screenwriter's notes on this conversation follow:

Mr. *M.* asked if I had thought over the problem. I told him it was difficult at times to think of anything else. He then asked if I had changed my mind. He said, "I think you owe it to the studio to write the letter. . . .

Mr. *M.* said they were beginning to put pressure on him — asking "what about *me?*" He said these groups were getting very violent. I asked if he meant that the American Legion would picket our pictures.

136

He said yes. *M.* then cited a case of an actor who was a day player — getting a salary of $150 a day. He was playing in a studio film. They gave him a few lines to say — next thing he knew the studio had a phone call telling them about this man. *M.* called the actor up to his office and showed him the list of political charges. The actor refused to answer — saying it was an invasion of his rights. The studio paid him off and he is out of the picture.

M. then spoke of what Mr. Brewer was doing about the writers who had gone to London and who were writing pictures there — he explained that these writers were Communists. The substance was that Brewer had written a letter to Mr. Sokolsky — that Mr. Sokolsky had commented on it and they hoped that there would be legislation to stop these films from playing in this country. He said that the IATSE operators could refuse to run those pictures. I then asked if they would picket a picture of mine which was about to go into production. Mr. *M.* said that he did not know, explaining that certain stories that they had bought before they knew of this trouble had been given an okay. He said that they now ask everyone who comes to work for them if they have been cleared for the Legion — that they would never have signed me now to the contract I have without that letter. He then asked about my contract, and I told him that I had one more picture to do after the present one I was working on.

He then said he was afraid the studio would have to ask me to give them a release. I said I would have to speak to my agent about any business things, and then asked what a release meant. He said, "Tear up the contract." He then said he wondered about the Un-American Activities Committee and what was my attitude about that. I reminded him that I had talked of that before and that naturally I would answer anything they wanted to know. He asked if I would go before the Committee voluntarily. I said that I did not think I could live through it.

He told me that writing a letter to Mr. *P.* was not a hard thing to do. "If you write saying 'I am not a Communist. I have never been and could never be,' and telling about the list of things that you were supposed to have been a member of and to have contributed to — that have been found to be Communistic fronts — that you did not know it and that if you had you would never have joined them."

An actor confronted with the American Legion's citations

against him who refused to answer the question of Communist Party membership had a different experience.

R. had worked in theater and motion pictures since 1925, both as actor and director. After serving in the Army for three and a half years during World War II, he came to Hollywood to study at the Actors' Laboratory under the G.I. Bill. In a short time he started getting small parts in motion pictures.

In 1952, he was called for a part in the M-G-M production of "Julius Caesar" and had been working on the picture for three days when he was summoned from the set to the office of a studio executive.

The actor went to the office wearing toga and make-up and was questioned at length. First the executive said that R should understand that the studio was owned by stockholders and it was the studio's job to protect the interest of stockholders by making certain that there would be no person in the studio's pictures who would cause the public to shun the box office. He then asked R. if he read the *People's World,* and in the same sentence gave the actor the date when he subscribed to the *People's World.* Next he asked if R. had signed the 1947 *Variety* advertisement. R. replied that if his name was on the advertisement, he must have signed it, though he could not recall signing it. The executive asked next if R. had belonged to the Actors' Laboratory, a Hollywood theater group listed as a "Communist venture" by the California Committee on Un-American Activities. R. replied that he had studied at the Actors' Laboratory under the G.I. Bill and later had joined the Theater. The executive then asked who invited R. to join the Actors' Laboratory. R. replied that no one had, he joined because he thought it was a good place to study. When the executive asked how he heard about the Actors' Laboratory, R. replied that he had read about in *Life* or *Time.* The executive then said, "You will write a letter to Mr. Schenck and explain your reason for these various activities and associations." When the actor replied that he

138

had no intention of writing such a letter to Schenck or anybody else, the executive said, "Then I will ask you, are you a member of the Communist Party?" R. answered, "You have no right to ask that question or any other like it, and I will not answer it." The executive concluded the interview. "Then you are no longer employed by M-G-M." After that, R. was called but not hired for one brief part at another studio, but he has not appeared in films since.

L., another actor, found himself "greylisted" because, though no one has charged him with being a Communist that he knows of, he has not denied Party membership. L.'s agent told him that until he makes such a denial he will not work again in motion pictures. L. says he refuses to "clear" himself, because he believes it impossible to be cleared without naming others.

In late 1953 L. went to interview a director who said he wanted L. for a part in one of the major Hollywood productions. A few weeks later, L. signed the contract for the part and started working on the film. Two days later his agent brought him the following memo from the desk of the casting director, with the news that L. would be removed from the cast if he did not write the letter requested. The citations were accompanied by a signed note from the casting director: "Would you please get an affidavit from L., answering each paragraph separately and whether or not he is a member of the Communist Party and have it notarized and sent to me as quickly as possible?" The following citations were charged against the actor:

In 1946 L. was in the Actors' Lab. On October 21, 1946, while at the Actors' Lab., he was the recipient of two scholarships: The Fiske Scholarship and the Apprentice Group. The latter was a select bunch of old-line comrades.

The Monday, November 3, 1947 issue of the *Hollywood Reporter* carries a full-page advertisement "contributed by the Actors Division of the Progressive Citizens of America." The ad is captioned "The Thomas-Rankin Committee must go." It is signed by L. and others.

On May 11, 1948, subject was on the Executive Board of the Actors'

Lab. On November 3, 1947, as a member of the Actors Division of the Progressive Citizens of America, he publicly endorsed the Hollywood "contemptuous Ten" — unfriendly witnesses.

On September 12, 1949, subject signed a public statement in defense of John Howard Lawson and Dalton Trumbo. On October 28, 1949, he signed a similar statement, this one called the "Hollywood Group."

On January 5, 1940, subject was a member of the Executive Board of the Los Angeles Negro Art Theatre, an organization connected with the Council of African Affairs, and similar organizations. On June 27, 1950, he was in the Actors' Lab. production of "Professor Mamlock."

In June, 1950, the Los Angeles Community (sic) party set up one of its characteristic defense organizations, this one called "The Jean Field Committee." The operations of this group were carried out by the Arts, Sciences, and Professions Council. The address of the Jean Field Committee was given on literature as the residence of subject, *L*.

L. said he would not sign any affidavit until he had talked to his lawyer. His lawyer told him the studio could not charge him with perjury if he disavowed the charge.

L. then wrote a letter to the studio saying that the document was full of half-truths and was unanswerable but adding that charges his name had appeared in the public advertisement and petitions listed were true. He would not, however, disavow any of the organizations listed since he believed in their purpose and there was nothing illegal with belonging to them.

The information compiled against him, he says, included several misstatements. For example, though he had belonged to the Actors' Lab., he never held a scholarship there. The charge that people in the group were "a select bunch of old-line comrades," in his opinion, was an unanswerable statement. Secondly, though he worked with the Negro Art Theater, he was not a member of the executive board of the group. He rehearsed with that group for a production of "Professor Mamlock" but the group never produced the play. He had nothing to do with the "Jean Field Committee," though he says a woman who moved into his house after he moved out was active in this group.

140

L. was told his answers were inadequate since he did not say anything about membership in the Communist Party. But *L.* did nothing more about it and continued to work on the film, though he received daily pleas from his agent to sign the disavowal, with a threat that his contract would be broken if he did not. *L.* was adamant in his refusal to sign it. He was permitted to finish the film, but after he finished it, his agent told him he would get no more jobs until he provided the requested statement. During this period his agent told him that the studio was "holding off," that the casting director hadn't sent *L.'s* name to other studios, but he would unless *L.* sent the "letter" in.

Since then, *L.* has had no work except one tv commercial, some tv films directed by a close friend who was brought in to Hollywood from New York, and one part in a movie made by an independent group. His agent has given up. *L.* now makes his living as a manual laborer.

L. has never been named as a Communist by anyone to his knowledge and has never appeared as a witness before the House Committee on Un-American Activities.

Other "greylist" cases indicate that if the subject answered the question, denying Communist Party membership, he was allowed to continue working, but this "clearance" only held true for that particular studio at that particular time. The charges, in one form or another, were brought up, with additional demands for disavowal, whenever it was announced that the "greylistee" had been signed for a particular movie. Typical of these cases was the experience of *T.*, apparently the target of free-lance investigators who follow the tradepaper announcements of job assignments.

A screenwriter since 1944, *T.* had an annual income of from $25,000 to $30,000 until 1954, when it fell to $12,000. Though he has denied Communist Party membership and cleared himself to the satisfaction of the employers who asked him to, *T.* finds that every time his name is announced in the industry papers for a writing job, someone calls his employer and makes a political charge against him. The last time it happened, the charge also included a criticism of his trade-union activity, with the implied threat that *T*. would be fired on the basis of the position he had taken on a union issue. *T*. had signed an *amicus curiae* brief submitted to the U.S. Supreme Court on behalf of the Hollywood Ten and also signed a petition for Lester Cole and Ring Lardner (two of the Ten) to run for members of the Screen Writers Guild Board of Directors, prior to the time they appeared before the Committee.

The first evidence *T*. had that he was being "greylisted" came in 1952, when he was offered a job polishing a screenplay for a studio notorious for its private blacklist. He had written ten pages on the job when the producer who hired him said that the studio had refused to put *T*. on the payroll. The reason, said the producer, was that *T.'s* name had appeared on a list published by *Alert,* a sporadically issued anti-Communist fact-sheet published in Los Angeles.

In January, 1954, *T*. was hired for work on a specific film at another studio. He was hired on a Friday afternoon. The following Monday his agent brought him a plain piece of paper on which it was stated that *T*. had signed a Hollywood Ten *amicus* brief, as well as the Guild nominating petition for Cole and Lardner. *T.'s* agent told him he would have to clear up the charges before he could take the new job. *T*. then wrote a letter stating he had never been a Communist and that his voting registration could be checked since he had been registered with one party since 1926. He said he had signed the *amicus* brief because he wanted to see the Constitutional issue clarified and added that he had signed the Lardner-Cole nominating petition because both writers were well thought of in the industry.

After signing this, *T*. was given a job writing the first draft of a screenplay. He was told that the studio liked his work but was not called back to complete the screenplay. A friend at this studio told him he knew the studio executive would not re-hire him and advised him to call on the studio vice-president in charge of "clearance." But *T.* did not do this. He says he felt he had "cleared" himself sufficiently and could do no more and still keep his honor. His next job was a tv assignment and he learned from the producer that he was on "some kind of a list in New York." He was allowed to do only the "pilot" film for the tv series, and though it was used to sell the series he was not hired to write it.

Through most of 1954, *T.* worked at screenwriting jobs that were not announced in the trade papers. He was not molested or asked to "clear" himself again. But late in 1954, one of the studios which had employed him earlier in the year announced that he had been assigned to write a film. The same day the announcement was made, his producer asked him, "What is all this about your being a Communist? Up front they have come to me and said there is talk you are a Communist."

In a conversation with a studio executive that followed, *T.* was charged with "leading the fight against the move to kick the Communists out of the Screen Writers Guild." *T.* denied the charge. He never made a speech at the Guild in his life and was out of town at the time the resistance meetings were supposed to have occurred. The executive refused to tell him who made these charges, and *T.* went on his way. He kept the job, but he feels very insecure and says that he is on the "ragged edge" of employment.

T. suspects that two of the cooperative witnesses before the House Committee whom he had known slightly in years past made the accusations, since he has been warned by an intimate of one that he should be more friendly toward these two men. His agent told him that regardless of how he feels, he should "crawl a little." If he does not do this, says his agent, "they can destroy you."

143

How to Write a Letter

SOME STUDIO WORKERS who were willing to "write the letter" had difficulty in preparing an explanation the executives would find satisfactory. If an employee belonged to an organization later identified as a Communist-front group, his "letter" had to include statements that he had not known the organization was a front, had clearly been "duped," and as a loyal American citizen violently opposed communism. Letters which did not include such statements were returned with the request that the signer try again.

Typical was the case of *B.,* a prominent character actor. When *B.* was about to be hired for a movie role in 1953, he learned through his agent that there was some question about his political reliability. On May 26 he wrote the following letter:

"To whom it may concern: I, *B.,* citizen of the United States, resident of the State of California, do hereby declare that I am not now and never have been a member of the Communist Party. Futhermore, that I am and always have been against the Communist philosophy and Communist Party line thinking. I am a loyal American citizen, believing in our democratic form of government and opposed to all forms of totalitarianism. I would be happy at any time to answer, to the proper authorities, any questions regarding past associations and activities."

But the letter was not satisfactory. The actor was then given a copy of the studio's report on him:

B., actor. . . . Questionable.

B. signed the ad appearing in the 11/3/47 issue of the *Hollywood*

Reporter, contributed by the Actors Division of the Progressive Citizens of America. The ad is captioned "The Thomas-Rankin Committee must go!" Progressive Citizens of America was cited as a Communist front by the California Committee on Un-American Activities in 1948.

According to information on the West Coast, *B.* was a member of the Actors Division of the Arts, Sciences and Professions Council in approximately 1947. The National Council of the Arts, Sciences and Professions was cited as a Communist front by the Congressional Committee on Un-American Activities in 1949.

Subject also endorsed the unfriendly witnesses who appeared before the HUAC in 1947.

B. wrote another letter: "To Whom it may concern: Supplementing my statement of May 26, 1953, to answer specifically the notations concerning my activities: I do not remember any such organization as Progressive Citizens of America, was never a member of its Actors Division. Concerning the Thomas-Rankin Committee, if my name appears in an ad in the *Hollywood Reporter,* I must have given some permission for its use, but I had no idea the organization was a Communist front as it was cited so to be in 1948. I belonged to the Independent Citizens Committee for a brief time in 1946-47, of which the Arts, Sciences and Professions Council was a part, I think, but I was never an active member of the Actors Division. I attended at the most three meetings during that period: one, a luncheon in honor of Mrs. Eleanor Roosevelt at the Beverly-Wilshire Hotel, a cocktail party at Ciro's at which Mr. James Roosevelt spoke, and a very large public meeting in Hollywood, at which time I decided the tone of the organization was too extremely left-wing for my views and I did not again attend any meetings or retain a membership in the organization. I never endorsed the unfriendly witnesses. I do remember at one time signing a petition that they have the right to petition the United States Supreme Court."

Cases like *B's* were comparatively easy for the studios to handle. File cabinets bulge with letters similar to the one he wrote. The studies were rarely asked questions about such people, yet if they were, the letters were kept as storm insurance. But for some others, providing an "explanation" that would satisfy the "experts" was not so easy.

A typical if especially difficult case was that of *X.Y.*, a prominent dramatist and scriptwriter. The studio was one of the largest, the "expert," Roy M. Brewer.

In July, 1952 Mr. *Y.* sent a letter answering the allegations against him. In his statement he not only discussed the details of the charges but also listed anti-Communist activities he had participated in and anti-Communist sentiments he had publicly expressed in the past. But this letter was unsatisfactory. Its tone was wrong. It did not sound repentant enough — nor humble enough. He was told that the letter he wrote did not accomplish the purpose for which it had been written.

Another letter was prepared. This one (dated January 6, 1953) was not as complete as the first but was meant to be supplemental to it. It was a letter of 17 single-spaced typewritten pages. It gave detailed answers to 53 items listed against the writer in Tenney reports from 1947 to '51. The charges ranged from sponsorship of Communist Party fronts to "support of Soviet Union" and "supported by individual Communists." Mr. *Y.*'s answers gave the history of his participation in some of the groups mentioned; he flatly denied certain of the other allegations. But the tone was still not repentant and in some answers *X.Y.* seemed to be defending the activities charged against him. The second letter was rejected as unsatisfactory.

A few weeks later he tried again. This letter included the statement that he was not then, and never had been, a member of the Communist Party. It pointed out that although he had permitted the use of his name and had been active in organizations later declared to be subversive, he had broken his connections with the groups before that declaration was made. The letter stated un-

146

equivocally that communism was a threat to world peace and that the House Committee's investigations had rendered an important service to the nation. *X.Y.* also placed his talents at the disposal of the United States in its fight against communism.

The answers given to the listed items were identical with those in his earlier letter, except for four significant changes. The January letter answering the charge that *X.Y.* had written a paper delivered at a conference on "Thought Control" said: "I did speak at the conference. A copy of my speech is available if you desire to read it. It expresses my thoughts then and now and I am sure it will express many of yours, too. . . ."

The February letter simply stated: "I did speak at this conference."

The second change dealt with a mass meeting in October, 1947, protesting the actions of the Thomas Committee. The January letter said: "The item is true. I did speak at the meeting. I do not remember who asked me to speak, but I obviously had no suspicion with reference to the nature of the meeting since all Hollywood was up in arms against the manner in which the Committee was functioning at that time. I distinctly remember that Eric Johnston spoke out against the manner in which Thomas was letting the Committee operate, as did Paul V. McNutt and various leaders of motion-picture industry. David O. Selznick and Samuel Goldwyn were among those aroused. This was the time when the Committee for the First Amendment was formed by a broad sector of Hollywood leaders. Likewise, at this time, the Thomas Committee was under attack from such conservative quarters as the New York *Times,* the New York *Herald Tribune,* the Washington *Post,* the Des Moines *Register,* St. Louis *Post-Dispatch,* and individuals such as Thomas L. Stokes, Edward R. Murrow, Congressman Sabath, etc."

The February letter said only: "The item is true. I did speak at the meeting. I do not remember who asked me to speak. At the time I had no reason to have any doubt about the meeting because of the reputable people who were actively participating in the discussions leading to that meeting."

The third charge dealt with the Committee for the First Amendment. In January, *X.Y.*'s letter said: "I permitted the use of my name by the Committee which represented a very broad front of people in Hollywood. I also helped write and produce two broadcasts over national networks for the purpose of presenting the then general Hollywood view of the manner in which the Thomas Committee was conducting its hearings. They are, of course, a matter of public record. Among those on the program were, besides four U.S. Senators. . . ." *X.Y.* then listed 40 well-known movie, radio, theater, literary and sports personalities. After listing these names, his January statement continued: "In addition to the cast of the broadcasts, the breadth of the Committee itself may be inducted by the following names among them. . . ." This list offered the names of 45 Hollywood personalities.

The February statement was precisely the same as the January one, except that it ended after the first sentence. No mention was made of the radio broadcasts, the participants in them or other members of the Committee for the First Amendment.

The last charge against him was concerned with criticism of the Tenney Committee. The January statement said: "My name is listed as having been one of the critics of the Tenney Committee. My answer is that this is entirely true. In my opinion the conduct of the Tenney Committee and the conduct of the Committee on Un-American Activities under the chairmanship of Dies, Rankin and Thomas did more to further the Communist cause in this country than all the acts of the Communist Party itself. I believe that contempt for the Tenney Committee's conduct is widespread among all who are familiar with its operation. This is not limited by any means to people who are Communists or of the extreme left. (See *The Tenney Committee,* an impressive book written on

148

the Committee by Edward L. Barrett, Jr., published by Cornell University Press, 1951.)"

In the February letter, the reference to this same item was changed to: "My name is listed as having criticized the Tenney Committee. This is true." (The letter, after all, was written for people outside the studios; these people did not want any of *X.Y.*'s political philosophy in his statement — they wanted their own.)

Even with all the changes and deletions, *X.Y.*'s statement failed to satisfy Brewer.

His next step was to file a 64-page document with the FBI, listing how his work had been received in the nation's press, his political advocacies, including his anti-Communist statements, and his political activities. The FBI document was given voluntarily in order to assist the Bureau if and when *X.Y.* returned to work for the UN.

He was still not hired in Hollywood. He was shut off from films, radio and tv. He had no income.

Throughout the whole period, there were conferences and luncheon meetings centered on the case. Some of the conferences were between studio officials and *X.Y.*'s attorney. *X.Y.* was present at times, absent at others. But always absent from the studio conferences was the man who really made the decisions — Roy Brewer. Brewer's presence, though, was always felt. It was for him that the statement had to be written and rewritten, it was he who decided that *X.Y.*'s "explanations" were not satisfactory. On two occasions Brewer and *X.Y.* met to discuss the problem. But both went away unsatisfied. *X.Y.* could not give Brewer what Brewer wanted. And *X.Y.* did not work in films again until 1955.

At least one prominent actress has paid a high price for refusing to cooperate fully with the "letter-writing" program. Marsha Hunt had been under contract at M-G-M for seven years before the first

149

investigation of Hollywood in 1947. She had appeared in more than 20 M-G-M films. Miss Hunt was one of the Hollywood figures who flew to Washington with other members of the Committee for the First Amendment. She was not under contract at the time. She went to New York to appear in a Broadway show shortly after the hearings and had no fear of blacklisting pressure. In 1949, she signed the *amicus curiae* brief in the Hollywood Ten case. That year she discovered she was in danger of being blacklisted.

Miss Hunt appeared in a "Studio One" television production directed and produced by Worthington Miner. Miner told her after the show that he had received a letter from a Catholic group on Long Island protesting her appearance. He knew she was not a Communist, Miner said, but he advised her to do something to clear the air. The actress, however, chose not to accept Miner's advice and was never again called to work for "Studio One," though she continued to appear regularly on television until *Red Channels* came out in June, 1950. When her picture was used on the cover of *Life,* the magazine described her as the motion-picture star most active in television. She appeared on Philco shows, on "The Show of Shows," and as a guest on a number of programs.

Red Channels listed six charges against her:

	REPORTED AS:
Amicus Curiae Brief	Signer. Petition to Supreme Court to review the conviction of Lawson and Trumbo
*Stop Censorship Committee**	Speaker by recording. Rally, Hotel Astor, N. Y. C. 3/23/48. *People's World* 3/30/48, p. 5
	N. Y. C., 3/23/48. *People's World,* 3/30/48, p. 5

---

* The Stop Censorship Committee is cited as a "Communist front" on the authority of *Counterattack,* the publisher of *Red Channels. Counterattack* "exposed" this Committee on July 1, 1949, 15 months after Miss Hunt's last activity in the organization.

150

Hollywood Independent Citizens Committee of the Arts, Sciences and Professions	Signer. Statement protesting Tenney's attack on John Garfield and Lewis Milestone. *People's World*, 6/3/46, p. 3
Progressive Citizens of America	Speaker. Rally against House Un-American Activities Committee and in honor of the "Hollywood Ten," Shrine Auditorium, Los Angeles, 10/16/47, Un-American Activities in California, 1948, p. 60
Committee for First Amendment	Member. *People's World*, 10/25/47, p. 3. Speaker. "Hollywood Fights Back" broadcast, 11/2/47. *People's World*, 11/8/47, p. 5
Statement Protesting House Un-American Activities Committee	Signer. UnAm. Act. in California, 1948, p. 210
Stop Censorship Committee	Participant. Rally against Cunningham Bill, N. Y. C. *Daily Worker*, 4/20/48, p. 16

After *Red Channels* appeared, Marsha Hunt says, "everything fell away." She continued to work on Broadway but television offers were few and some were withdrawn soon after they were made. In 1951 she and her husband were asked by Jinx Falkenberg to work as summer replacements on the Tex and Jinx show. Miss Hunt's agents told her later that the network vetoed the idea as a result of *Red Channels*.

In the winter of 1951, she received a call from Harry Ackerman, then a CBS vice-president. Ackerman asked her if she would take over the lead in the Lucille Ball radio show "My Favorite Husband" when it was transferred to television. Miss Hunt herself reminded the executive that she was listed in *Red Channels*. Ackerman said he knew that but CBS was handling the problem. The network was asking everybody to sign a non-Communist oath. Miss Hunt said she was against such oaths on principle but if it was the "price for work" she would sign. Though she decided not to take the "Favorite Husband" role because it was not suitable for her, she did write a statement denying she had ever been a Party member, had the statement notarized and distributed to the networks, ad agencies, packagers and New York radio-tv executives who might be in a position to offer her a job.

That year she was assigned to three-days work in an independent film made in Hollywood. No political questions were asked. Then, in the spring of 1952, she was signed for the Stanley Kramer-Columbia film production of "The Happy Time." After the contract was settled, she was asked to sign a loyalty oath and instructed her agent to give the Kramer company a copy of the non-Communist affidavit that had been distributed throughout the radio-television industry. The agent did this, but Miss Hunt was nevertheless asked by Sam Katz, chairman of the board of the Stanley Kramer Company, to sign another statement prepared by the company's legal department. Katz told the actress, "You don't have to sign to make this picture, but you'll never work again in films if you don't." The statement included a paragraph which declared she was sorry she had participated in the political activities cited by *Red Channels*, that she was guilty of bad judgment and would show more discretion in the future.

Miss Hunt refused to sign this statement. She offered another of her own which said: "If any of these activities furthered the cause of communism, I regret having done them." This was apparently acceptable to Katz. Then, after she had been through costume fittings, she got a call from an executive in the Kramer Company. The executive said that it had been made clear to Nate Spingold, vice-president of Columbia, that "The Happy Time" would be picketed if Marsha Hunt appeared in it. He would not say who had delivered the ultimatum but only that "they" demanded Marsha Hunt take out an advertisement in the trade papers saying she was not a Communist and expressing regret for her previous political activities. It was not enough never to have been a Communist, he told her.

Miss Hunt refused to buy such an ad. The arrangement, she insisted, would be a "deal" to prevent picketing and she would not make a "deal" with anonymous people. Thoughout the shooting of "The Happy Time," she was besieged with phone calls from the studio executive but put off seeing him until the picture was completed. Then in an interview the producer told her, "They want it now. This is a time for expediency, not integrity." Others talked to her. For three hours Sam Katz argued in favor of the ad. "If you don't, you will be hurting the only company that has employed you," he told her.

Miss Hunt said she would have no objections to the Kramer company's buying such an ad but would not do it herself. The company did not buy the ad. The picture was released and favorably reviewed. There was no picketing.

But Marsha Hunt did not get another motion-picture assignment for the next two and a half years. Television jobs came up but were quickly withdrawn. Her agent reported that when he suggested her for television parts he was told, "We're not allowed to use her," "The advertising agency says we can't have her," etc. In 1954 Miss Hunt went to Jack Dales, executive secretary of the Screen Actors Guild, for advice. Dales asked if she was a Communist. She said no. Dales then suggested that she consult with Roy Brewer.

The Hunt-Brewer meeting took place at the Guild office. Brewer's assistant, Howard Costigan, was on hand with Miss Hunt's dossier. The dossier included the charges found in *Red Channels* and a few other items. Miss Hunt says that there were one or two innacuracies among them.

The meeting lasted for three hours. The men talked about the dangers of Communist infiltration, but the actress would not agree to sign up for their "rehabilitation" course.

153

A second meeting was arranged. Brewer read her voluntary loyalty statement. At this meeting Brewer told Miss Hunt that he was *personally* satisfied but unfortunately nowhere in her statement was there any recognition that she had erred and been used by the Communists. Unless she admitted that fact, what assurance did he have that she would not repeat her folly in the future? Didn't it make sense, he asked, that she should demonstrate publicly her present understanding of past mistakes? Marsha Hunt agreed to sign the statement Brewer wanted if he could convince her that any of her activities had furthered the cause of communism. They reached a stalemate and the meeting ended. Brewer told her before they separated, "If you want me to, I will send your statement out to my people, but I can tell you now it won't do any good."

Miss Hunt continued to get occasional television offers. In the summer of 1953, she was signed for a Ford Theater show to be filmed in Hollywood at the Columbia studios. When she appeared at Columbia she was told to see B. B. Kahane, vice-president. Kahane said he had discussed her case with Roy Brewer, and asked for a copy of her loyalty statement. After reading it, he said he sensed a little "annoyance" in it. "They won't like that. Rewrite it, keep it to the denial, delete a few phrases." He suggested that she add a paragraph saying that since the days when she had been involved in the activities held against her, the political climate of the world had changed and she now understood the need for caution. Miss Hunt agreed and rewrote the letter, adding some other paragraphs suggested by Roy Brewer. Kahane accepted the letter and she completed her assignment. But she was not asked to appear in any other Ford Theater productions.

Later that summer, she went to New York. Philco and U.S. Steel, she learned, had wanted her for productions but the advertising agencies said no. A filmed show made in England June, 1954 was the last thing she did on television.

Later Miss Hunt received two offers for movie parts at Warner

154

Brothers. One fell through when the picture was cancelled. She could not accept the other because of a previous commitment to do a play. She concludes therefore that though she is probably acceptable now for motion picture work she is still blacklisted in television.

In the summer of 1955 Miss Hunt went to see Dore Schary and asked why she had not worked at M-G-M since 1947. Schary took her to the office of Benjamin Thau, vice-president of Loew's, Inc. Thau said that she had not worked at M-G-M because no director or producer had asked for her. M-G-M, he explained, does not begin its political investigation until a performer is requested; therefore he could not say for sure whether she was "clear" or not. Schary then took her to the office of Marvin Schenck, who read her non-Communist statement, said it sounded all right to him, with one exception: she should add that if she knew in 1947 what she does now about Communist activities, she would have behaved differently in the earlier period.

Brewer was firmly committed to his "rehabilitation" theory. He felt strongly, as he put it not long ago, that "one of the by-products of this problem is that we make heroes out of guys who are not heroes, and enemies out of people who ought not to be enemies. People who have social consciences are penalized, and guys who never helped anybody are way out in front. It was only the people who were trying to help others who got involved. And they ought not to be punished for this." In line with this idea he worked hard to find employment for movie people who had been in difficulty, after he was personally satisfied that they were no longer in the Communist Party or came within its orbit of influence.

But the "rehabilitated" had to meet Brewer's standards of what it meant to break with the Party — and for many Brewer's standards were hard to achieve. Brewer wanted them to see the political implications of their relationships with the Party and/or its front

155

groups as he saw them. To this end, both he and his assistant Howard Costigan gave freely of their time. Once Brewer felt the proper understanding had been achieved, he demanded that some public profession of the new anti-Communist faith be made. A man who wanted to be above suspicion might be wise, for instance, to join the Motion Picture Alliance for the Preservation of American Ideals. Nor could one go wrong by attacking the Communists or the "anti-anti-Communists" at a Motion-Picture Industry Council meeting. Various techniques were used to meet the Brewer-Costigan standards of what a "rehabilitated" ex-Communist, ex-fellow-traveler or merely ex-"dupe" should do to establish his ex-mess. The bigger the name, the more was required. At the time of his death one of the mass-circulation magazines was planning to publish an article by John Garfield called "I Was a Sucker for a Left Hook."

People who helped build up the Party, even though they were wholly innocent of subversive intent and had actually been motivated by high ideals, Brewer and Costigan held, were under special obligation to help smash the Party. Those who met Brewer's standards were assured of his support. Others were left out in the cold. For instance, Brewer felt he could do nothing for screenwriter $X.Y.$ "If I wasn't satisfied about somebody, I couldn't help him," he said not long ago.

Irving Pichel, an actor and director, was one of those who did satisfy Brewer. Pichel had never belonged to the Communist Party but had been involved in a number of alleged front groups. As a result, he could get no work from a major studio and was employed in the Department of Fine Arts at the University of California at Los Angeles. Brewer "worked with" Pichel and, when he felt that Pichel's break with his former thinking was complete, went out of his way to see that the movie man found work again in the industry. On November 26, 1953, Pichel sent Brewer a letter saying:

156

DEAR ROY BREWER:

I have learned of your call to Jerry Fairbanks on my behalf and I want to let you know of my deep gratitude to you. I can imagine no greater evidence of fairmindedness and generosity than you have shown toward me in the situation in which my own shortsightedness involved me. Please believe me when I assure you that I have found it very moving to receive from you and Mabel Willebrandt and Ward Bond such friendly understanding and help in my effort to assume my proper place as a loyal American citizen, devoted to the security and freedom of our country. I shall let no opportunity pass to make this clear.

Brewer's sources for the evaluations he made were varied. The reports issued by Senator Tenney's California Un-American Activities Committee, he believes, were "about 90 percent correct on factual material — but Tenney's conclusions weren't correct." Brewer also believes that the Tenney reports are dangerous in the hands of persons not politically "sophisticated" enough to interpret them. Similarly, he believes that the danger in a publication like *Red Channels* is that it puts information into the hands of "amateurs" who don't know how to use it. He says that from the *Counterattack* group in New York he accepted whatever information they had that was "reliable" — "But I never depended on it." Brewer insists he made his own evaluations, though he had "professional" help. Costigan, his chief aide, was an ex-Communist himself. Brewer also called on Richard Collins, Martin Berkeley and other "rehabilitated" former members of the Hollywood Party. The whole process was informal. The telephone was the usual medium for exchanging information.

Brewer denies that he kept people from working. But when he was not satisfied he would not help people find work, and many studio executives were loath to hire anyone who did not have his positive approval.

When Brewer was "sure," he did not hesitate to make his position clear. Jose Ferrer and director John Huston, for instance, got

157

Brewer's complete backing after an American Legion group had started picketing "Moulin Rouge," a film directed by Huston and starring Ferrer. Brewer had been "educating" Ferrer and Huston. (He convinced Huston that although the director did not know it at the time, he had been maneuvered by the Communists when he helped organize the Committee for the First Amendment.) But the Legion did not know the two men were in Brewer's hands when the picketing began. It was quite a shock to the Legion pickets, then, when Brewer entered the Los Angeles theater where "Moulin Rouge" was showing. When Legion officials complained, Brewer told them he was "working with" Ferrer and was convinced the actor was all right. At the time, he and Costigan were trying to find some way for Ferrer to make his anti-Communist position clear to the public. A speech by singer Paul Robeson provided the opportunity. Ferrer sharply criticized Robeson and was, in turn, attacked by the Communist Party. The Legion was satisfied then that Brewer was right about Ferrer and called off its picket line.

Whether or not Brewer actively prevented people from working is ultimately not very important. The only thing necessary was for him not to "back up" an individual and that person would remain on the Hollywood "greylist." The labor leader's influence extended far beyond Hollywood. There was the time, for instance, when Zsa Zsa Gabor phoned him from France and asked whether she should go ahead with plans to make a French film directed by Jules Dassin, a Hollywoodian who had been named as a Party member but had not made himself available to subpoena. "I made it clear I wasn't telling her whether she should go into the picture or not," Brewer said, "but I did answer her question." The next day Brewer got a wire from Irving Brown, European AFL representative, asking again about Dassin's politics. Brewer made his objection stronger and Dassin was dropped.

Why was such power invested in Roy Brewer? For one thing

his fight against rival union leadership (which he let it be known was inspired by his loathing for communism) was generally counted a resounding success. He had access to knowledgeable ex-Communists who could tell him who had and had not been in the Party, so he was able to let producers know in advance if an individual they considered hiring was likely to be named publicly in the future. Then Brewer's IATSE was the dominant union in Hollywood and its leader's support well worth wooing.

The dancing star Gene Kelly, who had been so harrassed that he went off to Europe, came home and commended Brewer at a AFL Film Council meeting as having had more to do with the unity of labor than any one man. Kelly then went on to note "Irving Brown's program in France in which he is doing an especially fine job of persuading members of French labor unions to the anti-Commie position of the American labor movement." The speech was accepted as a public announcement that Kelly's "list" troubles were over and that he now had Brewer's approval.

The talent guilds looked to Brewer for the support his IA could give them in their collective bargaining. He was on the best of terms with the leading figures in the anti-Communist power centers. James F. O'Neil of the American Legion, George E. Sokolsky and Victor Riesel, of the Hearst papers, the group centered around *Counterattack* in New York, all accepted Brewer's credentials as a "sophisticated," hard-headed anti-Communist. He dominated the Motion Picture Alliance for the Preservation of American Ideals and worked closely with its other leaders.

Finally, much of Brewer's power was directly conferred upon him by the movie producers themselves, though they remained ambiguous in their feelings toward him — at one and the same time they feared him as a possible threat and yet were happy that they could deal with him. The producers felt that he understood their problem and that it was possible to reason with him. He was not as rigid as some of his MPA admirers tended to be. Whenever a

159

difficult decision became necessary, the executives checked with him. And Brewer was careful not to make errors. Though he was quick to charge others with being "soft on communism," he was slow to charge anyone with actual Party membership. This was known to the studios and in the anti-Communist power centers, where Roy Brewer had become a name to be reckoned with.

In a word, Brewer dominated the motion-picture industry more than any individual had ever succeeded in doing. In 1954 he tried to unseat Richard Walsh as international president of IATSE. Brewer characteristically charged Walsh with being "soft on communism" during his campaign, but was nevertheless defeated in the union election and formally withdrew from the labor movement to become a film executive himself with Allied Artists. Since he moved to New York in the early months of 1955, no one in Hollywood has really taken his place.

Blacklisting: An Institution

THE LETTER-WRITING PROGRAM which began as a result of the American Legion's list was not limited to answering Legion charges. In time the studios began a program of "self-policing." The program opened the door to private accusations and lengthening lists. In some studios, private investigators were hired to run down every charge that might later be presented as reason why someone should not be employed. Several smaller studios pooled their resources to hire a single "clearance" man.

Other information was voluntarily submitted by busybody citizens and organizations. One young motion-picture worker who joined the industry long after the Legion list was submitted, for example, was called in, after he had been at work for 18 months. He was charged with having written an editorial for his college newspaper criticizing loyalty oaths. He was also asked to explain "active trade union work after having been at the studio for only six months." He refused to disavow these activities and was fired. The young man has no idea of who supplied the studio with this information.

It is apparent that studios now check the political record of their workers before placing them on the payroll. Another young man born about the time of the Spanish Civil War was rejected at one movie employment office on the grounds that he had fought for the Loyalists. When it was pointed out that he was in diapers at the time of the Spanish Civil War, the studio relented — but not before requiring him to sign a non-Communist oath. It turned out that the youth's name was identical with that of a man in another city who had never worked in the motion-picture industry but had been named in the voluminous lists published by the California Un-American Activities Committee.

Investigations, "clearances," and letters of "explanation" have been used by the industry since 1952 as a matter of routine practice. Some leaders of the industry view these procedures with distaste and assume the duties of a political policeman with reluctance — but the practices nonetheless are almost universally accepted as a fact of life. All the studios are now unanimous in their refusal to hire persons identified as Communist Party members who have not subsequently testified in full before the House Un-American Activities Committee. The studios are equally adamant about not hiring witnesses who have relied upon the Fifth Amendment before Congressional Committees.

The two powerful talent unions, the Screen Actors and the Writers Guilds, have differed in their attitudes toward blacklisting. The Communist Party never gained significant strength in the Screen Actors Guild. The three most prominent leaders of that Guild, Robert Montgomery, George Murphy and Ronald Reagan, were all conspicuously anti-Communist. Some of its officers were among the friendly witnesses at the 1947 hearings. Long before these hearings, anti-Communist resolutions had been introduced at its meetings. But in the first period after Parnell Thomas' probe, the Screen Actors were concerned with preventing the producers from developing a secret blacklist.

At the time of the 1951 hearings, Gale Sondergaard addressed the executive board of the Actors Guild through an ad in *Variety*. Miss Sondergaard asked the union to support her right to plead the Fifth Amendment and to make a public declaration that it would not tolerate any industry blacklist against any of its members.

The board answered Miss Sondergaard a few days later by stating

162

its belief that "all participants in the international Communist conspiracy against our nation should be exposed for what they are — enemies of our country and of our form of government." The statement concluded: "The Guild as a labor union will fight against any secret blacklist created by any group of employers. On the other hand, if any actor by his own actions outside of union activity has so offended American public opinion that he has made himself unsaleable at the box office, the Guild cannot and would not want to force any employer to hire him. That is the individual actor's personal responsibility and it cannot be shifted to his union."

In practice, this meant that the Actors Guild would do nothing about the blacklisting of those identified as Communists during the hearings, or of persons who "took the Fifth" when they were called to testify.

Following the 1953 hearings, the executive board of the Guild condemned by name, "in the strongest possible terms," all those among its members "who have been named as past or present Communist Party members and who on appearing before the House Committee on Un-American Activities refused to state whether they are or ever have been members of the Party." At the same time, the board recommended a change in the by-laws to provide that: "No person who is a member of the Communist Party or of any other organization seeking to overthrow the government of the United States by force and violence shall be eligible for membership in the Screen Actors Guild. The application for Guild membership shall contain the following statement to be signed by the applicant: 'I am not now and will not become a member of the Communist Party or of any other organization that seeks to overthrow the government of the United States by force and violence." The recommendation was accepted by the Guild's membership.

Spokesmen for the Screen Actors Guild claim that the union took this position for two reasons: (1) the Communist Party is an enemy of the United States and the Guild does not believe in feeding that enemy; (2) as a union, the Guild is interested in promoting public approval of the movie industry so that its members may have work. If the presence of Communists in the industry cuts down public acceptance of films and consequently hurts the actors' job-market, then the *economic* interests of the union alone demand that Communists be driven from the industry.

The Guild faces a serious problem in handling the difficulties confronting those of its members who have the same name as black-listed actors. If the performer is not a well-known personality, a name duplication may completely cut him off from employment when routine studio checks reveal that someone with the name is "suspect." If the actor is fortunate enough to discover he is being denied employment for this reason, the Guild tries to help him. The following is typical of the letters it has helped prepare in cases like this:

"To Whom it May Concern: I, XY, motion picture and television actress, residing at Beverly Hills, California, of my own free will and volition make the following affidavit: It has come to my attention that a person calling herself XY sent May Day Parade congratulations to the Communist publication, the *Daily Worker,* and that this fact was reported on page 19 of the April 27, 1947 issue of the *Daily Worker.* I wish to make it crystal clear that the XY who did this was not me. I have always had a hatred of the Communist ideology and totalitarianism and I also have an un-rivalled scorn for the Communist publication, the *Daily Worker.* I was in New York City in 1947 residing with my mother and brother at the *Blank* Hotel, but I never had correspondence of any nature with the *Daily Worker.*

"During the last ten years, I have encountered several other XY's and I recall that once, while working at a 20th Century-Fox studio in Hollywood, I received in error a check made out to an XY, who turned out to be a girl employed in the fan mail department there.

164

"I believe now, and I believed in 1947, that the American Communist Party is a conspiracy seeking to overthrow the government of the United States by force and violence and I am ready at all times to do whatever I can in my small way to combat the Communist traitors."

The Screen Actors Guild, following the last of Hollywood's strikes, aligned itself with Roy Brewer and the leadership of his IATSE. It has continued that support through the years since. An Actors Guild official was involved as a defendant in a law suit growing out of a libel charge made by Michael Jeffers, a former president of the Screen Extras Guild. During an Extras Guild election Jeffers was accused of having actively supported the "Communist-dominated" Conference of Studio Unions. Thereafter Jeffers found difficulty in getting employment in the studios. He has gone to court several times in an effort to remove the stigma placed upon him by the charge. During one of these trials the presiding judge specifically exculpated him from any charges of being a Communist. But at this writing Jeffers has yet to receive compensation for the mental anguish and unemployment he suffered.

The internal struggle against the left-wing faction in the Screen Writers Guild continued after the CSU strike was settled. The Guild's executive secretary resigned during the intra-union fracas in the CSU strike. In 1947 an economic program introduced and supported by many of those who later appeared as "unfriendly" witnesses was rejected by the Writers Guild membership. When the 1947 hearings were announced some members tried without success to have the Guild represented by the same lawyer who was handling the "unfriendlies" among its own members. On a number of other issues, the leftist faction lost out to the middle-of-the-roaders.

Following the 1947 hearings, however, the Screen Writers came to the defense of its blacklisted members in certain limited areas. For instance, it concerned itself with Paul Jarrico's demand to receive screen credit on "The Las Vegas Story" and filed suit against

165

the producers. But all kinds of pressures were exerted on the leadership. Those who led the middle-of-the-road group say that they were beset by the two extremes within the Guild — the Communists on the one hand and the partisans of the Motion Picture Alliance on the other. In time, these guildsmen say, the middle-of-the-roaders simply grew weary of holding off both sides. In any case, the suit against the producer was quietly dropped in 1952 and the Guild has taken no meaningful steps against blacklisting since that date. Yet the Writers have never gone so far in giving their active approval to blacklisting as the Actors. A few years ago, it was proposed that the Motion Picture Industry Council formalize and regularize political "clearance" procedures; the Writers refused to participate. Since all Industry Council decisions must be unanimous, their resistance was enough to block action on setting up a "clearance court."

When, during the early months of 1955, the Writers Guild failed by three votes to pass a proposed change in its new constitution which would outlaw those who invoked the Fifth Amendment before Congressional bodies, its leadership was under severe attack. A watered-down version of the proposal did finally pass, but since few persons who are likely to "take the Fifth" remain employed, neither version had much actual relevance.

Nevertheless the Writers Guild is still regarded with suspicion by groups like the Motion Picture Alliance for the Preservation of American Ideals, which seem to live in a world of yeas and nays, however rhetorical they may be.

When the letter writing "clearance" procedure began in 1952, the power of the Motion Picture Alliance for the Preservation of American Ideals rose enormously. It was, after all, to satisfy such groups as the MPA that the letters were written in the first place. What was more logical then, than to "check" these letters with prominent members of the Alliance? So, though Brewer remained the top evaluator, Ward Bond, Borden Chase and Martin Berkeley, all active members of MPA, were also called upon to sit in judgment.* That put them in the position of determining the "employability" of people who were competing for the same kind of jobs they themselves held.

Inevitably, differences between MPA members developed. The first serious division arose over the question of attitudes to be taken towards ex-Communists. Brewer and his supporters believed passionately in their "rehabilitation" program, while gossip columnist Hedda Hopper, for instance, continued to attack Edward Dmytryk long after he broke completely with the Communist Party. The difference was resolved in Brewer's favor. Miss Hopper and others holding her position dropped out of the MPA.

Another difference was centered about the standards used to judge the sincerity of ex-Communists and fellow travelers. Some MPA members felt that a certain number of the ex-Communists Brewer had accepted had been evasive in their appearances before the House Committee. Brewer himself was less of a stickler. "Nobody tells *all* the truth, and you can't expect it from everybody," he holds. But he was subjected to criticism within MPA for acting on the belief. There was some feeling that he was "clearing Communists," or at least people who were not truly repentant for their past political sins. Some MPA members were not satisfied, for instance, with the testimony of actor Lloyd Bridges. But Brewer raised no objections when Bridges was hired at Allied Artists. These differences among MPA members were generally kept "within the family." When MPA was attacked, its various factions put their personal feelings aside and banded together to defend the organization.

---

* As an organization the MPA did not "clear" people for employment, but the services of individual MPA members were enlisted and it is unlikely they would have had the power given them had they not been in the Alliance and invested with its new prestige.

The power and prestige that the MPA once enjoyed has been slipping away since Brewer left Hollywood. Its present leader, Ward Bond, does not inspire the confidence that the studios placed in Brewer. Since he is directly involved in the industry, Bond, of course, is vulnerable to the oft-heard charge that he has used his position to further his own career and eliminate competition in the casting offices.

Again, the MPA lost status during the early months of 1955 after a proposal to expel Fifth Amendment witnesses from the Writers Guild was defeated in referendum by three votes. The amendment was presented by Borden Chase, a prominent Alliance member. After the defeat was announced, the MPA publicly attacked the Writers Guild, claiming that it was under Communist influence, and called upon the studios to stop all contractual negotiations with the Guild not required by law. The Guild fought back and carried its fight to the Motion Picture Industry Council. The Council then issued a statement defending the union and, by implication, criticizing the MPA. A supplemental statement was subsequently issued by the Council to mollify the MPA. But, unquestionably, the Alliance suffered a setback when the Industry Council sided with the screenwriters.

Differences of opinion between the MPA and "clearance" powers in New York have also served to reduce the Alliance's effectiveness in Hollywood. The case of Abe Burrows was significant. The MPA was not satisfied with Burrows' testimony before executive sessions of the House Committee in 1951 and again in '52. Burrows was one of the authors and owners of the hit Broadway musical "Guys and Dolls." Paramount held an option on "Guys and Dolls" for which the studio had paid $75,000, but the fact that the MPA did not trust Burrows was considered sufficient reason by the Paramount executives to drop their option. Then Burrows — working through his lawyer Martin Gang ("I went over everybody's head — straight to Sokolsky," Gang explained not long ago.)

168

— was "cleared" by George Sokolsky in New York. After Burrows was armed with Sokolsky's approval, the way was open for the movie sale of "Guys and Dolls." Samuel Goldwyn bought it, to the chagrin of the Paramount executives, and MPA was put in a very embarrassing position: Paramount had lost $75,000 and its opportunity to make "Guys and Dolls," a movie which promised to be a gold mine. MPA was powerless to do anything but attack Goldwyn in its publication and warn the industry it was going to publicize the matter.

Yet neither Goldwyn, Joseph Mankiewicz, the director, nor the stellar cast of "Guys and Dolls" seemed worried.

It is years now since serious attention has been given to the legislative purpose of Congressional investigations of Communism. The notion that the hearings conducted by the House Committee on Un-American Activities are a means of "public exposure" has largely triumphed. The Committee's main function, in the minds of its members and staff, and in the opinion of the population at large, is to "expose" Communists and ex-Communists wherever they are. The Committee is not altogether ruthless and unfeeling in this aim. In recent years it has heard in executive session some witnesses whose physical and mental health could not survive the strain of a public hearing. In other cases, it has heard the private testimony of persons who needed to get that testimony on record in order to stay employed in the Hollywood studios. But generally speaking, the "public exposure" function requires it to operate under a spotlight; its hearings should have as wide an audience and receive as much publicity as possible.

But the years of recurrent hearings have meant that the publicity the House Committee can mine in the Hollywood hills has by now been largely used up. In its last West Coast hearing, during the summer of 1955, only two persons directly connected with the

169

movie industry were heard. Both testified that they had in the past been members of the Communist Party and were no longer, but refused, under the Fifth Amendment, to go further. The first of these "Fifth Amendment" witnesses, a cinema instructor at the University of Southern California at the time he was called, was suspended from his teaching post three hours after he appeared. The other, a character actress, was dropped by her studio the day she received her subpoena and announced that she would use the Fifth Amendment.

Blacklisted persons in the motion-picture industry include some who have won Academy Awards and many who have been nominated for the coveted Oscars at one time or another. Besides highly successful workers like Paul Jarrico, who was earning $2,000 a week at the time he was blacklisted, they number such well-established writers as Michael Wilson, who won an Academy Award for his part in writing the script of "A Place in the Sun"; Ring Lardner, Jr., who won an Academy Award for his screenplay of "Woman of the Year"; Dalton Trumbo, nominated for an Academy Award for his screenplay of "Kitty Foyle"; Albert Maltz, who won an O. Henry Award for the best American short story in 1938; Alvah Bessie, who has held a Guggenheim fellowship in creative writing; Donald Ogden Stewart, who wrote the screenplay for "The Philadelphia Story" and other hit films; Lillian Hellman, author of "Watch on the Rhine"; Sidney Buchman, writer-producer of "The Jolson Story"; Abraham Polonsky, writer-director, who wrote "Body and Soul"; Jules Dassin, director of "Naked City"; Ben Maddow, author of the screenplays for "Intruder in the Dust" and "Asphalt Jungle"; and many other highly talented persons.

It has been widely rumored that prominent blacklisted writers in Hollywood are making a living by selling their work on a blackmarket. Though there is doubtless some blackmarketing of scripts, the pressures and problems involved are great. In order to be active in motion pictures a writer must appear for conferences and work with others involved in production. This is largely impossible for those excluded from the industry. In addition, the Writers Guild can fine a member the entire payment received for work not registered with the Guild. The writer can be sued in civil court if he does not pay the fine. Recently the Guild moved to strengthen the enforcement of the rule. Blackmarketing is so difficult in Hollywood that a producer who wants to buy blackmarket writing usually will not permit any personal contact at all between himself and the writer. One producer when questioned about a script said: "It isn't true, but if it were true, I would still say it wasn't true. So it isn't true."

Blacklisting has invaded the field of manual labor in California. One blacklisted radio writer in Hollywood attempted to go into business with a Los Angeles baker. When the baker discovered that the writer had been an uncooperative witness before the House Committee, the deal was called off.

Most blacklisted persons interviewed were reluctant to say how they are making their living at present. Some have received phone calls from unknown persons who use various subterfuges to find out where they are working. Many believe that their telephones are tapped. Even those engaged in day labor are reluctant to say where they are employed for fear they will be dropped from their unions if it is discovered that they "took the Fifth."

During the winter of 1954-55, fear was especially keen because of the introduction in the California legislature of a bill which would have denied licenses to anyone who refused to testify before any Congressional committee investigating Communism. Had this bill passed, it would have made it impossible for blacklistees to work in California as contractors, barbers, beauticians, or at 150 other jobs requiring a license. It would have also made it impossible for a blacklistee to go into business on his own if he intended to hire helpers.

171

The difficulty blacklisted people face in getting any kind of work is illustrated by the case of an actor whose name, like that of others in this report, is withheld at his request.

M., born into a theatrical family, has been in show business since he was eight years old. Because he was one of the group of more than 160 people named by screenwriter Martin Berkeley as a Communist before the House Un-American Activities Committee, M. is blacklisted not only from acting, but from the electronics industry, a field in which he has years of experience.

M. came to Hollywood 20 years ago, when his father was under contract at Columbia studios as an actor. He started working as a "day actor" in the studios himself at that time. He was also a skilled radio operator, and alternated between these two fields. He worked for Cecil B. DeMille on three pictures, and for a time was control tower operator at Lockheed Air Terminal. During World War II he served as a radio operator in the U.S. Maritime Service, and after the war he went into television engineering. He left Los Angeles in 1950 to install equipment and train personnel for a new television station in Mexico City. While he was in Mexico, his father appeared as an uncooperative witness before the House Committee and invoked the First and Fifth Amendments. During the same period M. was named as a Communist before the Committee.

M. returned to Hollywood in the fall of 1953 and found a job as a design engineer with a television antennae manufacturing concern at Burbank, California. Shortly after he started work, he states, his employer was officially advised that M. was a "dangerous subversive" and should not be working there. This manufacturer had no defense contracts or government orders of any kind, and produced entirely for the domestic commercial market. Though he was sympathetic with M.'s plight, the employer fired him, and M. went into partnership with another blacklisted motion-picture worker to set up a television servicing business. The business did not thrive and

M. was forced to leave it. He then got a job working for a television station in Tijuana, across the Mexican border from San Diego, but he was told by an official of the Mexican Immigration office that the American Embassy had "pressured" the Mexican Immigration authorities not to renew *M.'s* working papers.

He returned to the United States after he got a warning that the Mexican government had issued a deportation order against him. Since his return, *M.* has learned that he cannot get a job as a salesman in the electronics industry because most companies hold defense contracts. He cannot teach his trade, for the schools in the area are accredited by the Veterans Administration. Thus *M.* finds he is cut off from the two careers in which he has experience.

The Legal Aspects

by HAROLD W. HOROWITZ*

The legal rights of the employee under the law governing the
employer-employee relationship (hiring practices of employers)

WHAT ARE THE LEGAL RIGHTS of an employee against his employer if he is
fired, or not hired, under circumstances in which (with varying degrees of
justification) suspicion of disloyalty or subversive activity is in some way
involved? The employee may be fired, or not hired, as a result of investigation under a private "loyalty program" of the employer, such as are apparently utilized by some motion-picture and radio-tv producers. Or, independently of any investigation of the employee's loyalty by the employer,
the employee may be fired, or not hired, as the result of the employer's
reaction to real or imagined pressures from consumer or other groups who
object to the employment of the particular individual on disloyalty grounds.
The underlying basis for the employer's or outside group's suspicion may rest
on refusal to answer questions before Congressional committees concerning
alleged Communist activities, or upon identification, from various sources,
in varying degrees, and with varying degrees of culpability, with what the
employer or private group classifies as Communist activity.

The employer may act from one or more of a number of motives: re-

---

* Mr. Horowitz is a member of the law faculty of the University of Southern
California. He has prepared a study of the legal aspects of blacklisting in the entertainment industry which is being published in the April, 1956, issue of the *Southern
California Law Review.* This paper was prepared as a popular summary of his
findings. It is divided into three parts:

(1) The legal rights of the employee under the law governing the employer-
employee relationship (hiring practices of employers);

(2) The legal rights of the employee under the law of defamation (*Red Channels* and similar publications);

(3) The legal rights of the employee under the law of interference with business relations (action of the American Legion, or similar groups, in objecting, in
one way or another, to the continued employment of the employee).

pugnance to hiring a person who may be disloyal; fear that the employee will utilize the entertainment medium for propaganda purposes; desire to eliminate unrest among other employees, who do not wish to work with the particular employee; a sense of duty which impels him to cut off the source of funds which the employee may be devoting to subversive activity; fear that he may lose patrons because he employs a suspected individual.

To the employee, his livelihood may be involved, for losing a job on such grounds may mean that he will not be able to find any employment in the industry. The action of employers, in ceasing to employ particular individuals on what, in the employers' or others' views, are ultimately disloyalty grounds, is the crux of the "blacklisting" problem. And the law does not offer any substantial means of redress to the employee who is the subject of such action.

Generally speaking, an employer may fire, or refuse to hire, an employee, in the employer's sole discretion, unless there is an applicable statute or other legal doctrine of some kind which narrows the employer's discretion, or unless the employer has by contract with the employee (or with the employee's union) agreed otherwise. Thus if an employer ceased to employ a particular employee for any of the reasons suggested, or for any other reason, he would, generally speaking, have no legal liability to the employee.

Discussion must be directed, then, to the question whether, in the entertainment industry, there are any factors which limit the free choice of an employer to hire and fire as he sees fit. Let us consider first, the statutes or other legal doctrines which may limit the employer, and, second, the limitations imposed by a contract between the employer and employee.

There is actually very little in the way of statutory or other legal doctrine which would limit an employer in ceasing to employ someone suspected of disloyalty. Some states have Fair Employment Practices Acts, which in general prohibit an employer's using standards based on race or religion; it is fairly clear, though, that such statutes would not be applied in cases where disloyalty or suspected disloyalty was the criterion. Some states have statutes similar to the following California act: "No employer shall coerce or influence or attempt to coerce or influence his employees through or by means of threat of discharge or loss of employment to adopt or follow or refrain from adopting or following any particular course or line of political action or political activity." The California Supreme Court has decided that this statute does not prohibit an employer's discharging employees whose loyalty to the nation has not been established to the satisfaction of the employer, because disloyalty or subversive activity is not a protected "political activity." It might be contended that this statute would require an employer at least to show good faith and establish reasonable grounds for suspecting the employee's loyalty before it is determined that the firing was not due to "political activity." But in the entertainment industry employers have rarely stated their reasons for ceasing to employ those suspected of disloyalty. Hence this statute, even if so construed, as a practical matter would not offer any effective means of redress.

A legal doctrine which may be applicable in this area is that of "conspiracy" — the employee who is refused employment may have some redress, in theory, if that refusal is the result of concerted action among a number of employers. This is probably the typical factual situation which comes to mind when the world "blacklist" is used. The theory here would be that though individual employers could lawfully refuse to hire a particular employee for any reason whatsoever, it would be unlawful for employers to combine to do the same thing.

There have been inconclusive law suits based on this theory.

In 1947, the motion-picture producers announced their agreement "not knowingly to employ a Communist or a member of any party or group which advocates the overthrow of the Government of the United States by force or by any illegal or unconstitutional methods." Three law suits arose after this "Waldorf-Astoria Policy Statement." Two of these were brought by the Hollywood Ten; neither was tried. The third was an action by the Screen Writers Guild in 1949 against the producers to restrain the studios from blacklisting employees on political grounds. This suit was dismissed by the Guild in 1953. In none of these actions were the legal problems involved in this conspiracy theory decided by the courts.

A more recent law suit based on this theory was filed in March, 1953, in a California state court by 23 persons who contended that the motion-picture companies and members of and investigators for the House Committee on Un-American Activities had conspired to

blacklist and to refuse employment to and exclude from employment in the motion picture industry all employees and persons seeking employment in the motion picture industry who had been or thereafter were subpoenaed as witnesses before the Committee on Un-American Activities of the House of Representatives and who, relying on their rights and privileges under the Constitution of the United States including the privilege against self-incrimination under the Fifth Amendment to said Constitution, refused to answer questions concerning their political affiliations, associations and beliefs, and all employees in the motion picture industry and persons seeking employment therein who were named before said Committee as Communists or who were subpoenaed as witnesses before said Committee or who were suspected of ever having been Communists or of ever having any associations with Communists and who refused or failed to appear before said Committee or its agents and waive and surrender their constitutional rights and

176

privileges and testify or give statements fully disclosing their own political affiliations, associations and beliefs and those of their family, friends, associates and acquaintances. . . .

This case, *Wilson* v. *Loew's, Inc.,* is presently before the California courts.

There is legal basis for the proposition that in general it may be wrongful for employers to agree to do in concert what they might do with impunity if they acted individually. But there is an unanswered question here whether on a balancing of all the social interests involved, employers could not, in the public interest and in their own self-interest, lawfully agree not to hire a person whose loyalty was suspect, or a person whose activities were in violation of the criminal law, or a person whose participation in the production of the industry's product might lead to loss of public patronage.

Another possible legal theory is the contention that such cooperation between employers would be a "combination . . . in restraint of trade" in violation of the Sherman Anti-Trust Act or of state anti-trust laws. This theory was the basis for one of the law suits by the Hollywood Ten which never came to trial. As far as I have been able to determine, there has been no application of the anti-trust laws to such a case as this.

Limitations on an employer may possibly be found in the contractual agreement the employer may have with the particular employee (or with the employee's union). For example, a collective-bargaining agreement between an employer and a union may provide that the employer can discharge employees *only* for "just cause" or for "good cause." Or a contract with an individual employee may contain a similar cause. This limitation found in contracts is applicable, in the present context, only with respect to employees who are discharged, as distinguished from the problem involving standards used by an employer in hiring prospective employees. (The latter problem is, of course, the more important in a practical sense.) There have been a few litigated cases in which a "blacklisted" employee in the entertainment industry who was discharged or suspended while under contract sought damages from his employer for breach of contract.

Most of these cases involved those of the Hollywood Ten who were under contract at the time the motion picture producers made their policy statement "not knowingly [to] employ a Communist," and to "discharge or suspend without compensation those in our employ, and . . . not re-employ any of the ten until such time as he is acquitted or has purged himself of contempt and declares under oath that he is not a Communist." In one of these cases, *Cole* v. *Loew's, Inc.,* the employee, a screenwriter, was suspended for his refusal to answer questions concerning membership in the Communist Party, under the following clause in his contract of employment:

The employee agrees to conduct himself with due regard to public conventions and morals, and agrees that he will not do or commit any

177

act or thing that will tend to degrade him in society or bring him into public hatred, contempt, scorn or ridicule, or that will tend to shock, insult or offend the community or ridicule public morals or decency, or prejudice the producer or the motion picture, theatrical or radio industry in general.

It was the employer's contention that the writer's refusal to answer these questions before the House Committee was a breach of this "morals" clause in the contract, giving the employer grounds under the contract to suspend him. The jury rendered special verdicts that the action did not breach the terms of the morals clause, but the judgment for the writer was reversed on appeal on other questions of law. This suit, and another breach of contract action by one other of the Hollywood Ten, were later settled out of court.

Two other breach-of-contract actions involving the Hollywood Ten were tried in 1952, and again there were jury verdicts that the employee's conduct before the House Committee in 1947 did not violate the provisions of the morals clauses. The judgment in one of these actions, *Lardner* v. *Twentieth Century-Fox Film Corp.,* was reversed on appeal to the federal court of appeals in California. The applicable morals clause in this case provided:

. . . if the artist shall conduct himself, either while rendering such services to the producer, or in his private life in such manner as to commit an offense involving moral turpitude under Federal, state or local laws or ordinances, or shall conduct himself in a manner that shall offend against decency, morality or shall cause him to be held in public ridicule, scorn or contempt, or that shall cause public scandal . . ., the producer may . . . terminate this contract . . .

The court of appeals said that the writer had breached this clause of the contract for two reasons: In his refusal to testify he was guilty of contempt of Congress, and this was a breach of his agreement not to "conduct himself in a manner that shall offend against decency, morality . . ." And his action before the House Committee constituted, the court said, the commission of "an offense involving moral turpitude."

A later legal action involving breach of contract arose out of the 1951 Committee hearings. This was a suit in 1952 in a California state court, *RKO* v. *Jarrico,* in which RKO studio sought a judgment that it was not bound by its contract to give Jarrico, a writer, screen credit on a picture he had worked on, because he had refused to answer questions in the 1951 hearings as to whether he was a member of the Communist Party. Jarrico's refusal to answer these questions did not constitute contempt of Congress because his refusal was based on the privilege against self-incrimination under the federal Constitution. (The Hollywood Ten had based their refusals, unsuccessfully, on the right of free speech guaranteed by the Constitution.) But the court found that Jarrico had breached the morals clause of his contract, having become an object "of public disgrace and ill will." This case, and the preceding ones involving the Hollywood Ten, marked, as far as I know, the first time that the morals clause in motion-picture contracts had become the subject of litigation.

I know of no cases in which an employee in the entertainment industry has been discharged under an individual contract, or under a collective bargaining agreement with his union, which would permit the employer to discharge for "just cause." But there are judicial decisions which indicate that if this question were to arise in the entertainment industry, an employer would be justified under such a clause in discharging an employee who refused, under the privilege against self-incrimination, to answer questions before a legislative committee concerning alleged Communist activities. And the employer would probably be justified in discharging an employee under a "just cause" provision in an employment contract if the employee were a member of the Communist Party, or if there were reasonable suspicion of disloyalty with respect to the employee, or if the employee carried on any kind of activities which caused his loyalty to be suspect in the view of consumer groups and thus raised the possibility of loss of patronage of the employer's product.

These contract questions all involve interpretation of the specific language used in the contracts. The wording of a contract setting forth the reasons which will justify an employer in discharging an employee is, of course, critical, and after the ambiguities in existing contracts were indicated in law suits, some employers made changes in the wording of the morals clauses. One such change would make clear that the employee would breach his contract, and give the employer grounds for discharging him, in this language:

> artist's refusal, even though in accordance with artist's legal rights, to testify before any court, congressional or other legislative committee, administrative board, or any other duly constituted governmental authority, federal, state or local, or the citation of artist for contempt by any such authority shall be deemed grounds for suspension.

A similar change was made in the collective-bargaining agreement between the motion-picture producers and the Screen Writers Guild after the Jarrico case. A clause was added to that agreement providing that if a writer makes a false statement that he has not been a member of the Communist Party, or refuses upon request of a producer to make a statement as to such membership, or refuses to testify as to such membership before the House Committee, the producer is relieved of its obligations to give the writer screen credit.

This discussion of the legal rights of an employee against his employer,

179

when the employee loses his employment in the industry because his loyalty is suspect, indicates that as far as legal controls are concerned an employer is substantially free, in the absence of contractual limitations and as long as he is not acting in concert with other employers, to use whatever employment standards he chooses. If the employer administers his own "loyalty program," and decides to cease employing a particular employee, the employee will generally have no available legal recourse, though the standard of "disloyalty" applied by the employer may be vague and unreasonable, and though the employee's activities may have been innocent of any subversive purpose.

The legal rights of the employee under the law of defamation ("Red Channels" and similar publications)

Defamation is the publication (if written, *libel,* and if oral, *slander*) of a falsehood which injures a person's reputation by holding him up to public hatred, contempt, scorn or ridicule, or causes him to be shunned or avoided, or which tends to injure him in his profession. It is fairly well settled today that the false charge that a person is disloyal, is a Communist, Communist-sympathizer, or fellow traveler, is defamatory. Defamatory statements of this kind with respect to particular individuals may possibly be found in some of the various actions and practices which have marked "blacklisting" in the entertainment field. For example, the question might be raised whether persons who are listed in *Red Channels* have been falsely charged with being disloyal or with being Communists or Communist-sympathizers. Though no individual is specifically called a Communist or Communist-sympathizer, it has been contended that as a practical matter the format of *Red Channels* does just that with respect to everyone listed. The cover contains the subtitle, "The Report of Communist Influence in Radio and Television," and a microphone surrounded by a red hand. And the preface to the list of names states that one of the purposes of the index of names is "to show how the Communists have been able to carry out their plan of infiltration of the radio and television industry." (As will be noted later, this contention, that everyone listed in *Red Channels* is in effect called a Communist, was rejected in recent litigation concerning *Red Channels.*)

Defamatory statements may possibly be found in such publications as an article, "Did the Movies Really Clean House?" in the December, 1951, *American Legion Magazine.* This article suggested that the motion picture industry had not at that time "cleaned house" of Communist infiltration, and named 66 persons then active in the industry, with their "Communist front" records, to illustrate the "extent to which recently-exposed Commu-

180

nists and collaborators with Communist fronts are still connected with the production of motion pictures." The "records" of some of the individuals named were somewhat less than conclusive evidence of subversive activity, and it might be contended that the overall effect of the article was to charge these individuals with being Communists or Communist-sympathizers.

Defamatory statements may possibly be made on the signs carried by pickets, or in literature distributed by pickets, protesting the appearance of a particular person in a motion picture or stage production. For example, in 1952 a group known as the Wage Earners Committee picketed a motion picture theatre in Los Angeles carrying two signs — one read: "Communists are killing Americans in Korea. Fellow travelers support Communists. Yellow travelers support fellow travelers. Don't be a yellow traveler," and the other urged that the motion picture not be patronized, and named an executive of the company which produced the picture, Dore Schary, with references to places his name appeared in the reports of the California Tenney Committee. It was later contended in a libel action by Schary against the Wage Earners Committee, which did not go to trial, that these signs defamed him. False charges against particular persons may possibly be found in the various publications "listing" allegedly disloyal, Communist or Communist-sympathizing theatrical personalities. There may be defamatory statements of this kind in communications, protesting the employment of particular individuals, which private groups or individuals may make to employers. And if an employer specifies his reasons for firing, or refusing to hire, a particular employee, he may possibly make defamatory statements concerning that employee.

The description of possible legal redress for the defamed individual is not complete with a listing of instances in which defamatory statements may be made, for other aspects of the law of defamation must be considered in describing the individual's legal rights.

One problem concerns whether the particular employee can show that an allegedly defamatory statement was made about him. This was the issue on which the trial judge ruled for the publishers of *Red Channels* in a defamation action brought by Joe Julian (*Julian* v. *American Business Consultants;* this case is now being appealed in the New York courts). *Red Channels* was sub-titled "The Report of Communist Influence in Radio and Television." It contained statements that the Communist Party, for purposes of indoctrination, uses not only members of the Party but also fellow-travelers and members of Communist adjuncts and periphery oganizations. Another statement read that "some fellow-travelers and 'reliables,' who are not members of the Communist Party, as well as many well meaning innocents, have unknowingly contributed to Party adjuncts and periphery organizations, as also must Party members." And another statement read: "In

181

screening personnel every safeguard must be used to protect innocents and genuine liberals from being unjustly labelled." *Red Channels* contained a list of 151 names with statements, taken mostly from various legislative committee reports, of Communist-front activities which each person listed had engaged in. An introduction to the list of names read:

The information set forth in the following report is taken from records available to the public. The purpose of this compilation is threefold. One, to show how the Communists have been able to carry out their plan of infiltration of the radio and television industry. Two, to indicate the extent to which many prominent actors and artists have been inveigled to lend their names, according to these public records, to organizations espousing Communist causes. This, regardless of whether they actually believe in, sympathize with, or even recognize the cause advanced. Three, to discourage actors and artists from naively lending their names to Communist organizations or causes in the future.

The listing with respect to Julian was that he was "reported" in a House Un-American Activities Committee publication as "speaker" at a "meeting" of Artists' Front to Win the War in 1942, and that he "attended meeting to abolish House Un-American Activities Committee," National Council of the Arts, Sciences and Professions, in 1949.

Julian contended in his libel action that the publication falsely conveyed to readers of the pamphlet that he was connected with the Communist Party, either as a "Communist," "dupe," "tool," "sucker," "colonist," "part of a transmission belt," or "fellow-traveler," or was sympathetic to the cause of Communism. The trial judge decided (affirmed by the intermediate New York state appellate court) that *Red Channels* made no specific reference to Julian as a Communist or fellow-traveler, or the like – *i.e.,* that there was no defamatory matter "of and concerning" Julian. The reasoning of the trial judge was that the introduction to the list of names indicated that some of those listed were Communists, and some were persons who associated with organizations espousing Communist causes "regardless of whether they actually believe in, sympathize with, or even recognize the cause advanced." And nothing in the pamphlet purported to indicate in which of the categories Julian belonged – *i.e.,* that Julian might as well be said from the form of the publication to have been one of the "innocents," as one of the "guilty."

It can certainly be argued with reason that a statement such as the introduction to the list of names in *Red Channels* – in effect saying some of the following are Communists and some are not – does not, as a practical matter, detract from the cloud cast on the reputation of all of the persons named. The problem is one of a matter of degree. A person who is not a Communist and whose name is listed in the Manhattan telephone directory

182

would not be able to recover in a defamation action from one who published the fact that some of the persons listed in the directory are Communists. But if it were published that one of three listed individuals was a Communist there would be a greater likelihood of a court's permitting those on the list who were not Communists to recover in defamation. The question of when a publication will be said to be "of and concerning the plaintiff" is not a settled one in American courts. As illustrated in the *Julian* case this issue may place a formidable obstacle in the path of an "innocent" person who seeks redress under the law of defamation against the publisher of a *Red Channels*.

The law of defamation is the end-product of a balancing of social interests — the interest of an individual in his reputation in the community, and the interest of the public in free discussion. Consequently there are circumstances in which harm to an individual may go uncompensated because a broader public interest in free discussion may be of greater social importance in a particular case. This balancing of interests has resulted in the recognition of various defenses in defamation actions. Three of these defenses are of particular relevance with respect to the publications described in this section which impute Communist sympathies or activities to an individual.

One of these defenses is "truth." In the *Red Channels* case it was apparently true that Julian did participate in the two activities listed with his name (Julian said that he had recited a poem at the 1942 meeting where he was listed as a "speaker"). But this would not have established the defense of truth to the defamatory statement Julian said was published about him — that he was a Communist, Communist-sympathizer, or fellow traveler. Had Julian been able to get by the "of and concerning" problem, the publishers of *Red Channels* could then have attempted to prove the truth of the defamatory statements about Julian. As a practical matter, proof of truth of such statements as these may be difficult, particularly with respect to statements such as "Communist-sympathizer," where the subjective state of mind of the person allegedly defamed would be so much in issue.

Another defense for the publisher of a defamatory statement is that of fair report of a legislative publication. Even if Julian did not "speak" at the meeting, as *Red Channels* reported, and assuming that a false statement to that effect (as distinguished from a statement that he was a Communist) would be defamatory, there would be no liability in defamation if *Red Channels* were simply reprinting (as it did) a publication of a legislative committee. This defense is based on the public interest in dissemination of information about governmental activities, even at the expense of uncompensated harm to an individual's reputation. Such a report must be "accurate," however, and in some cases the references in *Red Channels*

183

differed in varying degrees from the legislative documents. Some of these instances were of a sort in which *Red Channels* published that an individual "sponsored" an organization when the legislative report said he was "affiliated" with it. Unless there were a number of instances of this kind about a single individual it is doubtful that such a change in emphasis would result in a court's saying this was not an accurate report, and if the statement were defamatory, and were not true, decide consequently that the publishers of *Red Channels* would be legally responsible to the individual.

A third relevant defense here would be that of "fair comment." This doctrine permits a person to comment, in what may be defamatory terms, about a matter in the public interest. Examples of this defense are found in the broad area in which possibly defamatory statements may be made about candidates for public office, about books or plays submitted to the public for approval, and the like. In some states this privilege refers only to statements of "opinion," or inferences, drawn from stated facts, of the speaker or writer, as distinguished from statements of "fact." And the privilege extends only to the matter which is of public interest — for example, defamatory comment about the personal character of the author of a book would probably fall outside the area of fair comment, the matter of public interest being the contents of the book. In the *Julian* case the publishers of *Red Channels* contended that if indeed *Red Channels* did call Julian a Communist or Communist-sympathizer — *i.e.*, that there was such a defamatory statement "of and concerning" Julian — this was fair comment on a matter in the public interest, expressing the honest and fair opinion of the publishers, based on the contemporaneously published true facts about his Communist-front activities.

The contention here would be that a radio actor is a "public" person, and that there is a public interest in whether or not an actor is a Communist, because he may be using his position to propagandize for Communist ends, may be engaged in a plot to take control of the industry, may be using his income to finance subversive activities, or may be adding his prestige to Communist-front activities. This was fair comment, the publishers of *Red Channels* said, on a public matter (Communist infiltration of the entertainment industry) concerning a public man, an actor, and was an honest comment put forth for an honest purpose, to check the Communist infiltration of radio and television. The court in the *Julian* case, because of its ruling on the "of and concerning" problem, did not have occasion to decide on the merits of this defense.

There are at least three questions which would arise in determining whether the defense of fair comment would permit a person falsely to say of an actor or other employee in the entertainment industry that he is a Communist or Communist-sympathizer. The possible answers to these questions will indicate, I think, that even if there were a false publication "of and concerning" an actor, that he was a Communist or Communist-sympathizer, he might yet have difficulties in recovering damages in a defamation action.

One question is whether the political activity of an actor is a matter of public interest. Julian contended that any privileged comment about him could refer only to his professional activity as an actor, and that to call him a Communist or Communist-sympathizer, though it might be an honest and fair opinion or inference based on his associations with Communist-front organizations, would not be a comment on a matter of public interest. This has not been a much-litigated question, but in light of the interest there may be for the public to know that a person such as an actor may be devoting his professional activities and income to Communist ends, I think that a court might well decide that the loyalty of an actor *was* a matter of public interest.

A second question is whether calling someone a Communist can be said to be the "opinion" of the publisher, or his inferences, based on his evaluation of the true facts regarding the individual's possibly innocent Communist-front activities. The tendency has been for courts to decide that the labels of "Communist" and "Communist-sympathizer" are to be considered statements of "fact," not opinion, and thus not privileged as fair comment. To publish that a person is a Communist or Communist-sympathizer would most likely be considered privileged comment, and not statement of fact, where the publication included true facts such as association with Communist fronts, and made clear that the "Communist" or "Communist-sympathizer" appellation was the publisher's inference based on these facts. A contrasting situation, where publication that a person was a Communist or Communist-sympathizer would be least likely to be considered privileged comment, would be that where only the appellation was published, so that it appeared that the publisher was offering the statement as a matter of his own knowledge, rather than as opinion or inference from truthfully stated facts. It would be a close question as to how a court would categorize, as fact or opinion, a publication in the form of *Red Channels* — i.e., where assumedly true (and possibly innocent) Communist associations of individuals are listed, with statements that some of those listed as Communists and some are not.

A third question with respect to the defense of fair comment would be whether the comment on truly stated facts was "fair" — i.e., whether it was an honestly held and not reckless opinion drawn by the publisher. This is a vaguely defined, and probably not too stringent, requirement, but there is a point beyond which the social interest in free discussion of matters of public interest will not outweigh the harm which may be done to a defamed

185

individual. This principle might come into play in such a situation as that involving *Red Channels,* or similar publications, where it might well be decided that with respect to some individuals the true facts of Communist associations, on which the publisher's inferences or opinions were based, were so minimal that comment that the person was a Communist, based on such facts, would not be "fair."

An analogous legal doctrine to defamation should be mentioned at this point. This is the "right of privacy," the right of a person to be protected from truthful but unauthorized publications relating to his private affairs. Here again the scope of public interest is critical in outlining the reach of the doctrine. A person before the public generally cannot complain if his name, picture and life history become public property, and persons who become associated with matters of public interest lose their right of privacy with respect to publicizing their association with that activity. It could be contended in some situations in which there have been truthful publications of past Communist-front activities of a particular person, that these activities were in the past, that he is no longer engaged in that kind of activity, and that a legal wrong is committed against him in now publicizing them. An example of this might be the present publication of a person's association with a Communist activity in the early 1940's. Though such activity may have been a matter of legitimate public interest at that time, there might be a question whether past activity of this sort is a matter of present public interest.

The basis for suggesting this possibility of legal redress for an employee is found in such decisions as that of a California court in an action by a woman against the producers of a motion picture based on her life. She had been a prostitute and had been tried for murder and acquitted, and then had gone into obscurity, when seven years later the defendants made their motion picture without her consent and based on her past life. Everything portrayed was true, so there was no defamation action. And the court said that the mere use of the incidents from her life (a matter of public record) did not constitute an invasion of her right to privacy. But the producers had gone further and used her true name, and this was sufficient, the court said, to give her an action against them. In its decision the court said: "Any person living a life of rectitude has that right to happiness which includes a freedom from unnecessary attacks on his character, social standing or reputation . . . This change having occurred in her life, she should have been permitted to continue its course without having her reputation and social standing destroyed by the publication of the story of her former depravity with no other excuse than the expectation of private gain by the publishers."

The present public interest in publication of past Communist associations of employees in the entertainment industry is certainly greater than was any

186

public interest in the past life of the plaintiff in the California case, and the expectation of private gain is probably not as paramount in at least some of the publications concerning employees in the entertainment industry as it was in that case. Hence the legal basis for recovery by such an employee on a theory of invasion of his right of privacy may not be overly sound, but, in any event, it is a possible basis for recovery in those states which recognize the doctrine (the doctrine is not as extensively recognized in New York as in other states).

The legal rights of the employee under the law of interference with business relations (action of the American Legion, or similar groups, in objecting, in one way or another, to the continued employment of the employee)

The law recognizes a man's right to be protected from wrongful interference with his business or economic relationships with others. The question is whether under this doctrine of interference with business relations an employee who is fired, or not hired, due to the intercession in some way of a group like the American Legion, has any legal redress against the group. (In the following discussion I shall use the Legion as a shorthand reference to other individuals or groups which have engaged in activities similar to those of the Legion.) The question would be raised, for example, where an employer dropped an actor upon being informed by officials of the Legion that in the view of the Legion, the actor was disloyal and any movie he appeared in would be picketed. The employer might then fire, or not hire, the actor, either because of belief by the employer that the actor is disloyal, or without pursuing the matter further, simply because of threatened loss of patronage. Or the group's action with respect to an actor may take the form of communication to a theater owner that if a picture with the actor in it is exhibited the theater will be picketed. Or when the picture is exhibited the group may picket theaters in protest. And the result of threatened or actual picketing of a theater may be that the producer of the picture will cease to employ the actor who was the object of attack.

The potential legal action for an employee under the doctrine of interference with business relations would be based on the contention that the Legion, or similar group, had harmed the employee by inducing his employer or prospective employers not to employ him. In determining whether an employee should in such cases as these be given redress under the law, the injury suffered by the employee would have to be balanced against the public interest which might be advanced by these activities of the Legion. This balancing of interests in the law of interference with business relations

187

is illustrated in many familiar areas. In the field of labor law, for example, when a union calls a strike against an employer it probably causes loss to the employer by inducing other persons not to deal with the employer while the strike is in progress; if the union's objective is one of promoting the welfare of the members of the union, as, for example, the seeking of higher wages or better working conditions, the loss the employer may suffer gives way to the social interest being pursued by the union, and the employer's loss goes uncompensated. Or a businessman may successfully attempt to increase his sales, by inducing prospective customers to deal with him and not with his competitors, with the result that other businessmen may lose sales; any loss which may be suffered in this competitive process goes without compensation as long as the inducement of prospective customers is not carried on by means of what the law calls "unfair competition."

There is no specific precedent for the imposition of legal liability on the Legion, under the law of interference with business relations, where the Legion induces an employer to cease employing a particular employee. In deciding such a question it would be necessary to weigh the injury suffered by the employee against the public or other interest served by the Legion. There are a number of factors which a court could consider in making this balance of interests. In the discussion which follows I have attempted to categorize these factors, and to refer wherever possible to the decided cases I have been able to find which would be relevant in reaching decision as to the Legion's liability.

A. THE NATURE OF THE INJURY TO THE EMPLOYEE.

Experience in the entertainment industry has indicated that once employment ceases because an employee's loyalty is suspect in the view of the employer, or in the view of a group such as the Legion, the employee may well lose all opportunities for employment in the industry. This approaches a loose form of "economic outlawry" and would be an important factor in weighing the justification of the Legion in causing such loss to an employee by inducing employers not to employ him.

B. THE JUSTIFICATION FOR THE LEGION TO INDUCE THE EMPLOYER TO CEASE EMPLOYING THE EMPLOYEE.

(1) *The public interest advanced by the Legion.* The contention of groups such as the Legion in inducing employers not to hire particular individuals is that the group, as a patriotic organization, is sincerely attempting to advance the interests and security of the nation. This factor would, of course, be of great weight in determining the Legion's potential liability to a particular employee. To my knowledge there have been no decided cases in which a court has had occasion to weigh the conflicting interests involved

where an employee's employment is attacked, in the public interest, by the Legion. There are, however, analogous decided cases which illustrate the consideration which courts will give to the justification which may be offered as making privileged an interference with business relations.

Interference with business relations by inducing third persons not to deal with a person, in the form of union activities for lawful labor objectives and in the form of "fair" competition between business men, have already been mentioned. Other typical cases have been these:

(a) In an English decision it was held that union officials who persuaded theaters not to contract with a touring stage troupe which paid women performers so little that they were driven into plying "another and older trade," were not liable to the manager of the troupe for inducing theaters not to engage the troupe, because this inducement was made to protect the underpaid women and to protect public morals.

(b) A college established a rule that students could eat only in college-approved restaurants, and it was decided that the college committed no actionable wrong to a restaurant which was left off the list, because the college was administering a health measure for the protection of its students.

(c) There have been some decisions dealing with the contention that the business or other relationships of a person were justifiably interfered with because the acts were done in pursuance of the interests of a religious group. One such decision, for example, held that the owners of a newspaper could not recover damages against officials of the Catholic Church who had promulgated an edict forbidding church members to read the paper, with the result that former readers no longer purchased the newspaper.

In an analogous case, Catholic Church officials procured their parishioners to write letters and to make telephone calls to a radio station demanding that the station cease selling radio time to a commentator speaking for the Jehovah's Witnesses sect. It was decided that the commentator's had no legal redress against the church officials when the commentator's program was discontinued, because the officials were acting to protect the church against what they considered to be unfair attacks and misrepresentations of Catholic teaching.

(d) A New York decision held that there was no actionable legal wrong done to the owner of a meat market when pickets from a butchers' union carried signs in front of the market advising prospective patrons, truthfully, that the market sold only kosher poultry and did not sell kosher meat. This activity was justified on the ground that it was a "public service" though the market owner may thus have lost prospective customers.

(e) A final illustration is that of the cases in which Negroes have picketed a place of business asking that customers not patronize the establishment

189

until the owner adopted non-discriminatory hiring practices with respect to the employment of Negroes. The technical legal problem is one of considering on the one hand the justification of attempting to broaden employment opportunities for Negroes, and on the other the injury to the store owner and, as added by some courts, the possibility that such action, in the form of picketing, will possibly lead to "race riots." Many of the cases which have arisen on this issue have decided that such picketing is legally wrongful and will be enjoined.

(2) *The nature of the activity of the employee which is the basis for the Legion's action.* It is apparent from the public activities of the American Legion and similar groups that there are no clear "standards" by which such groups determine that the employment of a particular individual in the entertainment industry is not in the public interest. Such groups do not as a rule offer a forum to the employee to defend himself; indeed, the notion of private groups, acting independently of official governmental procedures, holding hearings to determine loyalty is not an attractive one. Thus, in practical effect, the Legion and other groups apply standards which may (1) be ill-defined and unreasonable (to the extent they are defined) in categorizing certain conduct as being inimical to the interests of the nation, and may (2) result in possibly unreasonable or reckless conclusions, leaving no means by which the determination of the group can be challenged by the employee. It is possible that if an action by an employee against the Legion were to arise, a distinction might be drawn, in determining the Legion's justification, between an employee with an apparently innocent and inconclusive Communist-front record, such as was cited with respect to a number of persons listed in the December, 1951, *American Legion Magazine* article, and an employee with a more serious "record" of front activity or other activity.

C. THE MANNER IN WHICH THE LEGION INDUCES THE EMPLOYER TO CEASE EMPLOYING THE EMPLOYEE.

Officials of the Legion have suggested that the Legion has engaged only in a program of truthfully publicizing the past Communist associations of employees in the entertainment industry, and has left to the recipients of the publicity the process of drawing conclusions from, or of acting on, the publicity. It is likely that if the Legion activity were limited to such publicizing (through the *American Legion Magazine* or a newspaper, for example) an employee could not reasonably claim that the Legion had unjustifiably interfered with his business relations. A public interest in such information would probably justify truthful publications of this nature. But the Legion's, and other groups', activity has on occasion gone further than this —for example, by notifying employers that motion pictures with a particular employee in them will be picketed, or by notifying theater owners that their theaters will be picketed, or by actually picketing such theaters, when a picture with a particular employee in it is exhibited. It is with respect to such activity that the employee has a stronger argument for contending that this is something more than simply "publicizing" his past activities, and that the Legion has directly, or indirectly through theater owners, unjustifiably induced employers to cease employing him.

Here the courts might draw a line between "persuasion" and "coercion." It might be decided that in the public interest the Legion would be privileged to "persuade" an employer not to employ a particular employee, or to "persuade" a theater owner not to exhibit a motion picture with a particular employee in it. Such "persuasion" might be by publication in the *American Legion Magazine,* or perhaps by direct communication with employers or theater owners. The Legion would likely be privileged to buttress that "persuasion" with a boycott of the picture by members of the Legion. But the employee's case would perhaps be meritorious enough to succeed if the Legion's action passed from "persuasion" to "coercion" of the employer or theater owner — *i.e.,* where by threatened or actual picketing of a picture, inducing consumers not to patronize the picture and inducing theater owners not to exhibit the picture, the employer's "free choice" in weighing the arguments disappeared, and he was in an economic sense coerced into ceasing to employ the employee.

A judicial decision which made such a distinction between "persuasion" and "coercion" was a Massachusetts case involving the Boston Watch and Ward Society. Members of this group read books and magazines looking for "unlawful" publications; when such publications were found, the society informed distributors of periodicals that in the group's opinion the specified publications were against the law, with the intimation that if those publications were sold the society would swear out criminal complaints against the distributors. If these warnings of the society were ignored, criminal prosecutions were instituted. That course was followed with respect to an issue of the *American Mercury* magazine, and the lawsuit, *American Mercury, Inc.* v. *Chase,* followed. The justification offered by the society for this interference with the business relations of the publishers of the magazine was that it was "actuated by a sincere desire to benefit the public and to strengthen the administration of the law." As a practical effect of the society's warnings many distributors did not purchase publications to which the society objected, so as to avoid the risk of even patently unjustified prosecution. In its decision, holding for the publishers of the magazine and enjoining the society from carrying on this activity, the court said:

> The injury to the persons affected does not flow from any judgment
> of a court or public body; it is caused by the defendants' notice, which
> rests on the defendants' judgment. The result on the other person is

the same, whether that judgment be right or wrong; i.e., the sale of his magazine or book is seriously interfered with. Few dealers in any trade will buy goods after notice that they will be prosecuted if they resell them. . . . The defendants know this and trade upon it. They secure their influence, not by voluntary acquiescence in their opinions by the trade in question, but by the coercion and intimidation of that trade, through the fear of prosecution if the defendants' views are disregarded. . . .

The defendants have the right of every citizen to come into the courts with complaints of crime; but they have no right to impose their opinions on the book and magazine trade by threats of prosecution if their views are not accepted. . . . The facts that the defendants are actuated by no commercial motive and by no desire to injure the plaintiff do not enlarge their rights in this respect. . . .

Of course, the distributors have the right to take advice as to whether publications which they sell violate the law, and to act on such advice if they believe it to be sound. The defendants have the right to express their views as to the propriety or legality of a publication. But the defendants have not the right to enforce their views by organized threats, either open or covert, to the distributing trade to prosecute persons who disagree with them.

It is possible that the approach taken in this decision involving the Watch and Ward Society might be followed in an action by a "blacklisted" employee against the Legion, where a court might say, paraphrasing the above-quoted provisions, that the members of the Legion are free to express their views as to the propriety of a particular employee's being employed in the entertainment industry, but they have not the right to enforce their views by threatening economic harm to an employer.

Assuming that a court might decide that at least to the extent that there was economic "coercion" of an employer (as distinguished from "persuasion") not to employ a particular employee and that the Legion had unjustifiably interfered with the business relations of the employee, the problem would arise as to the effect to be given, in the final decision, to the fact that the Legion may induce the employer by means of "speech." For example, where the Legion picketed a theater protesting the appearance of an actor, consideration would have to be given, in balancing the injury to the employee against the public interest in permitting the Legion's freedom of action, to the fact that speech is involved, and to the scope of constitutional protection of free speech as applied to the Legion's activity. The fact that the Legion activity were being carried on by speech would, of course, be an important factor in deciding whether the Legion should incur legal liability to the employee, to the end that a decision not be reached which would infringe upon the Legion members' rights of free speech. But it is clear, of course, that constitutional protection of free speech does not confer upon a speaker a blanket immunity from liability for the harm he may cause another by speech; the law of defamation is a familiar illustration of this principle. And to some extent, at least, it is fair to say that picketing by the Legion, as distinguished, for example, from publications in the *American Legion Magazine,* is more than the exercise of speech, in the sense of communication of ideas and seeking to persuade by argument.

This is illustrated most clearly with respect to labor-union picketing, where it has been pointed out in judicial decisions that picketing may exert an influence on the "viewer" or "hearer" as a "signal," enforced by union sanctions, for members of other unions not to deal with the person picketed. And to a lesser extent picketing may exert an influence on prospective customers of the person picketed not to patronize that person, not because they are persuaded to do so by the merits of the pickets' argument, but because they wish to avoid controversy. This principle was expressed in a recent decision of the United States Supreme Court:

> But while picketing is a mode of communication it is inseparably something more and different. Industrial picketing 'is more than free speech, since it involves patrol of a particular locality and since the very presence of a picket line may induce action of one kind or another, quite irrespective of the nature of the ideas which are being disseminated.' . . . Publication in a newspaper, or by distribution of circulars, may convey the same information or make the same charge as do those patrolling a picket line. But the very purpose of a picket line is to exert influences, and it produces consequences, different from other modes of communication. The loyalties and responses evoked and exacted by picket lines are unlike those flowing from appeals by printed word.

The problem of whether enjoining the Legion from picketing a theater protesting the employment of a particular performer would be an unconstitutional infringement of the pickets' rights of free speech would be a difficult one. However under present interpretations by the United States Supreme Court of the scope of the constitutional right of free speech, a court could probably, as a matter of constitutional law, validly decide, on a balancing of the various interests discussed above, that Legion activity in the form of picketing, or otherwise, which induced an employer to cease employing an employee was wrongful as against the employee, and could therefore hold the Legion members in damages for the harm suffered by the employee, and enjoin the picketing.

I do not know of any case in which an employee has brought an action against the Legion on a theory of interference with business relations. This theory was put forth in the suit by Dore Schary against the Wage Earners' Committee, which was referred to in the section on defamation. The case never came to trial, for the picketing was terminated by the Wage Earners Committee upon the issuance of an injunction against continuance of the picketing in a legal action brought by the theater.

Another theory on which an employee might seek to recover damages against the Legion would be under the federal or state anti-trust laws. The theory of such an action would be that members of the Legion had combined in restraint of trade by inducing employers not to employ the employee. There is little precedent for this kind of action under the anti-trust laws, and I think it sufficient for purposes of these notes simply to suggest the possibility of such an action.

In connection with activity of the Legion to induce an employer to cease employing a particular individual, it should be pointed out that if the activity is in the form of threatened or actual picketing of a theater exhibiting the employer's motion pictures, the producer and distributor of the motion picture and the theater owner may contend that the Legion has interfered with *their* business relations. The theory of the producer and distributor would be that the Legion was unjustifiably inducing the theater owner not to purchase their product, by economically "coercing" the theater owner. The theory of the theater owner would be that the Legion was unjustifiably inducing consumers not to patronize his theater. The same factors which were discussed with respect to the employee's possible action against the Legion would be relevant in balancing the injury done the producer, distributor, or theater owner against the public interest in permitting the Legion its freedom of action.

An additional factor would be present in considering the theater owner's possible action against the Legion, for the theater owner might contend that he was at least "partially neutral" in the "dispute" the Legion had with the employer and employee. The argument would be that the Legion was engaged in a "secondary boycott" against the theater, interfering with its business relations as a means of inducing the public not to patronize the producer's product. This theory was accepted by the court in a law suit arising out of the picketing by the Wage Earners Committee protesting the employment of Dore Schary; the court enjoined the picketing, as a secondary boycott, in an action brought by the theater.

SUMMARY

In broad outline the discussion indicates the following: (1) the employee will generally have no legal redress against his employer or prospective employers with respect to hiring practices which may result in the employee's losing his position in the industry; (2) under the law of defamation the employee may in some cases have some possibility of legal recovery, but there are unsettled problems in the law of defamation which may restrict the potential redress of the employee; (3) under the law of interference with business relations the employee may possibly have theories of recovery against third persons who induce his prospective employers not to hire him, but here the legal doctrine is so extensively unsettled, because of the breadth of interests which must be balanced in reaching a decision, that no precise description of the scope of the employee's rights is practical.

To the problems of legal doctrine there must be added, for a complete picture of the "legal aspects of blacklisting," the caution that for the employee who is faced with the loss of his employment, the expense and delay of litigation may be an all-important practical consideration in assessing his legal rights. Hence it may be said that to a very large degree "blacklisting" in the entertainment industry is a practice in an area in which the law, because of the countervailing social interests involved, does not offer any effective redress for an employee, and such controls as there may be must be found in the self-restraint of those whose actions contribute to the practices involved and in the public opinion within which the practices are carried on.

195

Communism and the Movies
A Study of Film Content
by DOROTHY B. JONES*

LEADERS of the Communist revolution in Russia were quick to realize the political importance of the motion picture. Lenin called it the most important of all the arts. From the outset, the Communist Party in the Soviet Union recognized the value of the motion picture medium not only as a weapon of propaganda within that country, but as a means of spreading the Communist idea of world revolution. Motion pictures approved by the Soviet Government have been distributed widely throughout the world since the 1920's. And there can be little doubt that Communist leaders have long looked with interest and envy upon the world position occupied by the American motion picture.

It was therefore pertinent to any investigation of Communist activity in the United States to explore the facts with respect to the infiltration of Communists into the Hollywood motion picture industry and to bring to light and examine objectively the facts with regard to the degree to which the Communist Party has been successful in utilizing the Hollywood movie as a means for spreading Communist propaganda. The task of studying the degree of Communist success in Hollywood was first undertaken by the Committee on Un-American Activities of the House of Representatives during the 80th Congress.

The degree of success or failure of the Communist Party in Hollywood can be measured in various ways. One index would certainly be the extent to which the Communist Party through its control or partial control of certain guilds and unions had succeeded in tying up production through strikes or by other means. The amount of financial support which the Party succeeded in obtaining from some members of the wealthy movie colony might provide another such index. What amount of money was paid into the Communist Party by Party members working in the motion picture industry over the past twenty-five years, and what sums reached the Party through the various front organizations to which other movie people unwittingly contributed support? Or the success or failure of the Communist

---

* Dorothy B. Jones served as chief of the film reviewing and analysis section of OWI during World War II.

196

Party in Hollywood may be measured by the degree to which the Communists were successful in adapting the content of Hollywood movies for their own purposes in furthering the spread of the Communist ideology throughout the world.

The end-product of the motion picture business is the completed film. Thus, while the degree of success achieved by the Communists in Hollywood can be evaluated by various standards, it is of primary importance that a careful examination be made of the extent to which the Communists were or were not successful in using the Hollywood movie, with its vast worldwide audience, for their own political purposes. Final judgment on this subject must be based on an objective analysis of the content of the motion pictures, themselves. Fortunately, the film is a relatively permanent form, which can be objectively analyzed. It is the central purpose of this report to examine and evaluate the content of Hollywood movies to find out whether or not they did contain such propaganda.

A year-long inquiry was undertaken which involved a search of story files at four major studios and an examination of the content of almost 300 films which were relevant to this question. The facts brought to light indicate that some Hollywood writers in some instances made attempts to adapt the content of the films on which they worked in a manner which would have been beneficial to the Communist Party and the Soviet Union. The facts also showed, however, that the very nature of the film-making process which divides creative responsibility among a number of different people and which keeps ultimate control of content in the hands of top studio executives; the habitual caution of moviemakers with respect to film content; and the self-regulating practices of the motion picture industry as carried on by the Motion Picture Association, prevented such propaganda from reaching the screen in all but possibly rare instances.

The second part of this study has been concerned with another question. Admittedly the necessary task of exposing Communist activity carries with it a certain element of risk to American freedom from some of the countermeasures directed against the internal Communist danger. Freedom of the screen is an important American freedom, and one which the Communists themselves only profess to support. (In this study it has been shown how the Communist Party while campaigning for freedom of the screen in support of one Hollywood movie which they were attempting to use for their own propaganda purposes, simultaneously fought the making of another film which would present an alternative point of view.) Furthermore, in the battle of ideas which has characterized the Cold War, the Hollywood movie (which provides an estimated 60 per cent of the screening time in theatres throughout the world) is and has been a medium of considerable importance.

In the light of these facts, this report has undertaken to explore the following questions: To what degree and in what manner, if at all, did Hollywood motion picture content appear to be affected by the exposures of Communist infiltration into Hollywood made by the House Committee on Un-American Activities in October, 1947 and by the Committee's widely publicized claims that the Communists had used the screen for propaganda purposes? (Before the opening of the 1947 Hearings the Committee had reported that it had in its possession "a complete list of all the pictures which have been produced in Hollywood in the past eight years which contain Communist propaganda," and this statement had been read into the Congressional Record.) What changes, if any, took place in the all-over content of the Hollywood product after 1947: what films were made dealing with communism, and what did these films say about the threat of communism, about Communist ideology and tactics, and about counter-measures for restricting the Communist movement in this country? The purpose of this second portion of the study has been to examine (1) what Hollywood films have actually said about communism, and (2) whether — and if so to what degree and in what manner — freedom of the screen was affected by the investigations conducted by the House Committee on Un-American Activities.

Summary of Methods and Source Materials Used in This Study

As noted above, this study has undertaken an examination of Hollywood films to determine the facts with regard to the question of whether Hollywood movies have or have not served as a vehicle for Communist propaganda. Many *opinions* have been given on this subject, and those made by persons appearing before the House Committee on Un-American Activities have been summarized in the body of this report. The study, however, has not primarily been concerned with opinions. Rather it has been devoted to a search for facts.

In examining whether or not there has been Communist propaganda in Hollywood movies, this study has concerned itself primarily with two bodies of data. First, and most important, has been an examination of the films of The Hollywood Ten. The films of these ten men (Alvah Bessie, Herbert J. Biberman, Lester Cole, Edward Dmytryk, Ring Lardner, Jr., John Howard Lawson, Albert Maltz, Samuel Ornitz, Adrian Scott, and Dalton Trumbo), totaling 159 in number which were released by motion picture companies over a period of 21 years (1929-1949, inclusive) have been studied with care. Although it has been impossible to screen all these 159 motion pictures (in some cases on films of the earlier years prints are even no longer available), 85 — or well over half of the total — have been examined at first hand, either by viewing a release print of the film or reading the cutting continuity of the completed movie. (A cutting continuity is a verbatim record of dialogue together with a shot-by-shot description of the action.) Of the remaining 74 films, the shooting script has been studied whenever possible and where the script could not be obtained a variety of secondary sources have been consulted with at least three different synopses, picture analyses, or reviews being covered on each film. However, with a few exceptions, every film of The Hollywood Ten which could in any way be called "controversial," or which was mentioned by any witness at the Hearings of the House Committee on Un-American Activities, has been examined at first hand (either by viewing the motion picture itself, or by checking through a cutting continuity of the film).

In identifying "Communist propaganda" in the 159 films of The Hollywood Ten thus studied, it was necessary to begin by defining propaganda and by establishing a set of criteria for recognizing and evaluating possible Communist-inspired content:

(1) Did any dialogue or any of the social, political or economic points of view expressed in a given film follow the line of the Communist Party current at the time when that film was being made?

(2) In instances in which dialogue or any other of the social, political or economic points of view expressed in a given film followed the Communist Party line, was this a viewpoint shared at that time by other large and identifiable non-Communist groups in the United States?

(3) In instances in which the social, political or economic viewpoint appeared to conform to that of the Party, were the symbols and phrases used the same as those employed at that time by the Communist Party?

(4) Did any of the films credited to The Hollywood Ten which purported to reflect reality depart from known facts beyond the point usually allowed for dramatic purposes, and if so, was it in a manner which was primarily advantageous to the Communist Party and the Soviet Union?

One or more of these four criteria were applied in evaluating the content of each of the 159 motion pictures studied. In the case of some films — for example a routine western — the subject matter of the film followed the usual formula in a manner which made it quickly obvious that these criteria could not conceivably apply, and that the answer to the first question was "no." (One can conceive of a western which would follow the Communist Party line, but it could hardly be one which could be described as "routine.")

An application of this method involved not only a careful summarizing of

199

the changing line of the Communist Party through five successive periods between 1929 and 1949 during which time the films credited to The Hollywood Ten were released, but also the making up lists of the 159 films so as to ascertain which films were made during which period of changing Communist policy.* These films were classified as falling into one of the five periods, for the most part, according to the date when the picture was completed (rather than the release date, which may be delayed months or in some period where there is a product backlog, even a year or more). With such film lists it was then possible consistently to compare the content of each film with the policy of the Communist Party in effect during the period when the film was in production. (In some cases a film was in the making over two periods, and in several such instances it was possible to go back into the story files of the studio and examine various stages of the script to observe whether changes in the Communist Party line were reflected in the successive versions of the script.) For purposes of this report, therefore, content of the 159 films of The Hollywood Ten have been examined separately for each of the five successive and changing periods of Communist Party policy.

In connection with films credited to The Hollywood Ten during the war years, the files of the Bureau of Motion Pictures, Office of War Information, now in The National Archives in Washington, were consulted in assessing the value of these films to the war effort as judged by the Office of War Information, with the evaluation of these films given in both Hollywood and New York taken into account. In addition to an examination of film content and an evaluation of this content in relation to its time and to each of the four criteria for identifying Communist propaganda already enumerated, certain general facts with regard to the 159 films of The Hollywood Ten have also been studied. These facts included: the various types of screen credits received by each of The Hollywood Ten on the 159 motion pictures; the number of writers working on each film (including all writers who received *any* type of screen credit on the picture); the proportion of "A" and "B" class features and the relative number found in each of the five periods; the year of release of the films credited to each of The Ten — showing the period during which the films of each man and the group as a whole reached the screen; and analyses of the 159 films of The Ten according to picture types, as distinguished from picture content.

Throughout this study also the story files of four major studios (Columbia, Twentieth Century-Fox, M-G-M and Universal-International) and cer-

---

* For lists of Hollywood Ten films according to the five successive periods of reorientation of Communist Party policy and propaganda, see Appendix I-B. For producer, director and writer credits on these films, see Appendix I-A.

tain files of the Production Code Administration of the Motion Picture Association were explored for relevant material on some controversial pictures. The purpose here was to determine, by an examination of original story materials and successive stages of treatment and script, whether *attempts* were made during the writing of certain films to inject ideas which would reflect the policy of the Communist Party.

The statistical and content analyses of the 159 films of The Ten were complemented by two case studies of films — namely BLOCKADE (Wanger-United Artists, 1938) which was based on an original screenplay by John Howard Lawson and which aroused widespread controversy at the time of its release, and WE WHO ARE YOUNG (M-G-M, 1940) which was based on an original screenplay by Dalton Trumbo and which, while reviewed unfavorably by many critics as an "uninteresting" movie, was never a controversial picture. In the case of both of these films, the writer named was the only writer to receive screen credit on the film. BLOCKADE was selected because it is the most controversial film credited to any one of The Hollywood Ten. And WE WHO ARE YOUNG was selected when it became clear from a study of the story files at M-G-M that it was a clear-cut instance in which an original screenplay contained material which was identifiable as Communist propaganda according to the criteria established in this study. (Such material did not appear in the finished film.) In each of these case studies the film has been analyzed in detail in a separate chapter of this report, and as many facts as possible presented regarding the film's production (as obtained from interviews with responsible studio personnel and a careful examination of story files and PCA records), as well as reviews and published comment appearing after release of the film in this country.

These analyses of the 159 films credited to The Hollywood Ten were followed by a less intensive study of a second body of data: namely the films credited to the self-declared ex-Communists. When the hearings of the House Committee on Un-American Activities were resumed in 1951, certain producers, directors and writers who had at one time belonged to the Communist Party, appeared before the Committee to give full testimony regarding their Communist affiliation and to answer questions regarding their activities as Communists in Hollywood. In every instance, one of the questions asked by the Committee was the period of membership, and these 29 ex-Communists, with only one exception, provided an answer. As supplementary evidence in evaluating the success of the Communist Party in influencing film content, I drew up a list of the films credited to this group of 29 ex-Communist producers, directors and writers during the years when they were members of the Communist Party (or in the year following membership, to allow for a possible time lag in release of the pictures). This group worked on a total of 124 films during the time when they belonged to the Communist Party, and those films, while not analyzed with anything like the thoroughness of those credited to The Ten, are reviewed and discussed in the body of the report.*

A wide range of source has been used in the second part of this study to determine what Hollywood films have actually said about Communism, and whether — and if so to what degree and in what manner — freedom of the screen was affected by the investigations conducted by the House Committee on Un-American Activities, particularly those held in 1947. The most important bodies of data used in answering these questions were:

(1) Over-all statistics from the Production Code Administration of the Motion Picture Association regarding the nature and content of films released 1947-1954 inclusive (see Appendix III-A);

(2) A compilation of lists of award-winning Hollywood motion pictures, 1947-1954, as judged by the New York Film Critics, the National Board of Review, *Film Daily,* and the Academy of Motion Picture Arts and Sciences (see Appendix III-B);

(3) Box-Office successes for the years 1946-1954, based on key city grosses for each year as compiled for *Fame,* Quigley publications, New York (see Appendix III-C);

(4) List of anti-Communist films of 1947-1954 and of earlier years compiled during this study with the help of studio Story Departments, the MPAA, and many other individuals and organizations (see Appendix III-D).

In addition, many of the anti-Communist films were specially screened and analyzed, although time did not permit any case studies of any of these motion pictures.

It goes without saying that throughout this study in addition to these data a wide range of secondary source material was covered with particular attention to published books and articles on the Communist question and to sources dealing with the motion picture.

Summary of Findings on Films of The Hollywood Ten

The Hollywood Ten are, for the most part, writers. Of the ten men, only Edward Dmytryk has never received a writing credit during his career in Hollywood. Two of the Ten (Biberman and Scott) have at one time or another received a producer credit — indeed half of Adrian Scott's screen credits have been as a motion picture producer, and the rest mostly as a writer. Three of The Ten (Biberman, Cole and Dmytryk) have received

---

* For a list of the 29 ex-Communists and the films credited to them during the period when they were Communist Party members, see Appendix II.

director credits — although only Dmytryk can be said to be a full-time motion picture director by profession. And six of the group (Bessie, Lardner, Lawson, Maltz, Ornitz and Trumbo) have never received anything but writer credits on Hollywood motion pictures. (*For complete figures on screen credits of these ten men, see Appendix I-C, Table 3.*)

As already noted The Hollywood Ten received credit on a total of 159 motion pictures which were released by the motion picture industry during the years 1929-1949, inclusive. That there was some overlapping of credits among The Ten on these pictures, is indicated by the fact that The Ten received a total of 179 screen credits on these 159 films. This does not necessarily mean that there were 20 films on which two of The Ten received credit, as it is possible for one man to receive two or more credits on a single movie — as was the case, for example, with THE MASTER RACE (RKO, 1944) for which Herbert Biberman received credit both as director and writer. However, in a number of instances two members of the group worked on the same motion picture — e.g., Dalton Trumbo wrote and Edward Dmytryk directed TENDER COMRADE (RKO, 1943); Albert Maltz and Ring Lardner, Jr. collaborated in writing the screenplay for CLOAK AND DAGGER (United States Pictures, 1946).

The most prolific members of the group were Lester Cole, with 36 films; Dalton Trumbo, with 27 films; Samuel Ornitz, with 25 films; Edward Dmytryk, with 24 films; and John Howard Lawson, with 16 films. These five men received a combined total of 136 or 75 per cent of the 179 credits received by the group as a whole. With the possible exception of Albert Maltz, who scripted several outstanding motion pictures, these five men are also the most important of the group in terms of their professional rating in Hollywood. Of the remaining five, none received credit on more than ten pictures during his career in Hollywood. Fifty-six of the 159 motion pictures on which one or more of The Ten received credit were A-pictures, as judged by the producers, directors and stars associated with these productions, and the types of billings which they received in the theatres as indicated in trade reviews. Thus it can be said that over one-third of the films on which The Ten received credit were A-Class features. (*For complete figures see Appendix I-C, Tables 3, 6 and 7.*)

Of the 179 screen credits received by The Ten, over 20 per cent or about one-fifth were credits for original story material; 60 per cent were credits for screen plays; less than 3 per cent were adaptation credits. It is notable that in the case of about one out of every 5 films credited to the group, one of The Ten was given sole credit for preparing the screenplay. In only four out of the 159 films was The Hollywood Ten writer the only scribe working on the picture. These four pictures were BLOCKADE (Wanger-United Artists, 1938) made from an original screenplay by John Howard

Lawson; and WE WHO ARE YOUNG (M-G-M, 1940), THE REMARKABLE ANDREW (Paramount, 1941), and TENDER COMRADE (RKO, 1943), the latter three all based on original screenplays by Dalton Trumbo. (*See Appendix I-C, Table 2.*)

An analysis of the types of pictures credited to The Ten has yielded some interesting results. The group appears to have been more concerned with subject matter of social relevance than was Hollywood as a whole. Thus if Social Theme, Prison and War Films are combined (and, indeed, war films can be regarded as films of social content, particularly when spy and espionage pictures are eliminated from the total, as was done in this case), then 49 movies or about 31 per cent of the pictures worked on by The Ten dealt with subject matter of social importance. This total is high when compared to the industry as a whole, for even during the war when the motion picture industry was making innumerable war films, no more than 20 or at the outside 25 per cent of the movies made dealt with the war or other social themes. Even in the postwar years, which have often been referred to as the period of "social realism" in Hollywood, the proportion of social theme and war films combined totaled 29.7 per cent of the product and this in 1947, which was undoubtedly an all-time high for films of this type.

On the other hand, the analysis by picture type of the 159 films of The Ten has shown that very few westerns, period pictures, horror films, or musicals were credited to the group. These four types combined accounted for only about 7 per cent of the total. Comparable figures are not available for the same period for the industry as a whole, but between 1947 and 1954 the proportion of total industry product falling into these same four categories accounted for from 23.2 to 35.3 per cent of the industry's output. Since these four picture types have appeared fairly consistently as a substantial part of the total industry product during the past twenty years, it is probably safe to say that the proportion of westerns, period pictures, horror films and musicals credited to The Ten was markedly less than the comparable figures for the industry as a whole during the 1929-1949 period.

In interpreting the above figures the question of the *motives* of The Ten will undoubtedly be raised — and the question asked as to whether or not these men were deliberately attempting to overemphasize the *problem* aspects of life under democracy. On the other hand, when confronted with these figures some Hollywood executives point to the fact that Hollywood has always dealt in some films with broad social themes, and that in this industry writers are "cast" for certain types of pictures (somewhat in the same manner as actors and directors are "cast"), and that it is only natural that The Ten, with their interest and knowledge of social problems, would be assigned to work on social theme movies (rather than on musicals, westerns, period pictures, etc.). It must be emphasized, however, that in any case we are not here concerned with the *motives* of The Ten, but rather with an objective analysis of the actual content of the finished films with which their names are associated. And obviously social theme movies cannot *per se* be said to be Communist propaganda, but must be examined individually as has been done in the present study.

The relatively large number of murder-mystery, mystery, spy and espionage pictures attributed to The Hollywood Ten is a matter of interest. These types of films rank first in number, accounting for 17.6 per cent of the 159 films of the group. It is interesting to speculate upon the possible factors of personality inherent in these ten men which may have attracted them to such themes, or may have caused their employers to assign them especially to the writing or directing of such motion picture material.

Most of the 159 films of The Hollywood Ten were, by and large, typical of the Hollywood product generally and the subject matter of the majority of their films could not reasonably provide a context for Communist ideas. For purposes of this intensive study, however, the 159 films were classified according to date of completion as falling into one of the five successive periods of re-orientation in the Communist Party line which governs all matters relating to Party policy and propaganda, with the following results:

24 or 15.1% were made during the New Revolutionary Period of Communist Party policy (January, 1929-August, 1935), a period of 6 years and 8 months

43 or 27.0% were made during the so-called Popular Front (August, 1935-August, 1939), a period of four years

27 or 17.0% were made during the Period of the Soviet-Nazi Pact (August, 1939-June, 1941), a span of 1 year and 10 months

49 or 30.8% were made during the Period of Soviet-American Collaboration (June, 1949-May, 1945), a four-year period

16 or 10.1% were made after World War II and during the Cold War (May, 1945 to date), for approximately 2½ years of which The Ten were employed in Hollywood.

These figures indicate that The Hollywood Ten were most active in film creation during the two periods when the Communist Party line was *not* directly at odds with the general policies being followed by the United States Government (i.e. during the so-called Popular Front Period and the period of Soviet-American collaboration during World War II). Ninety-two, or almost three out of every five, films credited to the group were made during one of these two periods, with the largest being made during the war years. These were the years when what the Communists had to say for their own reasons of expediency happened to come closest to what American liberals believed and stood for. Particularly during the war years (after Hitler's attack on the Soviet Union), the Communists in Hollywood, like those in the factories and on battlefields throughout the world, fought the war with a zeal second to none.

During the New Revolutionary Era of the Communist Party (1929-August, 1935) the Party strove internationally for the preservation of the world status-quo as a means of protecting the Russian oligarchy. During this period the Communists promoted a strongly revolutionary-sounding type of propaganda, which was, however, according to Sidney Lens and other students of Communist Party tactics, aimed primarily at harrying capitalism rather than destroying it since the regime in Russia was far too involved in its internal problems to be able to extend itself at that time.

In the United States, the Party called for "a Soviet America" as the only way out of the depression and for the defense of the Soviet Union as the "Fatherland of the workers of the whole world." At that time the Party branded the Socialists as the "twins" of the Fascists, and singled them out as the main enemy of the Communists. In the United States, the Communists demanded social insurance, free rent, free gas, electricity and water and public transportation for the unemployed during the depression. And they followed an independent trade-union policy, setting up separate Communist unions in this country through the Trade Union Unity League.

A study of the content of films of The Hollywood Ten made during this period shows that they were, in the main, routine Hollywood fare which followed time-worn patterns of content. The six or seven films having important social or economic content on which The Ten worked during this period spotlighted some of the contemporary problems of that day. However, these same problems — conditions of convict labor, the role of munition makers in World War I, corruption in municipal government, etc. — were all matters which were being currently aired in the American press as part of the backwash of the depression. Furthermore, at that time other films were being made in Hollywood which treated these same problems in much the same manner. In treating such problems, films of The Ten recommended no violent, unlawful or undemocratic means for correcting the conditions shown. On the contrary, these problems were shown as being resolved by democratic means — by newspaper exposés which result in the removal of corrupt officials from public office e.g. HELL'S HIGHWAY (RKO 1932, etc.), by court trials of those guilty of breaking or circumventing the law, e.g., AFRAID TO TALK (Universal, 1932), etc.

Actually these films, and others like them made throughout the industry, were a reflection of the times — and, on the part of the motion picture industry, an attempt to capitalize at the box-office on current public interest in exposés of graft and corruption. A careful examination of all material available on these early films shows that none of the symbols and phrases used in such films as Afraid to Talk or Success at Any Price were similar to those being employed at that time by the Communist Party. Indeed, at that time the Communist Party terminology and phraseology was so revolutionary-sounding that it would have been recognized immediately and would never have been able to make its way onto the screen. Also, the facts as to conditions pictured in films of this period were not exaggerated beyond the point usually allowed for dramatic purposes. On the contrary the films in question were based on newspaper accounts of factual investigations (Afraid to Talk on the Seabury investigations into corruption in municipal government, Hell's Highway on the "sweat box" trials being aired as part of the investigation into conditions of convict labor in the South, etc.).

In the Period of the so-called Popular Front that lasted for four years, from August, 1935, to August, 1939, the line which was to guide Communist Party policy and propaganda in the United States was first announced in the summer of 1935 at the 7th Congress of the Communist International. Reversing Party policies of the previous period, the Communists, dominated by a fear of the growing power of Nazi Germany, now called for a coalition of Communist, Socialist, democratic and progressive elements against all "fascist" and "reactionary" elements. During this period the Communists, following Soviet policy, supported the idea of collective security; intervened on the side of the Republic in Spain against General Franco, who was supported by Italy and Nazi Germany; and fought a brief but full-scale war with Japan along the Soviet-Manchurian border. As part of its strong anti-fascist policy during this period, the Communists in the United States urged a boycott of German, Japanese and Italian goods. They also urged a revision of the Neutrality Act in this country to allow shipment of arms to countries which were victims of Fascist attack (particularly Loyalist Spain).

During the Popular Front period of the Communist Party The Hollywood Ten were credited with 43 motion pictures; of this number 15 dealt one way or another with subject matter of social importance. Almost without exception, these films told stories about the underprivileged, the non-conformist, the disfranchised citizen, or the misunderstood person in our society, similar to those being widely published in this country at that time. The Hollywood Ten social theme films of the so-called Popular Front Period were more diversified both as to picture type and subject matter, than were themes of the New Revolutionary Era. Furthermore in this period, social-content films were concerned with presenting the personal stories of individuals rather than in exposing unsavory social and economic conditions. But again the overwhelming majority — about two-thirds — of the 43 movies on which The Ten worked between the summers of 1935 and 1939, were run-of-the-mill movies — murder mysteries, spy films, musicals, sports stories, action and adventure films. The total of 43 films included no less than 16 different picture types, a

207

greater diversification than that found in any other period, except the period of the Nazi-Soviet Pact which followed.

The 43 Hollywood Ten films of the Popular Front period were evaluated in relations to the four criteria established in this study for identifying Communist propaganda in motion pictures. In comparing the content of these films with the Communist Party line, it became evident that the social and economic content of this period was strongly pro-democratic rather than in any way supporting the Communist ideology as such. It was in accordance with the Communist Party line to the extent that the official Party line itself professed to be pro-democratic during this period, this reversal in policy having grown out of Communist fear of the rising tide of fascism in Europe, and particularly the growing strength of the Nazi State. It is significant, however, that with the exception of the film BLOCKADE there were no films credited to The Ten which in any way took sides in the battle between Fascism and communism fast shaping up on the European continent. An exhaustive study of the film BLOCKADE has shown that, while it was inherently partisan in its sympathy for the Loyalists, this attitude was one supported at the time by large and identifiable non-Communist groups in this country, even though it was at the same time one which was condemned by Catholic organizations. And since the film contained no symbols or terminology being used by the Communists, it cannot be said to have been Communist propaganda. Actually the primary theme of this movie was anti-war, a viewpoint widely endorsed at the time not only by liberals, but by conservative isolationists, who reviewed the picture favorably.

Communist policies of the Popular Front urged that the United States enter into a system of collective security along with the Soviet Union; sought opportunities for sharpening existing differences among European powers; urged the boycott of German, Japanese and Italian goods; and favored changing the Neutrality Act to allow shipment of arms to countries who were victims of Fascist attack. All of these and related policies of the Communist Party found no expression in the content of films credited to The Ten. Indeed, with the exception of BLOCKADE, their films of this period were notably non-political in content. Considered in detail by all four criteria, films of the Popular Front period were found to be devoid of Communist propaganda.

The third period of Communist orientation considered in relation to films of The Ten was the period of the Nazi-Soviet Pact, which lasted from August, 1939, to June, 1941. Of all the periods during which the Communist Party line in the United States twisted and turned under directives from the Comintern, the period of the Nazi-Soviet Pact is the one in which it was most transparently clear that Communist propaganda in the United States was emanating from the Soviet Union. Whereas prior to the Pact the Communist

Party had supported those who were fighting Hitler, Mussolini and the Japanese militarists, now that the Soviet Government had thrown in its lot with the fascist dictatorships, the Party began to refer to the war against Hitler as an "imperialist struggle" and to the defense program which had begun to develop in the United States as a "capitalist program fostered by Wall Street."

In keeping with this new policy the Communists opposed the draft and lend lease, and sought to defeat these measures by capitalizing on isolationist and pacifistic sentiments of all kinds within the United States. While there were others besides the Communists who opposed the draft and lend-lease, by August, 1939, public opinion had already begun to shift toward support of these measures. As was evident in the successive public opinion polls throughout this period, the Communist Party line was in many respects in direct contradiction to prevailing trends of public opinion in the United States. Furthermore, for the first time in a decade, the Party line was in direct opposition to the viewpoint increasingly held by the majority of liberals and intellectuals in the United States who strongly believed that the spread of fascism in Europe must be checked as it was becoming a major threat to all democratic nations, including our own. One would assume, therefore, that during this period, any efforts of the Communists to get the Party-line viewpoint into motion pictures would be clearly identifiable and unmistakably evident, providing, of course, such efforts had been successful.

There were only 27 motion pictures credited to The Ten during the Nazi Pact Period. Though this number is small, actually considering the relatively short time-span of the Pact, The Ten were credited with almost twice as many films as would have been anticipated. But if The Ten were more prolific than usual during the Pact Period, there were few observable differences in the kinds of films with which they were credited during that time. The 27 films which they turned out in these months were of no less than 16 different types including everything from routine murder-mysteries like THE LONE WOLF STRIKES (Columbia, 1940), racketeer films like HALF A SINNER (Universal, 1940) and UNDER AGE (Columbia, 1941), to horror films like THE DEVIL COMMANDS (Columbia, 1941), a Sports Picture entitled GOLDEN GLOVES (Paramount, 1940), career films like the Dr. Christian series and pure fantasies like THE INVISIBLE MAN RETURNS (Universal, 1940). Indeed, the variety of picture types during the Pact Period was greater than in any other period except the preceding one, which it matched.

About 30 per cent of films worked on by The Ten during this period had themes dealing primarily with social or economic problems and this proportion was approximately the same as that found in the two previous periods. The only respect in which the overall composition of films credited to The Ten during the Pact period appeared to differ from that of earlier periods was that proportionately there were fewer A-Class films. In the period of

209

the Pact, The Ten were credited with only four A-Class features, and these were credited either to Lawson or Trumbo.

On the whole, the social and economic points of view expressed in The Hollywood Ten films of this period were much the same as those found in the previous period, but there are a few observable differences. These differences are not so much in the kinds of films or their subject matter as in a shift in emphasis toward a more complete and forthright screen portrayal of contemporary economic problems. In The Popular Front Period, as already pointed out, Social Theme pictures and others portraying the American scene presented widely diversified stories about the little guy who, after many difficult and trying experiences, finally comes into his own. In these films economic problems were often presented but usually not as the central theme of the picture. By the late summer of 1939, however, economic themes had begun to be treated with a directness hitherto unknown on the screen. Among the films of The Ten which followed this trend were WE WHO ARE YOUNG (M-G-M, 1940), which has been analyzed in detail as a case study in this report, ACCENT ON LOVE (20th Century-Fox, 1941), and THEY SHALL HAVE MUSIC (Goldwyn-United Artists, 1939), etc. It was found in this study, however, that while films of The Ten showed greater frankness in treating contemporary economic problems than did their films of earlier years, this attitude was one which was increasingly evident in the product of the entire industry. For example, it will be recalled that this was the time when GRAPES OF WRATH (20th Century-Fox, 1940) was made, based on John Steinbeck's best-selling novel — and it was but one of a number of films treating the problems of dust-belt farmers or migratory workers (a film on this subject entitled THREE FACES WEST, starring John Wayne, was credited to Samuel Ornitz and three other writers).

The films of the Nazi-Soviet Pact Period were notably lacking in political content of any kind. There was nothing in the films which made reference to the draft, lend-lease, the defense program and other measures which the Communist Party was strongly opposing at the time. There were, however, two films in this period which dealt with what was happening on the European continent — MYSTERY SEA RAIDERS (Paramount, 1940), an adventure melodrama about Nazi sea raiders plying the Caribbean, and FOUR SONS (20th Century-Fox, 1940), an A-Class feature starring Don Ameche which pictured the experiences of one Czechoslovakian family through the days when Hitler threatened and finally took over Czechoslovakia. These two films were examined with care to see whether or not either or both of these movies contained anything which could be identified as Communist-line propaganda, and the results in the case of both films were entirely negative. An examination of the content of these films showed that these movies were not in keeping with the Party line, for even though FOUR SONS was an anti-war

210

picture, both movies pictured the Soviet Union's ally, Nazi Germany, as the heavy. Actually, however, both films tended to be less pointedly political in the handling of their war content than did some of the other Hollywood films of that time which treated similar subject matter. It is worthy of note that although the Communist Party line was strongly anti-war at the time these two films were made, both of these pictures were among those named during the Senate investigations of 1941 as being *pro-war* propaganda movies.

On June 22, 1941, Nazi legions crossed the borders of Poland and attacked the Soviet Union. Thus the Nazi-Soviet Pact ended. The American Communist Party, once more quickly reversing itself, immediately urged American participation in the war in Europe. What the Communists had scorned as an "imperialist war" against Nazi Germany, overnight became glorified in the Communist Press as "the People's War." Whereas, as we have seen, in the previous period they had opposed the draft and Lend-Lease and promoted the slogan "The Yanks Are Not Coming," now they urged that the nation enact draft legislation at once and carry on an all-out program of preparedness for war, revising their slogan to "The Yanks Are Not Coming Too Late." Public opinion polls taken throughout the United States show that during the entire period of Soviet-American collaboration (even in the six months prior to American entry into the war), the Communist Party line was, with a few specific exceptions, in keeping with the point of view held by the majority of Americans.

During the four-year period of Soviet-American collaboration there were a total of 49 feature films on which one or more of The Ten received screen credit, and this total is proportionately higher than that for any other period under study. Twenty-three or 47 per cent of all the films credited to The Ten during the war years were A-Class productions, as compared to only 15 per cent in the previous period. The increased activity of The Ten during the war years is also reflected in the fact that during this period, more than in any other, there was a tendency for a man to receive more than one screen credit on a single film, and also for various members of the group to collaborate in working on a single picture. And for the first time, all of the Hollywood Ten received one or more screen credits during this period.

Of the 49 films credited to The Ten during the period of Soviet-American collaboration, 57 per cent were primarily concerned with some aspect of the war. And it is significant that the proportion of war films made by The Hollywood Ten as a group was almost twice as high as that made by the industry as a whole during the war years.

A careful examination of the content of films credited to The Hollywood Ten during the period of Soviet-United Nations collaboration has shown that by all four criteria used there was nothing in the films of The Ten which could be identified as Communist propaganda. The Ten were credited with an impressive number of top-quality war films which made a positive contribution to the government's war information program. In any list of the ten outstanding Hollywood films of the war years, John Lawson's ACTION IN THE NORTH ATLANTIC (Warners, 1943), and his SAHARA (Columbia, 1943), Dalton Trumbo's THIRTY SECONDS OVER TOKYO (M-G-M, 1945), and Albert Maltz's PRIDE OF THE MARINES (Warners, 1945) would necessarily be among those included. Possibly, too, other films of The Ten might be included on such a list, for example, HITLER'S CHILDREN (RKO, 1942), DESTINATION TOKYO (Warners, 1943), COUNTER-ATTACK (Columbia, 1944), etc.

On the other hand, many films on which The Ten received credit did not follow the Communist Party line of this period which called for an all-out war effort, for some of the films of this group failed to give a useful handling of the war topics which they undertook to treat, and a few, though not related in any way to the Communist viewpoint, were judged by the OWI to be detrimental to the war effort abroad, mostly because of their inadequate portrayal of the American home front in wartime.

In instances where dialogue or any of the social, political or economic points of view expressed in a given film were in keeping with the Party line, it was because they gave support to the war-effort in a manner similar to that of most non-Communist groups. Furthermore, what the films of The Ten had to say about the war was in keeping with the official information policy of the United States government. There is no evidence in any of their films of appeals being made for a second front, nor was the role of the Soviet Union played up in any way. Only one picture, COUNTER-ATTACK, portrayed Russians in major roles, and this film was judged to be of positive value to the government's war information program. The New York OWI reviewer noted that "the Russians are shown to be brave, but not without faults." And there was no evidence in this study that films of The Ten made during the war years utilized the symbols or phrases currently in use by the Communist Party. However, a few films (notably TENDER COMRADE, THEY LIVE IN FEAR, TOMORROW THE WORLD, etc.) appeared to suffer from an over-zealous handling of their war content. So eager were these writers to arouse fellow-Americans to the issues of the war and the role which we in this country must play in it, that they outdid themselves and wrote films some of which were clearly propaganda-type pictures.

This survey of films made by The Hollywood Ten disclosed that one film produced during the war years departed from the facts which it purported to portray beyond the point usually allowed by dramatic license and in a manner which was of political significance. This film, OBJECTIVE BURMA (Warners, 1945), was one in which coincidentally two of The Ten received writing credits. A member of the War Department familiar with the China-India-Burma Theatre was the studio consultant on this film from its outset, but

212

unfortunately gave only technical advice. Furthermore, Warner Brothers received an OK on the completed film from the War Department before it was shipped abroad. This picture, which according to the British viewpoint pictured Errol Flynn as winning the battle of Burma practically single-handed, was greatly resented in England. Finally it was withdrawn because of the adverse sentiment it aroused toward the motion picture industry in particular, and the United States in general. However, the distortion of facts in this film was to the disadvantage rather than to the advantage of the Communist Party and the Soviet Union *at the time when this film was being written*. And, therefore, this film cannot be regarded as containing Communist propaganda, even though, when it was released abroad after the close of the war, the film tended to stimulate unfriendly feelings toward this country on the part of Great Britain, and thereby may be said to have served the purpose of the Soviet Union. Furthermore, OBJECTIVE BURMA was neither the first nor the last of several war films made in Hollywood in which a bumptious American hero won a military campaign virtually singlehanded, thereby arousing resentment among our allies.

During the Cold War the Soviet Union did everything possible to weaken the economic and political life of the Western countries, and in line with this general policy, the Communist Party in the United States opposed all political programs which would strengthen the Western democracies (e.g. The Truman Doctrine, the Marshall Plan, the Atlantic Pact, etc.). During this period, too, the Party conducted propaganda campaigns for peace and disarmament, while the Soviet Union steadily increased its preparations for war. American foreign policy in the period was labeled "American imperialism" by the Communists, and the United States was charged with being the "aggressor in Korea against the peoples of Asia," and an instigator of atomic war to destroy the Soviet world. Likewise, as already noted, during this period the Communist Party sought every possible means for sharpening differences between the United States and its allies.

Between May, 1945 and October, 1947, at which time The Hollywood Ten were arraigned before the House Un-American Activities Committee, The Ten were credited for work on 16 motion picture features (some of these films were not released until as late as June, 1949). A high proportion of these films (56 per cent) were A-Class features, a relatively higher proportion than in any of the previous periods.

My analysis of the content of films credited to The Hollywood Ten during the years immediately following the close of World War II and during the early years of the Cold War, showed that none of these reflected in any manner the current viewpoint of the Communist Party. On the contrary, the films of The Ten during these years were, with a few exceptions, escapist Hollywood fare. In the case of those films which undertook to treat social themes,

213

for example CROSSFIRE (RKO-Radio, 1947), dealing with the problem of anti-Semitism, and TILL THE END OF TIME (RKO, 1946), dealing with the postwar adjustment of a G.I., the ideas expressed were those being treated and discussed generally throughout the country in magazines, newspapers, postwar novels, etc., and were also similar to those being portrayed at that time in other Hollywood motion pictures. In fact, on the whole the films credited to The Ten in the years immediately following the war were less political and less concerned with contemporary social and economic problems than the films this group made in earlier periods (except, perhaps, those of the Nazi-Soviet Pact Period). Actually, the most important social document films of the immediate postwar years were written by people whose names have never been associated with the Communist cause.

Summary of Findings on Films Dealing with Communism, 1947–1954

Hollywood has traditionally steered clear of controversial screen material particularly of religious and political subject matter. Although the threat of communism has been treated in a few early Hollywood films (*see Appendix III-D 2*), these movies in several instances caused controversy — for example OUR LEADING CITIZEN (Paramount, 1939) was protested by some labor organizations, and a few theatres where it played were, reportedly, picketed by Communists. Even more important to Hollywood, the subject of communism has failed to arouse interest at the box-office and has generally been regarded by producers as uninteresting and unprofitable screen fare.

During the days of the Nazi-Soviet Pact, however, when sentiment throughout this country was strongly anti-Russian, Hollywood introduced a cycle of comedies in which Communists and their ideas were ridiculed, and several of these films did well at the box-office. These films included HE STAYED FOR BREAKFAST (Columbia, 1940), starring Melvyn Douglas and Loretta Young; COMRADE X (M-G-M, 1940), PUBLIC DEB NUMBER ONE (20th Century-Fox, 1940), etc. By far the most successful of these, however, was NINOTCHKA (M-G-M, 1939), starring Greta Garbo. These and other films of the 1939-40 period treated Communist theory and tactics to a not-so-gentle ribbing which was particularly devastating in its effectiveness because of the as yet unshaken assurance implicit in these comedies as to our own security in relation to communism and to the Soviet Union at that time. NINOTCHKA, sent into Italy at the behest of the State Department after the war, was credited with helping to swing an election in that country when the Communists were in danger of gaining control there. The other Hollywood films of this period also undoubtedly have done much for the democratic cause throughout the world.

214

In November, 1947, the month following the 1947 Hearings, M-G-M re-released NINOTCHKA, and between 1947 and 1954 there were thirty-five or forty anti-Communist movies. These films were of three types. The vast majority were anti-Communist spy thrillers. These spy melodramas followed the familiar timeworn pattern. Except for a change in the identity of the foreign power involved, they were indistinguishable from the Nazi and Japanese spy stories of World War II or from the endless stories about un-specified foreign powers whose spies and secret agents have peopled the Hollywood films of earlier years. The bulk of the anti-Communist films were thus spy thrillers which added nothing to public understanding of commu-nism, but instead merely utilized the Communist threat as a convenient and timely element in the usual spy-formula movie. While it can be argued that such pictures are harmless — that audiences the world over, long familiar with this type of film, simply do not take these stories seriously, yet these films appeared during the Cold War and it must be pointed out that their stereotyped portrayals of the Communist threat tended to minimize the im-portance of the very real and serious threat of Communist infiltration. Par-ticularly to overseas audiences, the anti-Communist spy thrillers must suggest that Americans do not take the Communist threat seriously — since they treat it, without thought or purpose, in a formula-type movie.

There were, however, a few films among this group which undertook to shed some light on the methods used by the Communists in infiltration and in obtaining information from citizens involved in secret defense projects in the United States. ATOMIC CITY (Paramount, 1952) was one of the better films of this group. But by far the best of such films was WALK EAST ON BEACON (Columbia, 1952) which gives a detailed case history of a Boston spy ring, and was reported in *Time* as being "loosely based on the real espionage case of Soviet Agent Harry Gold and Britain's atomic scientist Klaus Fuchs." Both of these films gave an unusually detailed portrayal of some of the countermeasures taken by the FBI in ferreting out and tracking down Com-munists engaged in espionage activity in the United States.

The second type of anti-Communist film released during this period at-tempted to depict and, in the case of a few films, to explain the growth and development of the Communist Party in the United States. Among such films were THE RED MENACE (Republic, 1949), THE WOMAN ON PIER 13 (RKO-Radio, 1939), I WAS A COMMUNIST FOR THE FBI (Warners, 1951), BIG JIM McLAIN (Warners, 1952), MY SON JOHN (Paramount, 1952) and others. These films in one manner or another set out to examine communism as it exists in the United States — the way in which the Party recruits and holds its membership, and the tactics by which it seeks to disrupt American life and to destroy American values.

In these films American Communist leaders were characterized in the gangster tradition as tough men who rule with an iron hand and use violence as their primary weapon. Like the Hollywood stereotype of the American gangster of yore, these Communist leaders are shown to live exceedingly well, to have their "yes" men and their stool pigeons who ferret out disloyal Party members. Most important, these Communist leaders follow the gangster pattern in that all opposition is met with violence and, whenever necessary, death to the person who dares to oppose their leadership.

On the other hand, these films suggest that for the most part those who are attracted to communism in the United States are the intellectuals. The reason why these Americans have been attracted to the Communist movement is rarely explained. But in more than a few instances (THE WOMAN ON PIER 13, THE RED MENACE, etc.) the main attraction is shown to be a woman, a formula which not only conforms to the Hollywood tradition, but often underscores the "free love" viewpoint associated with radical movements.

These films which picture communism in the United States gave erroneous and misleading portrayals of Communist tactics and some minimized the countermeasures being taken against Communist infiltration in this country, and thus, unwittingly, these films may well have benefitted the Communist cause abroad. American Communists as pictured in these films usually regret their entrance into the Party. However, if world audiences are to believe what they see in these films, they will learn that disaffected American Communists cannot escape party discipline and are often forced to suicide (THE RED MENACE, WALK EAST ON BEACON, etc.), or are murdered by the Communist Party (I WAS A COMMUNIST FOR THE FBI, THE RED MENACE, MY SON JOHN, etc.). Actually, in point of fact, the Communists in practice rarely put themselves in direct opposition to the law by such extreme measures. The subtlety of Communist methods is almost completely overlooked in these films about communism. This oversimplification is misleading so that these films have the effect of underestimating the damage which the Communist can inflict upon American democracy.

While the purpose of some of these films may have been to awaken Americans to the threat of communism, in retrospect it is clear that these films, particularly as looked at abroad, grossly misrepresented the methods of the Communist Party in the United States and often made the countermeasures of the United States government against Communist espionage look weak or ineffectual. This impression is augmented by the large number of spy pictures which show Communists in high places able to lay hands on top-secret information invaluable to the Kremlin. Thus, for example, in WALK A CROOKED MILE (Edward Small Productions-Columbia, 1949) an American scientist gathers top-secret data for the Communists while the FBI is portrayed as incompetent. J. Edgar Hoover, replying to a letter of protest about FBI portrayal in this film, made public in a letter to *The New York*

216

Times (October 21, 1948) that the FBI had not participated in the making of the film and had no way to restrain the producer from using the term FBI since this term is in the public domain. Likewise, in WHIP HAND (RKO, 1951) agents of the Soviet government are shown to have built a laboratory for the development of diseases for use in bacteriological warfare in a midwestern ghost-town, unbeknown to the FBI. These and similar films (PROJECT X, BELLS OF CORONADO, etc.), while recognized by Americans as purely fanciful, cannot always be judged realistically by overseas audiences, and certainly do nothing for American prestige abroad.

A third group of anti-Communist films of the 1947-54 period dramatized events of the Cold War which had taken place abroad. Some of these films are laid behind the Iron Curtain — GUILTY OF TREASON (Eagle-Lion, 1949) deals with the recent trials of Cardinal Mindszenty; ASSIGNMENT PARIS (Columbia, 1952) presents a story closely paralleling the Vogler and Otis cases in Hungary; MAN ON A TIGHTROPE (20th Century-Fox, 1953) tells the escape of a Czech circus from behind the Iron Curtain; etc. The reference to reality implicit in these and similar movies is heightened by the fact that most of them were photographed in Europe, in settings which cannot but be recognizable to many Europeans. These films by and large portray the Russian enemy as blindly obedient to his government, inhuman toward his fellowman, and on the whole lacking in intelligence. This stereotyped portrayal has been modified in a few films — notably in MAN ON A TIGHTROPE, directed by Elia Kazan and based on a screenplay by Robert Sherwood, which is unquestionably one of the best anti-Communist films of this period. Also in THE IRON CURTAIN (20th Century-Fox, 1948), a film which tells the experiences of Igor Gouzenko, former code clerk at the Russian Embassy at Ottawa, there is some modification in the usual stereotype of the Russian Communist.

Of the many motion pictures about communism produced by Hollywood, only one took the form of a documentary — namely THE HOAXTERS (M-G-M, 1952). This film in its indictment of communism and other forms of totalitarianism uses actual newsreel footage portraying the real words and deeds of the dictators in exposing the many switches in the Communist Party line toward the United States which have taken place over a period of years. It also expresses a warning against those who use slander, gossip, hate and innuendo to crucify individual citizens of a particular race or creed, and points out that these tactics when used to fight communism are as un-American as communism itself. The HOAXTERS while it may be criticized for its oversimplification of the Communist problem nevertheless is notable as one of the few efforts made by Hollywood to give any serious consideration to the question of communism.

None of the so-called anti-Communist films of the 1947-1954 period did well at the box-office. With a few exceptions, these films were not good motion pictures as judged by one of the industry's own main criteria — box-office success. Yet there is no reason to doubt that a good anti-Communist film can be made. Indeed TRIAL (M-G-M, 1955) has been generally reviewed as a good movie and the public appears to have borne out the opinion of the critics in this case. And it is undoubtedly no accident that the first postwar anti-Communist film to do reasonably well at the box-office is the most honest and accurate in its treatment of communism in the United States.

Summary of Findings on Changes in Hollywood Film Content, 1947–1954

Following World War II there was evident in Hollywood an increasing interest in social themes. During the war, Hollywood producers, directors and writers had undertaken to dramatize some of the serious problems of the war years. At the same time quite a few prominent film-makers had spent part or all of the war in combat photography in some branch of the armed forces; others had made training films for the armed services; and still others had been active in helping to produce for the Overseas Branch of OWI, motion pictures which would tell the world about American democracy and the American way of life.

When these film-makers returned to Hollywood they brought with them new ideas about picture-making. After the war, documentary technique came into use in the production of Hollywood films as never before, and writers, producers and directors began to experiment with the telling of stories which would dramatize some of the social problems of the post-war period. Many of those who had served in the service had come to see at first-hand the tremendous sacrifice of life and the widespread human suffering which the war had brought with it, and felt that the motion picture could help to bring greater understanding of the many problems which remained to be solved at the war's end.

World War II came to a close in 1945, and it was not until about a year and a half later that the bulk of the social document films began to appear. Thus it was that the 1947 Hearings of the House Committee on Un-American Activities came in the year when social realism in Hollywood was just beginning to come into its own. THE BEST YEARS OF OUR LIVES (Goldwyn-RKO, 1946) had won wide critical acclaim, and had done big business at the box-office. Documentary-type films like THE NAKED CITY (Hellinger-International, 1947) and BOOMERANG (20th Century-Fox, 1947), both shot almost entirely on location, were attracting the enthusiastic interest of critics and public alike. In 1947, the anti-Semitic problem was explored on the screen in GENTLEMEN'S AGREEMENT (20th Century-Fox) and CROSSFIRE

218

(RKO). And since the public had shown its interest at the box-office in this more adult kind of movie fare, the industry began to move ahead on other productions of this kind, which would explore social problems through the personal story of a few individuals. That this type of movie had reached what was undoubtedly an all-time high, is suggested by PCA figures for the last half of 1947, which show that 28 per cent of the industry product was being devoted to social theme movies, or to films dealing with psychological problems (a very popular type of movie at that time).

From the standpoint of change in movie content the years 1947-1954 appear to fall into three periods. In the first of these, roughly 1947-1949, social and psychological themes in movies began to decline, dropping from 28.0 per cent of the product in the last half of 1947, to 20.2 per cent in 1948 and to 17.7 per cent in 1949. Although throughout this period – and to a lesser extent throughout the period that followed – some social theme movies continued to be made, there was an ever-smaller number of them. Still, in this initial period, 1947-1949, there were many outstanding productions of this type – for example, THE SNAKE PIT (20th Century-Fox, 1948), which treated mental illness; ALL THE KING'S MEN (Columbia, 1949) and a number of films treating the Negro problem in the United States, including Kazan's PINKY (20th Century-Fox), INTRUDER IN THE DUST (M-G-M), and HOME OF THE BRAVE (Screen Plays – U.A.), the latter all released in 1949. And in this same year – the first year in which Hollywood began to be seriously concerned about the effects of television upon box-office receipts, a new cycle of war films began to appear. The first of these was BATTLEGROUND (M-G-M), which surprised many in the industry by turning out to be a top box-office success, and was soon followed during the same year by TWELVE O'CLOCK HIGH (20th Century-Fox), with many other war stories going into production, and many old war films being pulled out of the vaults for hasty re-issue.

It was in the second period, however, 1950-1952, that the most clear-cut change in the content of Hollywood films occurred. The 1950-1952 years were characterized not only by more war films (of the sure-fire patriotic variety) but by fewer social theme movies, by a greater emphasis throughout the industry on what is sometimes called "pure entertainment" – and by a large number of anti-Communist films.

The number of pictures dealing with social and psychological problems, which had been declining in the previous several years, now took a sharp drop – from 17.7 per cent in 1949 to 11.7 per cent and 12.5 per cent in 1950 and 1951 respectively. This drop is even more evident if psychological stories are eliminated from the totals: the social problem film in 1949 accounted for 16.5 per cent of the product; in 1950 this figure dropped to 8.9 per cent and in 1951 to 9.0. Films dealing with crime or crime investigations also increased somewhat representing one-fifth of all films receiving code approval in 1950 (a high for the 1947-1954 years). It cannot be said that during the early 1950's the social problem type of film disappeared entirely from the Hollywood screen. In 1950 THE MEN (Kramer – U-A) which treated the postwar adjustment of the G.I., and NO WAY OUT (20th Century-Fox) another film on the Negro problem, were named among the best films of the year by the National Board of Review. In 1951, BRIGHT VICTORY (Universal-International), which dealt with both of the aforementioned problems in a single film, and DEATH OF A SALESMAN (Kramer-Columbia) won critical acclaim. And DECISION BEFORE DAWN (20th Century-Fox) which examines the concept "What is a traitor?" and A STREETCAR NAMED DESIRE (Warners) a social problem movie which *Time* Magazine described as a "grown up, gloves off drama of real human beings" were among the top films of the year as judged both by the critics and by American audiences at the box-office. Also there were, for example, a number of films dramatizing the work of American school teachers (WOMAN OF DISTINCTION, Columbia, 1950; CONFIDENTIAL CONNIE, M-G-M, 1953, etc.). But films of this type were far fewer in number after 1949.

The switch to escapist fare is reflected in the type of films which won top acclaim from the critics in these years. And not least significant in describing the 1950-1952 change in content is the fact that Hollywood itself, voting for the best film of the year through the Academy of Motion Picture Arts and Sciences, named "pure entertainment" films as the best in each of these years: ALL ABOUT EVE (20th Century-Fox), a story about an ambitious young actress' rise to fame on Broadway, in 1950; AN AMERICAN IN PARIS (M-G-M), a musical, in 1951; and THE GREATEST SHOW ON EARTH (Paramount) in 1952. Even though AMERICAN IN PARIS came in as a "dark horse" against two other runners-up (A PLACE IN THE SUN and A STREETCAR NAMED DESIRE), the choices for these years are not without significance.

As for the anti-Communist films, these had begun to appear immediately after the Hearings with the re-issue of NINOTCHKA (M-G-M) in November of 1947. In 1948, three anti-Communist spy melodramas made their appearance, and in 1949 a half dozen more now including several on communism in America (THE WOMAN ON PIER 13, THE RED MENACE) and on the Cold War in Europe (THE RED DANUBE and GUILTY OF TREASON). But this cycle of films reached its height in 1952 when no less than 13 anti-Communist films of this type were released, this number representing over 37 per cent of all those made in the eight-year period under study (1947-1954).

Thus the years 1950-1952 can be described as a period when the industry radically reduced the number of social theme movies, and devoted itself to escapist fare of various kinds. And it was the period when the bulk of the anti-Communist films came to the screen.

220

The third period of change actually began toward the end of 1952, but became clearly evident in 1953. Trends of the previous period continued to some extent. But the prime motivating factor which effected the product as a whole was the change in the film form. Cinerama was introduced in September, 1952, and it proved to have phenomenal appeal and was soon followed by the introduction and equally sudden popularity of 3-D and large screen. In September, 1953, the first cinemascope production *The Robe,* was previewed in New York and this and the pictures which followed in this new form did a landslide business at the box-office. There followed Vista Vision and other big-screen formats designed to give third-dimensional effects. All these changes had notable effect on film content.

Social and psychological themes continued to fall in number (from 12.7 per cent in 1952, to 9.2 per cent in both 1953 and 1954). On the other hand, subject matter and types of films which were suited for wide screen presentation, increased in number — westerns, adventure films, and the number of historical, biographical and historical-fiction movies.

It is interesting, however, that in both 1953 and 1954 the top film of the year was once more inclined toward the tradition of "social realism." In 1953 FROM HERE TO ETERNITY (Columbia) was selected as the best film of the year not only by the Academy of Motion Picture Arts and Sciences, but by the New York Film Critics and the *Film Daily,* and was included among the 10 best of the year named by the National Board of Review. In 1954, ON THE WATERFRONT (Columbia) likewise made a clean sweep of the honors. On Academy Award night it was revealed not only as the industry's choice as the best picture of the year, but won an Oscar apiece for its writer, director and producer. This film was likewise voted best picture of the year by the New York Film Critics and the National Board of Review, and named as one of the Ten Best by *Film Daily.*

CONCLUSIONS

This study of COMMUNISM AND THE MOVIES has thrown considerable light on a number of questions. Some of these questions were raised at the outset of this study; other pertinent questions naturally arose as the findings began to take shape. Thus, for example, while the first part of this study was to have been simply with the question of whether or not there was Communist propaganda in films of The Ten, as the results began to point consistently toward a negative answer to this question, we were impelled to ask further questions. Did the Hollywood Ten make any *attempt* to incorporate in their pictures content which appeared to serve the Communist cause? If so, were such efforts made by all or only by some of this group? And were such attempts consistent throughout the work of a given writer, in evidence only at certain periods? If such attempts had been made at all, what persons or processes intervened which prevented this content from coming through in the completed film? In these conclusions, we shall indicate what our findings have shown wtih respect to these and other questions.

Did Hollywood Writers Attempt to Inject Communist Propaganda into the Films on which they Worked?

From the material collected and analyzed in this study, and from an examination of story files at four of the major studios and at the Motion Picture Association, it can be stated definitely that some Hollywood Ten writers did, in the case of certain pictures, attempt to incorporate in their films ideas which paralleled those of the Communists. There are instances which provide definite proof that such efforts were made. Thus, for example, a detailed analysis of the original screenplay submitted by Dalton Trumbo for the movie, WE WHO ARE YOUNG (M-G-M, 1940), indicates that this script's unequivocal condemnation of the American way of life would have served the Communist cause if it had been produced as originally written. However, this script underwent a thorough-going revision under the direction of the producer and the studio, and when released never raised controversy of any kind. That such attempts were made by some other writers in shown by our study of the films of the self-declared ex-Communists as well as by the files of the Code Administration of the Motion Picture Association of America.

However, the facts collected in the course of this study indicate that this effort was made by relatively few writers, and was not made consistently even by the most ardent and politically-minded of the group. Actually, this study has shown that the overwhelming majority of the films on which The Hollywood Ten or the self-declared ex-Communists worked, were rarely suitable as vehicles for Communist propaganda — routine westerns, murder mysteries, etc. And even in the case of pictures which might have afforded possibilities for injecting party-line content, there was for the most part, little effort made to do so. Thus, for example, John Howard Lawson worked on the original screenplay for an anti-war and anti-Nazi motion picture entitled FOUR SONS (20th Century-Fox, 1940) and his writing on this film covered the period January, 1939 — March, 1940. Yet a careful comparison of various stages of script over this period of time shows that the material prepared prior to the Nazi-Soviet Pact did not differ in any significant respect from versions of the same material prepared three months after the signing of the Pact (although the political emphasis was ultimately minimized due to the wishes of the producer who wanted to play up the personal story.)

However, in another instance story file material strongly suggested that in preparing a script Lester Cole, by revising characterizations, attempted to portray big industrialists, and the idle rich, as well as a United States Senator,

222

in an unfavorable light. SINNERS IN PARADISE (Universal, 1938), an original screenplay by Harold Buckley, had described a group of people who had boarded a plane bound for the Orient which had been forced to land on a deserted south sea island. These people, facing the same problems of securing food and shelter, had all reacted quite differently to the situation. Harold Buckley's script included, among others, a beautiful girl named Doris Dodd, who is described as the "richest girl in the world," an amusing but harmless U. S. Senator, and two representatives of large oil companies competing for business in the Far East.

Two writers, Lester Cole and another writer worked on the second script, which when completed about six months later had revised these characters as follows: Miss Dodd had become Miss Thelma Chase, traveling incognito, who was given an unfavorable portrayal and identified as "heiress to the Chase millions and one of the richest girls in the world . . . who was going abroad to absent herself from the growing labor troubles at one of her great auto plants, which was closed on strike." The Senator was shown to be less amusing and more pompous, and was also shown using his governmental influence in making "private deals" on war supplies in the Far East ("it's easy for the government to wink an eye" on such deals). And the oil men in this second script had become munitions salesmen, who "with a fortune at stake were hastening to the Orient to close gigantic deals for the sale of munitions" ("when these gentlemen dump their munitions in the Orient, they'll be responsible for . . . approximately 100,000 lives"), and were vying with each other to make a deal with the Senator.

This script provides an example of what might be called the "politicalizing" of film content which, our study indicates, was in a number of instances attempted by The Hollywood Ten writers. (It should be noted in the case of the script on SINNERS IN PARADISE that many revisions were made in the above-noted content prior to the making of the film.)

According to testimony given before the Committee, The Ten have not always been in agreement as to what they say in motion pictures or as to how it should be said. Edward Dmytryk testified that CORNERED (RKO-1945), which Adrian Scott produced and he directed, and on which John Wexley had prepared the original script — aroused considerable controversy among The Ten, controversy which involved John Howard Lawson and Albert Maltz and others. John Wexley, whom Dmytryk described as being at that time a party member, claimed that the script which Dmytryk had used in shooting (which had been written by a non-Communist writer) had resulted in their turning out a "pro-Nazi" picture. Dmytryk, who testified that his major interest in this case was to turn out a good movie, reported that he and Adrian Scott were "startled" to learn that Wexley, John Howard Lawson and others considered that they had turned out "a pro-Nazi instead of an anti-Nazi picture."

All of the above statements, it will be noted, have been made with respect to Hollywood *writers*. It is much easier to examine the work of writers — which takes the form of concrete and accurately dated story outlines, treatments and successive versions of script — than it is to search out the unrecorded decisions and possible influence of producers and directors. Movie directors, by their role in the movie-making process, are not in a position to influence content directly to the same extent as the writers are. Producers, on the other hand, can have even more influence than the writers. All that can be said on this subject is that there has been no evidence turned up in the course of this study which indicates that producers or directors attempted to influence film content in a manner which would serve the Communists. However, it must again be stressed that this study has been basically concerned with an examination and evaluation of *completed films,* rather than with a consideration of factors influencing the content of the earlier stages of film production.

Did motion picture studios or the Motion Picture Association attempt to prevent writers from using the screen for Communist purposes?

This study has indicated that the degree of political awareness about the Communists and about the desire of some writers to influence film content along party lines has varied greatly not only from one studio to another, but even within a given studio. On the whole, however, writers working with a studio producer have had little or no opportunity to distort screen content in a way which would serve the Party line. The tailoring of a script for film production is a rigorous, stream-lined process which does not readily allow the introduction of extraneous material. There have been relatively few stories which could have lent themselves to the propaganda purposes of the Party, and this study has shown that even when such have been submitted by The Hollywood Ten writers, an average of three writers have worked on a picture, with the work of all these writers being done under the supervision and guidance of the picture producer, and with the final script being checked by the "front office" prior to production.

As has been revealed in this study, even in instances in which The Hollywood Ten writers had an ideal vehicle for propaganda purposes (as in BLOCKADE or WE WHO ARE YOUNG), and an ideal writing situation (in the case of each of these films, the Hollywood Ten writer was the only one working on the script), the producer of the film and the studio exercised such complete control that it was impossible for the writer to turn out a shooting script that would express Communist ideas.

The high degree of control over content exercised by the producer was also brought out during the hearings in the testimony of some of the ex-Communists. Thus, Richard Collins testified that he and Paul Jarrico, who,

224

he states, were both Party members at that time, were highly pleased when they were assigned to do the screenplay for SONG OF RUSSIA. However, before the picture was shot, the question of whether it might conceivably be too pro-Russian in its effect was fully discussed in a conference attended by the producer, the director and others as well as the head of the Studio. And finally, after it was decided that the picture could be made "without any trouble," Richard Collins testified that he and Paul Jarrico were put to work "cleaning up" the script by eliminating references to "collective farms" and, one gathers, all other items in the script which had even remotely referred to communism. This same kind of revision was done in the case of WE WHO ARE YOUNG, when Dalton Trumbo made two revisions of this script before the studio agreed to purchase it, and then was put to work under the direction of the producer, to revise the story along lines which the studio wished it to follow.

The Code Administration of the MPAA, in its reviews of story and scripts prior to production, and in its screening of completed films for Code approval, has also kept a watchful eye out for any Communist-inspired content. An intra-office summary on various subjects compiled by a staff member of the Code Administration of the MPAA prior to World War II indicates that as far back as the middle 1930's the industry was aware that there were some communistically-inclined writers in Hollywood who occasionally attempted to inject propaganda into their films:

"This (communism) is a very dangerous subject as screen material. Some Hollywood writers are Communists, and try to inject communistic propaganda speeches into scripts they write. These take the form of speeches condemning the capitalistic system, and wealthy people, or bemoaning the plight of the poor, and suggesting this condition would not exist under communism. The PCA watches, closely, for this propaganda, and suggests inflammatory speeches to be deleted or modified."

This PCA summary then cites a total of 20 motion pictures submitted to the Code Administration between 1935 and 1941 in the form of properties considered for production, screenplays, or completed films which from the viewpoint of the MPAA raised some kind of problem because of the "communistic angle" in their content. Not all these instances were cited as having contained Communist propaganda. Some were questioned as being attacks against American institutions believed to have been inspired by Communist writers. At least one script (submitted in 1939) was not produced because in the opinion of MPAA officials it was "obviously Communist-inspired." A few were anti-Communist films which encountered censorship difficulties in this country or overseas. Most, however, were motion pictures (including a few anti-Communist films) which contained speeches of Communist agitators that the MPAA found questionable. This material provides further evidence of the fact that the motion picture industry itself has long been aware that Communists might try to influence film content, and the MPAA has in some instances recommended the elimination or revision of material which it believed to be Communist-inspired.

Thus it can be stated that the evidence produced in this study shows that the production process itself, and the review of story material, scripts and completed films by the Code Administration of the MPAA, have tended greatly to restrict what efforts have been made by writers to utilize the screen for Communist propaganda.

Was there Communist propaganda in the films credited to The Ten?

The films of The Hollywood Ten have been analyzed in great detail in this study with the following results:

(1) *It was found that none of the 159 films credited over a period of years to The Hollywood Ten contained Communist propaganda,* judged according to the objective criteria set up at the outset of this study as described above. Furthermore, it should be stated that *the files of the MPAA, which indicate films which the Code Administrator felt contained possible Communist propaganda, confirm the findings of this study with regard to films of The Ten, in that none of the pictures cited are those on which any members of this group received screen credit.*

(2) *The Communist Party has, on occasion, once the picture was released, utilized films credited to The Ten for purposes of propaganda.* The detailed analysis and evaluation of BLOCKADE (Wanger-United Artists, 1938) made during the course of this study shows that this film reflected a viewpoint which was held at that time by strongly pro-democratic (anti-Communist and anti-Fascist) groups in this country, and did not contain Communist propaganda as judged by any of the four criteria used in this study. Nevertheless, BLOCKADE was used as a springboard for a propaganda campaign by the Communists once it was released. In this case the picture was tossed squarely into the political arena by the studio at the time of its release when Walter Wanger wired Cordell Hull, then the Secretary of State, that Franco's agents were in Hollywood investigating the film and might protest its release. (Actually, of course, no one from Franco's government had even heard of the picture, much less having seen it.) And the controversy over BLOCKADE resulted in a public debate on freedom of the screen which the Communist Party did its utmost to exploit. How sincere the Communists were then (or are now) about freedom of the screen may be judged by the howls of protest they put up at that same time when it was reported that 20th Century-Fox was considering making THE SIEGE OF ALCAZAR, which told the other side of the story with respect to the controversy in Spain.

226

(3) *The content of the films of The Hollywood Ten appears to change in a manner which is in keeping with changes in the content of Hollywood films generally, with the exception of the fact that films of The Ten deal more with social themes.* For example, one of the major studios for its own purposes made an analysis of all the films produced by the industry during the twenty-year period, 1920-1940, and found that 16 per cent of the pictures which were made during these two decades had themes of international, political or economic significance — or related to some event of current importance. The proportion of social theme, war and prison pictures etc. credited to The Hollywood Ten during the period 1929-1940 was over 30 per cent, and while it is obvious that there were probably more films of this type made by the industry generally during the 1930's than during the 1920's, still the figure for The Ten is high enough to indicate a special interest in stories of social consequence.

Of The Ten, John Howard Lawson was the most consistently concerned with the social and economic problems of society, and, particularly during the earlier part of his Hollywood career, Dalton Trumbo also reflected such concern in the stories which he wrote for the screen. However, the films of all ten men reflect a sincere concern with social and economic problems, and a large number of the films with which these men were associated championed the cause of the underdog, the underprivileged, the social outcast — e.g., the criminal or the person with criminal associations who tries to go straight and finds himself an outcast of society (I STOLE A MILLION, Universal, 1939, THE MAN IN BLUE, Universal, 1937, etc.); the unwed mother (PORTIA ON TRIAL, Republic, 1937); the hobo (HITCH HIKE LADY, Republic, 1935); the department store basement clerk or the newsboy who aspire to a better life (HEAVEN WITH A BARBED WIRE FENCE, Twentieth, 1939, KING OF THE NEWSBOYS, Republic, 1938, etc.); people who live in the tenements and want to improve their living standards (LITTLE ORPHAN ANNIE, Colonial-Paramount, 1938, ACCENT ON LOVE, Twentieth Century-Fox, 1941); underprivileged children aspiring to a greater opportunity to develop their musical talents (THEY SHALL HAVE MUSIC, Goldwyn-United Artists, 1939); the devoted physician, unappreciated in his home community, inadequately rewarded, economically, for his untiring efforts (ONE MAN'S JOURNEY, RKO, 1933; A MAN TO REMEMBER, RKO, 1938; MEET DR. CHRISTIAN, RKO-Stephen-Lang, 1939, etc.); the lot of the criminal, his mistreatment in prisons and on chain gangs (ROAD GANG, First National-Warner Brothers, 1936; HELL'S HIGHWAY, RKO, 1932; ONE WAY TICKET, Columbia, 1935); the alcoholic (SMASH-UP, Universal, 1947); one could go on with such a list, for it is a lengthy one. These subjects were being treated in some other films written by other writers (I WAS A FUGITIVE FROM A CHAIN GANG, SATURDAY'S CHILDREN, GRAPES OF WRATH, etc.). But, as Bosley

227

Crowther pointed out in *The New York Times* (November 9, 1947), it can hardly he said that "the age-long struggle for social betterment is a treasonable bid for revolution."

(4) *Finally, it is worthy of comment that none of the films credited to The Ten were laid in Russia or dealt primarily with that country.* Indeed, in only one motion picture — COUNTER-ATTACK (Columbia, 1945) — were Russian characters given a leading role. This war film, depicting a combat incident on the Russian-Nazi front, was judged both in the Hollywood and New York offices of OWI as making a valuable contribution to the war information program, and was recommended for distribution overseas.

Was there Communist propaganda in films credited to the self-declared ex-Communists?

The types of films made by the ex-Communists were, for the most part, entertainment films of the kind that allowed little opportunity to introduce social, economic or political content of any kind.

Two films credited to the ex-Communists — namely SONG OF RUSSIA and NORTH STAR — came under attack at the 1947 Hearings because of their favorable portrayal of the Soviet Union, then our ally in World War II. It was also pointed out during the Hearings that these films gave a highly inaccurate portrayal of the Soviet Union. However, as has been shown in this report, these films were produced during World War II as friendly tributes to a fighting ally, and the OWI, while neither condoning nor overlooking the gross inaccuracies in these and other films about our various allies, indicated to the producing studios that despite their shortcomings such films served a useful purpose in the war effort by strengthening the bonds of friendship between peoples of the United Nations. Furthermore, it is doubtful whether either SONG OF RUSSIA or NORTH STAR was more inaccurate in its portrayal of Russia than THE MOON IS DOWN was inaccurate in its representation of life in occupied Norway; or even than MRS. MINNIVER was inaccurate in its portrayal of middleclass life in wartime England. However, it must be stressed that these films were not among those intensively studied at this time and thus it cannot be definitely stated whether or not they did contain Communist propaganda.

Probably there were rare instances in which the Communists were successful in getting their propaganda onto the screen during the middle thirties, before the country had become alerted to the extent of Communist infiltration and before the motion picture industry had become fully aware of the intentions of some Communist-minded writers to use the screen for Party purposes. Thus, for example, in 1935 Clifford Odets, by his own testimony then a member of the Communist Party, wrote the screenplay for THE GENERAL DIED AT DAWN (Paramount, 1936). The movie, dealing as it

228

did with the confused situation then existing in China about which little was known or understood in this country at the time, was one of a cycle of warlord pictures about China then currently being made in Hollywood. THE GENERAL DIED AT DAWN was described in studio publicity releases as being "based on the struggle between modern China and the predatory war lord who is laying the country waste. On the side of oppression is General Wang, ambitious war lord intent upon crushing China under his iron heel. On the other is a growing people's movement. Gary Cooper is in the ranks of this movement."

Quite clearly the studio had no awareness whatever that the events or characters portrayed in the picture could be interpreted as having any relationship to events then taking place in China. Nevertheless, certain politically-acute reviewers in this country suggested that the American hero was, by inference, identified with the Communists. This idea was underscored by the fact that the film was laid in Shanghai where, in 1927, a bitter encounter had taken place between Chang Kai-Chek and the Communists, and the war lord General Wang in this picture could have been an attempt to characterize Chang Kai-Chek.

Although this picture with its potential propaganda value abroad for the Communists was released without industry awareness of its possible political implications, Paramount, at the request of the Chinese Nationalist government, did not distribute this picture outside the United States. And an examination of many reviews on this film suggest that in this country probably 99 per cent of the people who saw the picture were unaware of its parallel to the historical events of Shanghai. While it cannot be said positively that Odets deliberately used the screen to portray the Communist viewpoint of events in China, considering his affiliations at that time it is difficult to believe the above-noted content was accidental.

There may have been a few instances in which writers were successful in injecting Communist propaganda into scripts which were produced and released without either the studio or the industry being aware of the fact. But instances like this are so rare that, even with a careful combing of the product, they are extremely difficult to find.

There can be little doubt, as indicated by this study, that the 1947 hearings of the House Committee on Un-American Activities, which focused attention primarily upon Hollywood film content, were not without their effect in influencing the subject-matter and the types of films made in Hollywood, particularly between November, 1947 and the end of 1952, a period of five years. That the rumblings and occasional press headlines which preceded the hearings had little effect upon films in production up to the actual opening of the hearings, can be attributed to the confidence which the industry felt about its own film content, for the motion picture industry believed that there had been no Communist propaganda in Hollywood films, and that none would be found. While the producers did not want the hearings, with their attendant headlines and publicity (they had been through this kind of thing before more than once), yet they were in no way fearful about the outcome.

The producers were, apparently, unprepared for the two-pronged approach of the Committee in the fall of 1947, which was to call witnesses who testified as to their opinions that there had been Communist propaganda in Hollywood films, and to question witnesses repeatedly as to why more anti-Communist films had not been made. The industry demanded and failed to get a public examination of the motion pictures included on a list which the Committee had in its possession and had described as including "pictures which have been produced in Hollywood in the past eight years which contain Communist propaganda" (this list had been mentioned in the report of the sub-committee which had been read into the Congressional Record recommending that public hearings on this matter be held in Washington at the earliest possible time). Furthermore, at the close of the 1947 Hearings the industry was promised that there would be a continuation of the Committee's investigation of film content "in the near future," although actually such investigations if made were never publicly reported. These facts, together with the headline-making performances of The Hollywood Ten before the Committee at the October 1947 Hearings, had a tremendous impact upon an industry which even under normal conditions is inordinately sensitive about what the public thinks about it and its product.

It is impossible to assess the degree of influence which the 1947 Hearings had on the change in film content which followed without considerably more research into story files to determine productions which were dropped and others which were begun in the months immediately following the hearings. From the record of films released, however, it is certain that even though anti-Communist films had traditionally proven to be poor box-office (as a number of witnesses had testified before the Committee in October, 1947), yet the motion picture industry immediately put into production a large number of such films. In some instances perhaps producers thought they could capitalize on current newspaper headlines about the Communist threat; in other instances, however, studios frankly did not expect these films to make money, but regarded them as being necessary for public relations. Several years later some producers (notably Leo McCarey with MY SON JOHN and John Wayne with BIG JIM McLAIN, both films released in 1952) were sincerely concerned with making what they felt to be effective films about communism.

That the hearings were, however, an important factor in the production of the anti-Communist film cycle is indicated by the fact that even although

230

the initial 1947-1949 cycle proved unprofitable, the Committee's 1951 hearings (and the closed sessions which preceded them) brought forth an even larger number of such films in 1952; no less than 13 anti-Communist films were released that year. Probably never before in the history of Hollywood had such a large number of films been produced which the industry itself doubted would prove really profitable at the box-office. During the years 1947-1952 only one major studio, Universal-International, did not make any so-called anti-Communist films, and studio sources indicate that story material submitted and available did not fit into the program of what this studio regards as suitable and profitable entertainment for international audiences.

The circumstances under which the anti-Communist films were made undoubtedly had much to do with the way they turned out. A study of these films reveals that, with a few notable exceptions, these movies can have added little or nothing to American understanding of the true nature of communism — the ideology, shifting strategy and subtle tactics of the Communists. And there is a real possibility that most of these films had an unfavorable effect abroad during the Cold War, since they suggested that Americans have little understanding of the true dangers inherent in the Communist threat to the free world, and because of the unfavorable picture which many of these films gave of the effectiveness of our government's counter-measures against Communist espionage in this country. There were among these 35-40 films, however, a few noteworthy exceptions — including WALK EAST ON BEACON, MAN ON A TIGHTROPE, THE HOAXSTERS, and, more recently in 1955, TRIAL. It is undoubtedly significant that all these latter films were made in 1951 or later, by which time moviemakers in Hollywood were beginning to recover from the confusion and panic which followed the hearings.

As indicated in this report, there were other changes in film content during the five years which followed the 1947 hearings. Social-problem movies which had represented 20.9 per cent of the industry's product in 1947, dropped to 9 per cent in 1950 and 1951. And the industry was increasingly inclined toward pure escapist-type films, except for sure-fire patriotic war pictures which increased from 1.7 per cent of the product in 1947 to 7 per cent or over in 1951 and 1952, with many World War I and II war films being re-issued to swell this number to an impressive postwar high. Hollywood's predisposition toward escapist fare during these years was also reflected in the fact that in voting for the best film of the year through the Academy of Motion Picture Arts and Sciences, the motion picture industry named "pure entertainment" films as the best productions in 1950, 1951 and 1952, when ALL ABOUT EVE, AMERICAN IN PARIS, and THE GREATEST SHOW ON EARTH were given top honors.

231

From the end of 1952 on, Hollywood film content was influenced primarily by the new film forms which made their appearance — Cinerama, 3-D, Cinemascope, Vista Vision, etc. — with subject-matter and types of films best suited for wide-screen presentation showing a marked increase — westerns, adventure films, biographical and historical-fiction, etc. Although the social theme film continued to decline in number in 1953 and 1954, this type of movie once more began to come into prominence. In both 1953 and 1954 the top films of each year tended more toward the tradition of "social realism," which had been evident in the post-war years prior to the investigations. In these years FROM HERE TO ETERNITY and ON THE WATERFRONT made almost a clean sweep of Academy and critic awards. As has been pointed out earlier in this study it is perhaps of considerable significance that in a period when social problem movies were still declining in number, when "escapist" fare was the order of the day, when the "big" films were being made in technicolor in a variety of impressive wide-screen processes, the critics should agree almost unanimously upon these two pictures photographed in black and white on a conventional-size screen, but films which, returning to the traditions of social realism characteristic of the post-war years, attempted to treat seriously social problems of the contemporary world.

After a year's study of this entire subject, the writer cannot but question to what extent the attack made by the House Committee on Un-American Activities on the content of Hollywood films was the result of a fear (also reflected in earlier Congressional inquiries) that motion pictures — the most popular medium of our time — were beginning to devote themselves seriously to an exploration of some of the social, economic and political problems of our time. There have long been some people — both in Washington and Hollywood — who regard these new trends in film subject matter as both unfortunate and dangerous. And it is possible that this was one of the factors which influenced the manner in which the 1947 hearings were conducted, and which led to the emphasis in these hearings upon film content.

It is one of the basic tenets of democracy that the truth — whatever it may prove to be — is one of the greatest resources of mankind, that unbiased information is one of the ways in which we are continually able to renew the freedom which is so essential to our way of life. During recent years, doubts and unsubstantiated opinions have blurred our vision with respect to the role which the motion picture can play in our society. Claims and counterclaims that the Communists have subverted the Hollywood film (and conceivably could in the future), have aroused fears and suspicions, and hampered a free screen. It has been one of the purposes of the present study to examine dispassionately the *facts* about what the Communists tried to do and what they actually accomplished in relation to Hollywood film content, in the hope that such an inquiry might help to clear the air and accelerate an already evident trend toward making it possible for movie-makers to speak freely on the screen on what-ever subjects they please, just as our newspaper writers, our novelists, our public speakers, our TV lecturers and commentators feel free to speak their minds. If this study can help in any respect to accomplish this, it will have served a useful purpose.

APPENDIX I-A

Films of "The Hollywood Ten," 1929-1949: Complete Lists
of Films with Release Dates, Credits, Etc.*

1. Hollywood Feature Films for which ALVAH BESSIE
   Received Screen Credits.

November, 1943 — NORTHERN PURSUIT (Warners)

> Producer, Jack Chertok. Company Executive in General Charge, Jack L. Warner. Director, Raoul Walsh. Adopted from short story "Five Thousand Trojan Horses" by Leslie T. White. Screenplay by Frank Gruber and Alvah Bessie.
>
> (Film completed July, 1943.)

November, 1944 — THE VERY THOUGHT OF YOU (Warners)

> Producer, Jerry Wald. Company Executive in General Charge, Jack L. Warner. Director, Delmer Daves. Devoloped from an original screen story by Lionel Wiggam. Screenplay by Alvah Bessie and Delmer Daves.
>
> (Film completed May, 1944.)

February, 1945 — OBJECTIVE BURMA (Warners)

> Producer, Jerry Wald. Company Executive in General Charge, Jack L. Warner. Director, Raoul Walsh. Developed from an original screen story by Alvah Bessie. Screenplay by Ranald MacDougall and Lester Cole.
>
> (Film completed August, 1944.)

March, 1945 — HOTEL BERLIN (Warners)

> Producer, Lou Edelman. Company Executive in General Charge, Jack L. Warner. Director, Peter Godfrey. From the novel "Hotel Berlin," 1943, by Vicki Baum. Screenplay by Jo Pagano and Alvah Bessie.
>
> (Film completed January, 1945.)

April, 1948 — SMART WOMAN (Allied Artists)

> Producer, Hal E. Chester. Associate Producer, Bernard W. Burton. Director, Edward A. Blatt. Original screen story by Leon Gutterman and Edwin V. Westrate. Screenplay by Alvah Bessie, Louis Morheim and Herbert Margolis. Adaptation, Adela Rogers St. John.
>
> (Film completed November, 1947.)

---

* Credits listed have, for the most part, been either recorded from the film itself or taken from the official credit records of the Academy of Motion Picture Arts and Sciences, except for credits on films released prior to 1938 which have mostly been taken from *The Film Daily Yearbook*. Information as to the date when the film was completed was obtained from Academy records, but was not available on most films released prior to 1938.

234

2. Hollywood Feature Films for which HERBERT BIBERMAN
Received Screen Credits.

December, 1935 — ONE WAY TICKET (Columbia)
Producer, B. P. Schulberg. Director, Herbert Biberman. Adapted from novel
"One Way Ticket" by Ethel Turner. Screenplay by Vincent Lawrence and
Joseph Anthony. Contributors to screenplay construction, Oliver H. P. Garret
and Grover Jones.
(Film completed October, 1935.)

July, 1936 — MEET NERO WOLFE (Columbia)
Producer, B. P. Schulberg. Director, Herbert Biberman. Adapted from novel
"Fer der Lance" by Rex Stout. Screenplay by Howard J. Green, Bruce Man-
ning and Joseph Anthony.
(Film completed April, 1936.)

March, 1939 — KING OF CHINATOWN (Paramount)
Associate Producer, Stuart Walker. Director, Nick Grinde. Developed from
original screen story by Herbert Biberman. Screenplay by Lillie Hayward and
Irving Reis. Contributors to screenplay construction, Gladys Ungar, Stuart
Anthony and Robert Yost.
(Film completed October, 1938.)

February, 1944 — ACTION IN ARABIA (RKO)
Producer, Maurice Geraghty. Director, Leonide Noguy. Developed from an
original screen story by Philip MacDonald and Herbert Biberman. Screenplay
by Philip MacDonald and Herbert Biberman.
(Film completed December, 1943.)

September, 1944 — THE MASTER RACE (RKO)
Producer, Robert Golden. Director, Herbert Biberman. Developed from an
original screen story by Herbert J. Biberman. Screenplay by Herbert J. Biberman, Anne Froelich and Rowland Leigh.
(Film completed June, 1944.)

December, 1944 — TOGETHER AGAIN (Columbia)
Producer, Virginia Van Upp. Director, Charles Vidor. Developed from an
original screen story by Stanley Russell and Herbert Biberman. Screenplay by
Virginia Van Upp and F. Hugh Herbert.
(Film completed October, 1944.)

April, 1947 — NEW ORLEANS (Jules Levy, United Artists)
Producer, Jules Levy. Associate Producer, Herbert J. Biberman. Director,
Arthur Lubin. Original screen story by Elliott Paul and Herbert J. Biberman.
Screenplay by Elliott Paul and Dick Irving Hyland.
(Film completed October, 1946.)

3. Hollywood Feature Films for which LESTER COLE
Received Screen Credits.

1932 — IF I HAD A MILLION (Paramount)
Directors, Ernest Lubitsch, Norman Taurog, Stephen Roberts, Norman McLeod,

James Cruze, William A. Seiter, H. Bruce Humberstone. Story credits, Claude Binyon, Whitney Bolton, Malcolm Stuart Boylan, John Bright, Sidney Buchman, Lester Cole, Isabel Dawn, Boyce DeGaw, Walter DeLeon, Oliver H. P. Garrett, Harvey Gates, Grover Jones, Ernest Lubitsch, Lawton MacKail, Joseph L. Mankiewicz, William Stevens McNutt, Seaton I. Miller, Tiffany Thayer. Original story, Robert D. Andrews.

1933 — CHARLIE CHAN'S GREATEST CASE (FOX)
Director, Hamilton MacFadden. Based on a novel by Earl Derr Biggers. Adaptation by Lester Cole and Marian Orth.

1934 — PURSUED (FOX)
Producer, Sol M. Wurtzel. Screenplay by Lester Cole and Stuart Anthony. Based on original story by Larry Evans.

1934 — SLEEPERS EAST (FOX)
Director, Kenneth MacKenna. Screenplay by Lester Cole. Based on the novel by Frederick Nobel.

1934 — WILD GOLD (FOX)
Director, George Marshall. Story by Dudley Nichols and Lamar Trotti. Adaptation by Lester Cole and Henry Johnson.

February, 1935 — UNDER PRESSURE (FOX)
Producer, Robert T. Kane. Director, Raoul Walsh. Screen play by Borden Chase, Noel Pierce and Lester Cole. From the novel by Borden Chase.

December, 1935 — HITCH HIKE LADY (Republic)
Director, Aubrey Scotto. Screenplay by Gordon Rigby and Lester Cole. Story by Wallace MacDonald.

December, 1935 — TOO TOUGH TO KILL (Columbia)
Director, D. Ross Lederman. Story by Robert D. Speers. Adaptation by Lester Cole and J. Griffin Jay.

1936 — FOLLOW YOUR HEART (Republic)
Director, Aubrey Scotto. Screen play by Nathaniel West, Lester Cole, Samuel Ornitz. Story by Dana Burnet. Additional Dialogue, Olive Cooper.

1936 — THE PRESIDENT'S MYSTERY (Republic)
Director, Phil Rosen. Producer, Nat Levine. Story conceived by Franklin D. Roosevelt. Written for Liberty Magazine by Rupert Hughes, Samuel Hopkins Adams, Anthony Abbot, Rita Weiman, S. S. Van Dine and John Erskine. Screen play by Lester Cole and Nathanael West.

1937 — THE MAN IN BLUE (Universal)
Director, Milton Carruth. Screen play by Lester Cole. Based on an original screen story by Kubec Glasmon.

1937 — AFFAIRS OF CAPPY RICKS (Republic)
Associate Producer, Burt Kelly. Director, Ralph Starb. Original screen play by Lester Cole. Suggested by a story of Peter B. Kyne.

1937 — SOME BLONDES ARE DANGEROUS (Universal)
Director, Milton Carruth. Screen play by Lester Cole. Based on a story by W. R. Burnett.

1938 — THE CRIME OF DR. HALLET (Universal)
Associate Producer, Edmund Grainger. Director, D. Sylvan Simon. Original screen story by Lester Cole and Carl Dreher. Screenplay by Lester Cole and Brown Holmes.

1938 — MIDNIGHT INTRUDER (Universal)
Director, Arthur Lubin. Screen play by George Waggner and Lester Cole. Based on the novel by Channing Pollock.

1938 — THE JURY'S SECRET (Universal)
Producer, Edmund Grainger. Story by Lester Cole. Screen play by Lester Cole and Newman Levy.

April, 1938 — SINNERS IN PARADISE (Universal)
Associate Producer, Ken Goldsmith. Director, James Whale. Developed from original screen story by Harold Buckley. Screenplay by Lester Cole, Harold Buckley and Louis Stevens.
(Film completed March, 1938.)

December, 1938 — SECRETS OF A NURSE (Universal)
Associate Producer, Burt Kelly. Director, Arthur Lubin. Screenplay by Tom Lennon and Lester Cole. Based on the story "West Side Miracle" by Quenten Reynolds.
(Film completed October, 1938.)

July, 1939 — WINTER CARNIVAL (Wanger-United Artists)
Producer, Walter Wanger. Director, Charles Riesner. Adapted from the story by Bud Schulberg. Screenplay by Bud Schulberg, Maurice Rapf and Lester Cole.
(Film completed July, 1939.)

July, 1939 — I STOLE A MILLION (Universal)
Associate Producer, Burt Kelly. Director, Frank Tuttle. Developed from an original screen story by Lester Cole. Screenplay by Nathanael West.
(Film completed July, 1939.)

November, 1939 — THE BIG GUY (Universal)
Associate Producer, Burt Kelly. Director, Arthur Lubin. Screenplay by Lester Cole. Based on a story by Wallace Sullivan and Richard K. Polimer.
(Film completed November, 1939.)

January, 1940 — THE INVISIBLE MAN RETURNS (Universal)
Producer, Ken Goldsmith. Director, Joe May. Suggested by novel "The Invisible Man" by H. G. Wells. Developed from original screen story by Kurt Siodmak and Joe May. Screenplay by Lester Cole and Kurt Siodmak.
(Film completed November, 1939.)

April, 1940 — THE HOUSE OF SEVEN GABLES (Universal)
Associate Producer, Burt Kelly. Director, Joe May. Dialogue Director, Lester

Cole. Screenplay, Lester Cole. Adaptation by Harold Greene. Based on the novel by Nathaniel Hawthorne.

(Film completed January, 1940.)

March, 1941 — FOOTSTEPS IN THE DARK (Warners)

Producer, Hal B. Wallis. Associate Producer, Robert Lord. Company Executive in General Charge, Jack L. Warner. Director, Lloyd Bacon. Adapted from play by Laszlo Fodor, Bernard Merivale and Jeffrey Dell. Screenplay by Lester Cole and John Wexley.

(Film completed November, 1940.)

December, 1941 — AMONG THE LIVING (Paramount)

Producer, Sol C. Siegel. Associate Producer, Coldert Clark. Director, Stuart Heisler. Authors, Brian Marlowe, Lester Cole. Screenplay, Lester Cole, Garrett Fort.

(Film completed June, 1941.)

January, 1942 — PACIFIC BLACKOUT (Paramount)

Associate Producer, Burt Kelly. Director, Ralph Murphy. Developed from an original screen story by Franz Spencer and Kurt Siodmak. Screenplay by Lester Cole and W. P. Lipscomb.

(Film completed September, 1941.)

January, 1943 — NIGHT PLANE FROM CHUNGKING (Paramount)

Executive Producer, Walter MacEwen. Associate Producer, Michael Kraike. Director, Ralph Murphy. From an unpublished story by Harry Hervey. Screenplay by Earl Felton, Theodore Reeves and Lester Cole. Adaptation, Sidney Biddell.

(Film completed September, 1942.)

August, 1943 — HOSTAGES (Paramount)

Executive Producer, B. G. deSylva. Associate Producer, Sol C. Siegel. Director, Frank Tuttle. Adapted from novel by Stefan Heya. Screenplay by Lester Cole and Frank Butler.

(Film completed April, 1943.)

February, 1944 — NONE SHALL ESCAPE (Columbia)

Executive Producer, Samuel Bischoff. Associate Producer, Burt Kelly. Director, Andre DeToth. Developed from an original screen story by Alfred Neumann and Joseph Than. Screenplay by Lester Cole.

(Film completed October, 1943.)

February, 1945 — OBJECTIVE BURMA (Warners)

Producer, Jerry Wald. Company Executive in General Charge, Jack L. Warner. Director, Raoul Walsh. Developed from an original screen story by Alvah Bessie. Screenplay by Ronald MacDougall and Lester Cole.

(Film completed August, 1944.)

June, 1954 — BLOOD ON THE SUN (Cagney Productions Inc.-United Artists)

Executive Producer, William Cagney. Producer, William Cagney. Director, Frank Lloyd. Original screen story by Garret Fort. Based on an idea by Frank Melford. Screenplay by Lester Cole. Added scenes by Nathaniel Curtis.

(Film completed December, 1944.)

238

September, 1945 — MEN IN HER DIARY (Universal)
Executive Producer, Howard Welsch. Associate Producer, Charles Barton. Director, Charles Barton. From an original screen story by Kerry Shaw. Screenplay by Hugh Herbert and Elwood Ullman. Adaptation by Lester Cole. Additional dialogue, Stanley Davis.
(Film completed March, 1945.)

May, 1946 — STRANGE CONQUEST (Universal)
Producer, Marshall Grant. Director, John Rawlins. Story by Lester Cole and Carl Dreher. Screenplay by Roy Chanslor.
(Film completed January, 1946.)

July, 1947 — FIESTA (M-G-M)
Producer, Jack Cummings. Director, Richard Thorpe. Original screenplay by George Bruce and Lester Cole.
(Film completed April, 1946.)

August, 1947 — THE ROMANCE OF ROSY RIDGE (M-G-M)
Producer, Jack Cummings. Director, Roy Rowland. Screenplay by Lester Cole. Based on a story by MacKinlay Kantor.
(Film completed December, 1946.)

February, 1948 — HIGH WALL (M-G-M)
Producer, Robert Lord. Director, Curtis Bernhardt. Screenplay by Sidney Boehm and Lester Cole. Suggested by a story and play by Alan R. Clark and Bradbury Foote.
(Film completed August, 1947.)

4. Hollywood Feature Films for which EDWARD DMYTRYK Received Screen Credits.

1935 — THE HAWK (Herman Wohl)
Producer, Herman Wohl. Director, Edward Dmytryk. Author, James Oliver Curwood. Screenplay by Griffin Jay.

October, 1939 — TELEVISION SPY (Paramount)
Executive Producer, William LeBaron. Associate Producer, Edward T. Lowe. Director, Edward Dmytryk. Developed from an unpublished story by Endre Bohem. Screenplay by Horace McCoy, William R. Lipman and Lillie Hayward. Contributor to screenplay construction, Irving Reis.
(Film completed June, 1939.)

January, 1940 — EMERGENCY SQUAD (Paramount)
Executive Producer, William LeBaron. Associate Producer, Stuart Walker. Director, Edward Dmytryk. Developed from original idea by Robert Musel and Michael Raymond. Screenplay by Garnett Weston and Stuart Palmer.
(Film completed September, 1939.)

August, 1940 — GOLDEN GLOVES (Paramount)
Executive Producer, William LeBaron. Associate Producer, William Thomas. Director, Edward Dmytryk. Developed from original story by Maxwell Shane. Screenplay by Maxwell Shane and Lewis R. Foster.
(Film completed December, 1939.)

239

August, 1940 — MYSTERY SEA RAIDER (Paramount)
Executive Producer, William LeBaron. Producer, Eugene J. Zukor. Director, Edward Dmytryk. Developed from an unpublished story by Robert Grant. Screenplay by Edward E. Paramore, Jr. Contributor to dialogue, Agnes Christine Johnston.
(Film completed June, 1940.)

December, 1940 — HER FIRST ROMANCE (Chadwick-Monogram)
Producer, I. E. Chadwick. Associate Producer, Herman Wohl. Director, Edward Dmytryk. Adapted from novel by Gene Stratton Porter. Screenplay by Adele Comandini.
(Film completed December, 1940.)

February, 1941 — THE DEVIL COMMANDS (Columbia)
Executive Producer, Irving Briskin. Producer, Wallace MacDonald. Director, Edward Dmytryk. Adapted from novel "The Edge of Running Water" by William Sloane. Screenplay by Robert D. Andrews and Milton Gunzberg.
(Film completed December, 1940.)

April, 1941 — UNDER AGE (Columbia)
Executive Producer, Irving Briskin. Producer, Ralph Cohn. Director, Edward Dmytryk. Developed from an original idea by Stanley Roberts. Screenplay by Robert D. Andrews.
(Film completed February, 1941.)

June, 1941 — SWEETHEART OF THE CAMPUS (Columbia)
Producer, Jack Fier. Director, Edward Dmytryk. Author, Robert D. Andrews. Screenplay by Robert D. Andrews and Edmund Hartman.
(Film completed April, 1941.)

October, 1941 — THE BLONDE FROM SINGAPORE (Columbia)
Executive Producer, Irving Briskin. Producer, Jack Fier. Director, Edward Dmytryk. Developed from an original screen story by Houston Branch. Screenplay by George Bricker. Contributor to dialogue, David Silverstein.
(Film completed June, 1941.)

November, 1941 — SECRETS OF THE LONE WOLF (Columbia)
Executive Producer, Irving Briskin. Producer, Jack Fier. Director, Edward Dmytryk. Developed from an original screen story by Stuart Palmer. Based on the character by Louis Vance. Screenplay by Stuart Palmer.
(Film completed August, 1941.)

January, 1942 — CONFESSIONS OF BOSTON BLACKIE (Columbia)
Executive Producer, Irving Briskin. Producer, William Berke. Director, Edward Dmytryk. Developed from an original screen story by Paul Yawitz and Jay Dratler. Based on a character created by Jack Boyle. Screenplay by Paul Yawitz.
(Film completed September, 1941.)

September, 1942 — COUNTER ESPIONAGE (Columbia)
Executive Producer, Irving Briskin. Producer, Wallace Macdonald. Director,

240

Edward Dmytryk. Developed from an original screen story by Aubrey Wisberg, based on the character created by Joseph Vance. Screenplay by Aubrey Wisberg. (Film completed January, 1942.)

January, 1943 — SEVEN MILES FROM ALCATRAZ (RKO)
Producer, Hermon Schlom. Director, Edward Dmytryk. Adapted from an unpublished story "Sou'west Pass" by John D. Klorer. Screenplay by Joseph Krumgold.
(Film completed August, 1942.)

March, 1943 — HITLER'S CHILDREN (RKO)
Producer, Edward A. Golden. Director, Edward Dmytryk. Adapted from book "Education for Death," by Gregor Ziemer. Screenplay by Emmet Lavery.
(Film completed October, 1942.)

May, 1943 — THE FALCON STRIKES BACK (RKO)
Producer, Maurice Geraghty. Director, Edward Dmytryk. Screenplay by Edward Dein and Gerald Geraghty. Story by Stuart Palmer.
(Film completed February, 1943.)

June, 1943 — CAPTIVE WILD WOMAN (Universal)
Executive Producer, Jack Gross. Associate Producer, Ben Pivar. Director, Edward Dmytryk. Developed from an original screen story by Ted Fithian and Neil P. Varnick. Screenplay by Griffin Jay and Henry Sucher.
(Film completed December, 1943.)

July, 1943 — BEHIND THE RISING SUN (RKO)
Director, Edward Dmytryk. Adapted from book by James B. Young. Original screenplay by Emmet Lavery.
(Film completed May, 1943.)

December, 1943 — TENDER COMRADE (RKO)
Producer, David Hemstead. Director, Edward Dmytryk. Original screen story by Dalton Trumbo. Screenplay, Dalton Trumbo.
(Film completed October, 1943.)

December, 1944 — MURDER, MY SWEET (RKO)
Executive Producer, Sid Rogell. Producer, Adrian Scott. Director, Edward Dmytryk. Adapted from novel "Farewell My Lovely" by Raymond Chandler. Screenplay by John Paxton.
(Film completed July, 1944.)

May, 1945 — BACK TO BATAAN (RKO)
Executive Producer, Robert Fellows. Associate Producer, Theron Warth. Director, Edward Dmytryk. From an original screen story by Aeneas MacKenzie. Screenplay by Ben Barzman and Richard H. Landau.
(Film completed February, 1945.)

December, 1945 — CORNERED (RKO)
Producer, Adrian Scott. Director, Edward Dmytryk. From a screen story by John Wexley. Screenplay by John Paxton. Adaptation, John Wexley.
(Film completed August, 1945.)

August, 1946 — TILL THE END OF TIME (RKO)
Producer, Dore Schary. Director, Edward Dmytryk. From the novel "They Dream of Home" by Niven Busch. Screenplay by Allen Rivkin.
(Film completed January, 1946.)

August, 1947 — CROSSFIRE (RKO)
Executive Producer, Dore Schary. Producer, Adrian Scott. Director, Edward Dmytryk. From the novel "The Brick Foxhole" by Richard Brooks. Screenplay by John Paxton.
(Film completed March, 1947.)

5. Hollywood Feature Films for which RING LARDNER, JR.
Received Screen Credits.

June, 1939 — THE KID FROM KOKOMO (Warners)
Executive Producers, Jack L. Warner and Hal B. Wallis. Producer, Sam Bischoff. Director, Lew Seiler. Developed from an original screen story by Dalton Trumbo. Screenplay by Jerry Wald and Richard Macaulay. Contributor to treatment, Ring Lardner, Jr.
(Film completed January, 1939.)

November, 1939 — MEET DR. CHRISTIAN (Stephens-Lang-RKO)
Producer, William Stephens. Associate Producer, Monroe Shaff. Director, Bernard Vorhaus. Developed from an original screen story by Harvey Gates. Screenplay by Ian McLellan Hunter, Ring Lardner, Jr., and Harvey Gates.
(Film completed October, 1939.)

April, 1940 — THE COURAGEOUS DR. CHRISTIAN (Stephens-Lang-RKO)
Producer, William Stephens. Associate Producer, Monroe Shaff. Director, Bernard Vorhaus. Original screenplay by Ring Lardner, Jr. and Ian McLellan Hunter.
(Film completed March, 1940.)

January, 1941 — ARKANSAS JUDGE (Republic)
Associate Producer, Armand Schaefer. Adapted by Ian Hunter, Ring Lardner, Jr. and Gertrude Purcell from the novel "False Witness" by Irving Stone. Screenplay by Dorrell and Stuart McGowan.
(Film completed December, 1940.)

February, 1942 — WOMAN OF THE YEAR (M-G-M)
A George Stevens' Production. Producer, Joseph L. Mankiewicz. Director, George Stevens. Original screenplay by Ring Lardner, Jr. and Michael Kanin.
(Film completed October, 1941.)

January, 1944 — THE CROSS OF LORRAINE (M-G-M)
Producer, Edwin Knopf. Director, Tay Garnett. Based on a story by Lilo Damert and Robert Aisner and "A Thousand Shall Fall," by Hans Habe. Screenplay by Michael Kanin, Ring Lardner, Jr., Alexander Esway and Robert D. Andrews.
(Film completed July, 1943.)

December, 1944 — TOMORROW THE WORLD (United Artists)
Producer, Lester Cowan. Associate Producer, David Hall. Director, Leslie
Fenton. From the play by James Gow and Arnaud D'Usseau. Screenplay by
Ring Lardner, Jr. and Leopold Atlas.
(Film completed August, 1944.)

September, 1946 — CLOAK AND DAGGER (United States Pictures, Inc.-Warners)
Executive Producer, Milton Sperling. Producer, Milton Sperling. Director,
Fritz Lang. Original screen story by Boris Ingster and John Larkin. Suggested
by the book by Corey Ford and Alastair McBain. Screenplay by Albert Maltz
and Ring Lardner, Jr.
(Film completed June, 1946.)

October, 1947 — FOREVER AMBER (20th Century-Fox)
Executive Producer, Darryl F. Zanuck. Producer, William Perlberg. Director,
Otto Preminger. From the novel by Kathleen Winsor. Screenplay by Philip
Dunne and Ring Lardner, Jr. Adaptation, Jerome Cady.
(Film completed March, 1947.)

June, 1949 — THE FORBIDDEN STREET (20th Century-Fox)
Producer, William Perlberg. Director, Jean Negulesco. From the novel "Britan-
nia Mews" by Margery Sharp. Screenplay by Ring Lardner, Jr.
(Film completed October, 1948.)

6. Hollywood Feature Films for which JOHN HOWARD LAWSON
Received Screen Credits.

1929 — DYNAMITE (M-G-M-Pathe)
Producer, Cecil B. DeMille. Director, Cecil B. DeMille. Story by Jean
MacPherson. Dialogue by Jean MacPherson, John Howard Lawson and
Gladys Ungar.

1930 — SHIP FROM SHANGHAI (M-G-M)
Director, Charles Brabin. Scenario by John Howard Lawson. Theme based
on Dale Collins' novel "The Ordeal."

1930 — OUR BLUSHING BRIDES (M-G-M)
Director, Harry Beaumont. Scenarists, Bess Merydth and John Howard
Lawson. Dialogue by Bess Meredyth and Edwyn Justice Mayer.

1930 — SEA BAT (M-G-M)
Director, Wesley Ruggles. Story by Dorothy Yost. Scenario by Bess Meredith
and John Howard Lawson. Dialogue by Bess Meredith and John Howard
Lawson.

1931 — BACHELOR APARTMENT (RKO)
Director, Lowell Sherman. Original story by John Howard Lawson. Scenario
and adaptation by J. Walter Ruben.

1934 — SUCCESS AT ANY PRICE (RKO)
Director, J. Walter Ruben. From the play by John Howard Lawson, as pro-
duced by the Group Theatre. Adaptation by John Howard Lawson and
Howard J. Green.

1935 — PARTY WIRE (Columbia)
   Director, Erle Kenton. Based on a story by Bruce Manning. Adaptation by
   Ethel Hill and John Howard Lawson.

June, 1938 — BLOCKADE (Wanger-United Artists)
   Producer, Walter Wanger. Director, William Dieterle. Original screenplay by
   John Howard Lawson.
      (Film completed March, 1938.)

August, 1938 — ALGIERS (Wanger-United Artists)
   Producer, Walter Wanger. Director, John Cromwell. Adapted from the novel
   "Pepe le Moko" by Detective Ashelbe. Screenplay by John Howard Lawson.
   Additional dialogue by James N. Cain.
      (Film completed July, 1938.)

August, 1939 — THEY SHALL HAVE MUSIC (Goldwyn-United Artists)
   Producer, Samuel Goldwyn. Associate Producer, Robert Riskin. Director,
   Archie Mayo. Screenplay by Irmgard Von Cube and John Howard Lawson.
      (Film completed October, 1939.)

June, 1940 — EARTHBOUND (20th Century-Fox)
   Executive Producer, Sol M. Wurtzel. Producer, Darryl F. Zanuck. Director,
   Irving Pichel. Adapted from short story "The Ghost's Story" by Basil King.
   Screenplay by John Howard Lawson and Samuel G. Engel.
      (Film completed February, 1940.)

June, 1940 — FOUR SONS (20th Century-Fox)
   Executive Producer, Darryl F. Zanuck. Associate Producer, Harry Joe Brown.
   Director, Archie Mayo. Suggested by short story "Grandmother Bernle Learns
   Her Letters" by I. A. R. Wylie. Screenplay by John Howard Lawson. Addi-
   tional dialogue, Milton Sperling.
      (Film completed May, 1940.)

June, 1943 — ACTION IN THE NORTH ATLANTIC (Warners)
   Producer, Jerry Wald. Executive in General Charge, Jack L. Warner. Director,
   Lloyd Bacon. Developed from an unpublished story by Guy Gilpatric. Screen-
   play by John Howard Lawson. Additional dialogue by A. I. Bezzerides and
   W. R. Burnett.
      (Film completed December, 1942.)

October, 1943 — SAHARA (Columbia)
   Director, Zoltan Korda. From an original screen story by Philip MacDonald.
   Screenplay by John Howard Lawson and Zoltan Korda. Adaptation: James
   O'Hanlon.
      (Film completed April, 1943.)

April, 1945 — COUNTER-ATTACK (Columbia)
   Director, Zoltan Korda. From the play by Janet Stevenson and Philip Stevenson. Based upon "Pobydea" by Ilya Vershinin and Mikhail Ruderman. Screenplay by John Howard Lawson.
      (Film completed December, 1944.)

244

March, 1947 — SMASH-UP (Universal)
Producer, Walter Wanger. Associate Producer, Martin Gabel. Directed by
Stuart Heisler. Screenplay by John Howard Lawson. Original story by
Dorothy Parker and Frank Cavett.
(Film completed August, 1946.)

7. Hollywood Feature Films for which ALBERT MALTZ
Received Screen Credits.

1932 — AFRAID TO TALK (Universal)
Director, Edward L. Cain. Screenplay by Tom Reed. Adaptation from the
play "Merry-Go-Round" by Albert Maltz and George Sklar.

March, 1942 — THIS GUN FOR HIRE (Paramount)
Executive Producer, B. G. deSylva. Associate Producer, Richard Blumenthal.
Director, Frank Tuttle. Adapted from novel by Graham Greene. Screenplay
by Albert Maltz and W. R. Burnett.
(Film completed, December, 1941.)

January, 1944 — DESTINATION TOKYO (Warners)
Producer, Jerry Wald. Company Executive in General Charge, Jack L. Warner.
Director, Delmer Daves. Developed from an original screen story by Steve
Fisher. Screenplay by Delmer Daves and Albert Maltz.
(Film completed September, 1943.)

October, 1944 — THE MAN IN HALF MOON STREET (Paramount)
Producer, Walter MacEwen. Director, Ralph Murphy. Adapted from play by
Barre Lyndon. Screenplay by Charles Kenyon. Adaptation, Garret Fort.
Contributor to screenplay construction, Don Hartman and Albert Maltz.
(Film completed October, 1943.)

September, 1945 — PRIDE OF THE MARINES (Warners)
Producer, Jerry Wald. Company Executive in General Charge, Jack L. Warner.
Director, Delmer Daves. From the non-fiction book, "Al Schmidt, Marine" by
Roger Butterfield. Screenplay by Albert Maltz. Adaptation, Marvin Borowsky.
(Film completed February, 1945.)

September, 1946 — CLOAK AND DAGGER (United States Pictures, Inc.-Warners)
Executive Producer, Milton Sperling. Producer, Milton Sperling. Director,
Fritz Lang. Original screen story by Boris Ingster and John Larkin. Suggested
by the book by Corey Ford and Alastair McBain. Screenplay by Albert Maltz
and Ring Lardner, Jr.
(Film completed June, 1946.)

March, 1948 — THE NAKED CITY (Universal)
Producer, Mark Hellinger. Director, Jules Dassin. Written by Albert Maltz
and Malvin Wald.
(Film completed September, 1947.)

8. Hollywood Feature Films for which SAMUEL ORNITZ
Received Screen Credits.

245

1929 — CASE OF LENA SMITH (Paramount)
Director, Josef von Sternberg. Adapted by Jules Furthman from a story by Samuel Ornitz.

1929 — CHINATOWN NIGHTS (Paramount)
Director, W. A. Wellman. From Samuel Ornitz' story "Tong War." Adapted by Oliver H. P. Garrett. Scenario by Ben Grannan Kohn. Dialogue sequences by William B. Jutto.

1930 — SINS OF THE CHILDREN (Cosmopolitan Productions-Metro)
Director, Sam Wood. From a story by Elliott Nugent and J. C. Nugent. Adaptation by Samuel Ornitz. Dialogue by Elliott Nugent and Clara Lipman.

1932 — HELL'S HIGHWAY (RKO)
Executive Producer, David O. Selznick. Director, Rowland Brown. Story by Samuel Ornitz, Robert Tasker and Rowland Brown.

1932 — SECRETS OF THE FRENCH POLICE (RKO)
Director, Edward Sutherland. Based on "Secrets of Surete" by H. Ashton-Wolfe and Samuel Ornitz. Screenplay by Samuel Ornitz and Robert Tasker.

1933 — MEN OF AMERICA (RKO)
Director, Ralph Ince. Story by Humphrey Pearson. Adaptation by Henry McCarthy and Samuel Ornitz.

1933 — ONE MAN'S JOURNEY (RKO)
Director, John Robertson. Screenplay by Samuel Ornitz. From the story "Failure," by Katherine Haviland Taylor.

1934 — ONE EXCITING ADVENTURE (Universal)
Director, Ernst L. Frank. Screenplay by William Hurlburt. Dialogue by Samuel Ornitz. Based on a story by Frank Schultz, and Billie Wilder.

1935 — THE MAN WHO RECLAIMED HIS HEAD (Universal)
Director, Edward Ludwig. Based on a play by Jean Bart. Adaptation by Jean Bart and Samuel Ornitz.

1935 — THREE KIDS AND A QUEEN (Universal)
Producer, Ben Verschleiser. Director, Edward Ludwig. Story by Harry Poppe and Chester Beecroft. Screen play by Barry Trivers and Samuel Ornitz.

1936 — FATAL LADY (Wanger-Paramount)
Producer, Walter Wanger. Director, Edward Ludwig. Screenplay by Samuel Ornitz. Additional dialogue by Tiffany Thayer. Original story by Harry Segall. Adapted by William R. Lipman.

1936 — FOLLOW YOUR HEART (Republic)
Nat Levine Production. Director, Aubrey Scotto. Screenplay by Nathanael West, Lester Cole, Samuel Ornitz. Story by Dana Burnet. Additional dialogue, Olive Cooper.

1937 — A DOCTOR'S DIARY (Paramount)
Producer, B. P. Schulberg. Director, Charles Vidor. Screenplay by David Boehm. Story by Samuel Ornitz and Joseph Anthony.

1937 — THE HIT PARADE (Republic)
Nat Levine Production. Director, Gus Meins. Screenplay by Bradford Ropes and Samuel Ornitz.

1937 — IT COULD HAPPEN TO YOU (Republic)
Leonard Fields Production. Directed by Phil Rosen. Adapted by Samuel Ornitz and Nathanael West from a story by Nathanael West.

1937 — PORTIA ON TRIAL (Republic)
Director, George Nicholls, Jr. Based on an original story by Faith Baldwin. Screenplay by Samuel Ornitz. Adaptation and added dialogue by E. E. Paramore, Jr.

1937 — TWO WISE MAIDS (Republic)
Director, Phil Rosen. Based on an original screen story by Endre Bohem. Screenplay by Samuel Ornitz.

March, 1938 — KING OF THE NEWSBOYS (Republic)
Associate Producer, Bernard Vorhaus. Director, Bernard Vorhaus. Developed from an original screen story by Samuel Ornitz and Horace McCoy. Screenplay by Louis Weitzenhorn and Peggy Thomson.
(Film completed February, 1938.)

July, 1938 — ARMY GIRL (Republic)
Executive Producer, Sol C. Siegel. Associate Producer, Armand Schaefer. Director, George Nicholls, Jr. Based on the published story by Charles L. Clifford. Screenplay by Barry Trivers and Samuel Ornitz.
(Film completed May, 1938.)

December, 1938 — LITTLE ORPHAN ANNIE (Colonial-Paramount)
Producer, John Speaks. Director, Ben Holmes. Story by Samuel Ornitz and Endre Bohem, based on the comic strip "Little Orphan Annie" by Harold Gray. Screenplay by Budd Schulberg and Samuel Ornitz.
(Film completed December, 1938.)

October, 1939 — THE MIRACLE ON MAIN STREET (Columbia)
Producer, Jack H. Skirball. Director, Steve Sekely. Developed from an original screen story by Samuel Ornitz and Boris Ingster. Screenplay by Frederick Jackson.
(Film completed November, 1939.)

July, 1940 — THREE FACES WEST (Republic)
Producer, Sol C. Siegel. Director, Bernard Vorhaus. Original screenplay by F. Hugh Herbert, Joseph Moncure March, and Samuel Ornitz. Contributor to screenplay construction, Doris Anderson.
(Film completed April, 1940.)

June, 1944 — THEY LIVE IN FEAR (Columbia)
Producer, Jack Fier. Director, Josef Berne. Developed from an original screen story by Wilfred Pettit. Based on an idea by Hilda Stone and Ruth Nussbaum. Screenplay by Michael Simmons and Samuel Ornitz.
(Film completed March, 1944.)

December, 1944 — LITTLE DEVILS (Monogram)
  Executive Producers, Grant Withers. Producer, Grant Withers. Director, Monta Bell. Unpublished story by Richard Davis. Screenplay by Samuel Ornitz.
  (Film completed August, 1944.)

March, 1945 — CIRCUMSTANTIAL EVIDENCE (20th Century-Fox)
  Producer, William Girard. Director, John Larkin. From an original screen story by Nat Ferber and Sam Duncan. Screenplay by Robert Metzler. Adaptation, Samuel Ornitz.
  (Film completed November, 1944.)

9. Hollywood Feature Films for which ADRIAN SCOTT
Received Screen Credits.

December, 1940 — KEEPING COMPANY (M-G-M)
  Producer, Samuel Marx. Director, S. Sylvan Simon. Developed from an original screen story by Herman J. Mankiewicz. Screenplay by Harry Ruskin, James H. Hill and Adrian Scott.
  (Film completed November, 1940.)

June, 1941 — THE PARSON OF PANAMINT (Sherman, Paramount)
  Producer, Harry Sherman. Associate Producer, Lewis J. Rachmil. Director, William McCann. Author, Peter B. Kyne. Screenplay, Harold Shumate and Adrian Scott.
  (Film completed June, 1941.)

September, 1941 — WE GO FAST (20th Century-Fox)
  Producer, Lou Ostrow. Director, William McGann. Adapted from story by Long Welch. Screenplay by Thomas Lennon and Adrian Scott.
  (Film completed June, 1941.)

May, 1943 — MR. LUCKY (RKO)
  Producer, David Hempstead. Director, H. C. Potter. Original story by Milton Holmes' "Bundles for Freedom." Screenplay by Milton Holmes and Adrian Scott.
  (Film completed January, 1943.)

November, 1944 — MY PAL WOLF (RKO)
  Director, Alfred Werker. Adapted from short story "The Pumpkin Shell" by Frederick Hazlitt Brennan. Screenplay by Lillie Hayward, Leonard Praskins and John Taxton.
  (Film completed July, 1944.)

December, 1944 — MURDER, MY SWEET (RKO)
  Executive Producer, Sid Rogell. Producer, Adrian Scott. Director, Edward Dmytryk. Adapted from novel "Farewell My Lovely" by Raymond Chandler. Screenplay by John Paxton.
  (Film completed July, 1944.)

December, 1945 — CORNERED (RKO)
  Producer, Adrian Scott. Director, Edward Dmytryk. From a screen story by John Wexley. Screenplay by John Paxton. Adaptation by John Wexley.
  (Film completed August, 1945.)

248

March, 1946 — Miss Susie Slagle's (Paramount)
Associate Producer, John Houseman. Director, John Berry. From the novel by Augusta Tucker. Screenplay by Anne Froelick and Hugo Butler. Adaptation by Anne Froelick and Adrian Scott. Additional dialogue by Theodore Strauss.
(Film completed November, 1944.)

March, 1946 — Deadline at Dawn (RKO)
Executive Producer, Sid Rogell. Producer, Adrian Scott. Director, Harold Clurman. Screenplay by Clifford Odets. From novel by William Irish.
(Film completed July, 1945.)

August, 1947 — Crossfire (RKO)
Executive Producer, Dore Schary. Producer, Adrian Scott. Director, Edward Dmytryk. From the novel "The Brick Foxhole" by Richard Brooks. Screenplay by John Paxton.
(Film completed March, 1947.)

10. Hollywood Feature Films for which DALTON TRUMBO
Received Screen Credits.

1936 — Love Begins at Twenty (First National-Warner Brothers)
Director, Frank MacDonald. Screenplay, Dalton Trumbo and Tom Reed. From a play by Martin Flavin.

1936 — Road Gang (First National-Warner Brothers)
Director, Louis King. Story by Abem Finkel, Harold Buckley and Dalton Trumbo.

1936 — Tugboat Princess (Columbia)
Director, David Selman. Original screen story by Dalton Trumbo and Isador Bernstein. Screen play by Robert Watson.

1937 — Devil's Playground (Columbia)
Producer, Edward Chodorov. Director, Earl C. Kenton. Original screen story by Norman Springer. Screenplay by Liam O'Flaherty, Jerome Chodorov and Dalton Trumbo.

September, 1938 — Fugitives for a Night (RKO)
Producer, Lou Lusty. Director, Leslie Goodwins. Developed from an unpublished story by Richard Wormser. Screenplay by Dalton Trumbo.
(Film completed July, 1938.)

October, 1938 — A Man to Remember (RKO)
Executive Producer, Lee Marcus. Producer, Robert Sisk. Director, Garson Kanin. Adapted from short story by Katherine Haviland Taylor. Screenplay by Dalton Trumbo.
(Film completed August, 1938.)

February, 1939 — Everything Happens to Ann (Arcadia, Grand National)
Producer, Jack Skirball. Director, Al Christie. Adapted from story by Dalton Trumbo. Screenplay by Fred Jackson.
(Film completed March, 1939.)

March, 1939 — THE FLYING IRISHMAN (RKO)
Executive Producer, Pandro Berman. Producer, Pandro Berman. Director, Leigh Jason. Screenplay by Ernest Pagano and Dalton Trumbo.
(Film completed December, 1938.)

May, 1939 — SORORITY HOUSE (RKO)
Executive Producer, Lee Marcus. Producer, Robert Sisk. Director, John Farrow. Adapted from short story "Chi House" by Mary Coyle Chase. Screen play by Dalton Trumbo. Contributors to treatment: Aleen Wetstein and Gladys Atwater.
(Film completed March, 1939.)

June, 1939 — FIVE CAME BACK (RKO)
Producer, Robert Sisk. Director, John Farrow. Developed from original screen story by Richard Carroll. Screenplay by Jerry Cady, Dalton Trumbo and Nathanael West. Contributor to treatment, Lionel Fouser.
(Film completed April, 1939.)

June, 1939 — THE KID FROM KOKOMO (Warners)
Executive Producers, Jack L. Warner and Hal B. Wallis. Producer, Sam Bischoff. Director, Lew Seiler. Developed from original screen story by Dalton Trumbo. Screenplay by Jerry Wald and Richard Macaulay. Contributor to treatment, Ring Lardner, Jr.
(Film completed January, 1939.)

July, 1939 — CAREER (RKO)
Producer, Robert Sisk. Director, Leigh Jason. Adapted from a novel by Phil Strong. Adaptation by Bert Granet. Screenplay by Dalton Trumbo.
(Film completed May, 1939.)

November, 1939 — HEAVEN WITH A BARBED WIRE FENCE (20th Century-Fox)
Executive Producer, Sol M. Wurtzel. Director, Ricardo Cortez. Developed from original screen story by Dalton Trumbo. Screenplay by Dalton Trumbo, Leonard Hoffman and Ben Grauman Kohn.
(Film completed July, 1939.)

January, 1940 — THE LONE WOLF STRIKES (Columbia)
Producer, Fred Kohlmar. Director, Sidney Salkow. Adapted from novel by Louis Joseph Vance. Developed from an unpublished story by Dalton Trumbo. Screenplay by Harry Segall and Albert Duffy.
(Film completed December, 1939.)

April, 1940 — CURTAIN CALL (RKO)
Executive Producer, Lee Marcus. Producer, Howard Benedict. Director, Frank Woodruff. Developed from an original screen story by Howard J. Green. Sole screenplay, Dalton Trumbo.
(Film completed February, 1940.)

April, 1940 — HALF A SINNER (Universal)
Director, Al Christie. Developed from original screen story by Dalton Trumbo. Screenplay by Frederick Jackson.
(Film completed March, 1940.)

May, 1940 — A BILL OF DIVORCEMENT (RKO)
Executive Producer, Lee Marcus. Producer, Robert Sisk. Director, John Farrow. Adapted from play by Clemence Dane. Screenplay by Dalton Trumbo. (Film completed January, 1940.)

July, 1940 — WE WHO ARE YOUNG (M-G-M)
Producer, Seymour Nebenzahl. Director, Harold S. Bucquet. Original screenplay, Dalton Trumbo.
(Film completed June, 1940.)

December, 1940 — KITTY FOYLE (RKO)
Executive Producer, Harry E. Edington. Producer, David Hempstead. Director, Sam Wood. Adapted from the novel by Christopher Morley. Screenplay, Dalton Trumbo. Contributor to treatment, Robert Ardrey. Screenplay construction, Donald Ogden Stewart. Additional dialogue, Donald Ogden Stewart. (Film completed November, 1940.)

July, 1941 — ACCENT ON LOVE (20th Century-Fox)
Associate Producers, Walter Morosco and Ralph Dietrich. Director, Ray McCarey. Developed from an original screen story by Dalton Trumbo. Screenplay by John Larkin.
(Film completed April, 1941.)

October, 1941 — YOU BELONG TO ME (Columbia)
Producer, Wesley Ruggles. Director, Wesley Ruggles. Developed from an unpublished story by Dalton Trumbo. Screenplay by Claude Binyon. (Film completed August, 1941.)

January, 1942 — THE REMARKABLE ANDREW (Paramount)
Executive Producer, B. G. deSylva. Producer, Richard Blumenthal. Director, Stuart Heisler. Adapted from novel by Dalton Trumbo. Screenplay by Dalton Trumbo.
(Film completed August, 1941.)

December, 1943 — TENDER COMRADE (RKO)
Producer, David Hemstead. Director, Edward Dmytryk. Original screen story by Dalton Trumbo. Screenplay by Dalton Trumbo. (Film completed October, 1943.)

March, 1944 — A GUY NAMED JOE (M-G-M)
Producer, Everett Riskin. Director, Victor Fleming. Developed from an unpublished story by Chandler Sprague and David Boehm. Screenplay by Dalton Trumbo. Adaptation by Frederick Hazlitt Brennan. (Film completed September, 1943.)

January, 1945 — THIRTY SECONDS OVER TOKYO (M-G-M)
Producer, Sam Zimbalist. Director, Mervin LeRoy. Based on the book and Collier's story by Capt. Ted W. Lawson and Robert Considine. Screenplay by Dalton Trumbo.
(Film completed June, 1944.)

July, 1945 — JEALOUSY (Republic)
Executive Producer, Howard Sheehan. Associate Producer, Gustav Machaty.

251

Director, Gustav Machaty. Based on an original idea by Dalton Trumbo. Screenplay by Arnold Phillips and Gustav Machaty.

(Film completed June, 1945.)

September, 1945 — OUR VINES HAVE TENDER GRAPES (M-G-M)

Producer, Robert Sisk. Director, Roy Rowland. Screenplay by Dalton Trumbo. Based on the book *For Our Vines Have Tender Grapes* by George Victor Martin.

(Film completed December, 1944.)

APPENDIX I-B

Films of "The Hollywood Ten," 1929-1949: Listed According to Date of Completion* in the Five Successive Periods of Reorientation of Communist Party Policy and Propaganda

1. Films Released During the "New Revolutionary Era" of the Communist Party (1929-August, 1935)

1929 — CASE OF LENA SMITH (Paramount)
Adapted from a story by Samuel Ornitz.

1929 — CHINATOWN NIGHTS (Paramount)
From Samuel Ornitz' story "Tong War."

1929 — DYNAMITE (M-G-M-Pathe)
Dialogue by John Howard Lawson (jointly with two other writers).

1930 — SHIP FROM SHANGHAI (M-G-M)
Scenario by John Howard Lawson.

1930 — SINS OF THE CHILDREN (Cosmopolitan Productions-Metro)
Adaptation by Samuel Ornitz.

August, 1930 — OUR BLUSHING BRIDES (M-G-M)
Scenario by John Howard Lawson (jointly with one other writer).

October, 1930 — SEA BAT (M-G-M)
Scenario by John Howard Lawson (jointly with one other writer).
Dialogue by John Howard Lawson (jointly with one other writer).

March, 1931 — BACHELOR APARTMENT (RKO)
Original story by John Howard Lawson.

1932 — AFRAID TO TALK (Universal)
Adapted from the play "Merry-Go-Round" written by Albert Maltz (jointly with one other writer).

1932 — HELL'S HIGHWAY (RKO)
Story by Samuel Ornitz (jointly with two other writers).

1932 — IF I HAD A MILLION (Paramount)
Story by Lester Cole (jointly with seventeen other writers).

1932 — SECRETS OF THE FRENCH POLICE (RKO)
Story by Samuel Ornitz (jointly with one other writer).
Screenplay by Samuel Ornitz (jointly with one other writer).

---

* Since for the most part, completion dates on films were not available for motion pictures released prior to 1938, dates given on these films are *release dates,* except where otherwise indicated.

1933 — CHARLIE CHAN'S GREATEST CASE (Fox)
Adaptation by Lester Cole (jointly with one other writer).

1933 — MEN OF AMERICA (RKO)
Adaptation by Samuel Ornitz (jointly with one other writer).

September, 1933 — ONE MAN'S JOURNEY (RKO)
Screenplay by Samuel Ornitz.

1934 — ONE EXCITING ADVENTURE (Universal)
Dialogue by Samuel Ornitz.

1934 — PURSUED (Fox)
Screenplay by Lester Cole (jointly with one other writer).

1934 — SLEEPERS EAST (Fox)
Screenplay by Lester Cole.

1934 — SUCCESS AT ANY PRICE (RKO)
From the play by John Howard Lawson. Adaptation by John Howard Lawson
(jointly with one other writer).

1934 — WILD GOLD (Fox)
Adaptation by Lester Cole (jointly with one other writer).

January, 1935 — THE MAN WHO RECLAIMED HIS HEAD (Universal)
Adaptation by Samuel Ornitz (jointly with one other writer).

February, 1935 — UNDER PRESSURE (Fox)
Screenplay by Lester Cole (jointly with two other writers).

May, 1935 — PARTY WIRE (Columbia)
Adaptation by John Howard Lawson (jointly with one other writer).

July, 1935 — THE HAWK (Herman Wohl)
Director, Edward Dmytryk.

2. Films Released During the "Popular Front" Period of the
Communist Party (August, 1935-August, 1939)

October, 1935 — THREE KIDS AND A QUEEN (Universal)
Screenplay by Samuel Ornitz (jointly with one other writer).

October, 1935 — ONE WAY TICKET (Columbia)
Director, Herbert Biberman.
(Film released December, 1935).

December, 1935 — HITCH HIKE LADY (Republic)
Screenplay by Lester Cole (jointly with one other writer).

December, 1935 — TOO TOUGH TO KILL (Columbia)
Adaptation by Lester Cole (jointly with one other writer).

1936 — FATAL LADY (Wanger-Paramount)
Screenplay by Samuel Ornitz.

1936 — FOLLOW YOUR HEART (Republic)
Screenplay by Lester Cole and Samuel Ornitz (jointly with one other writer).

254

1936 — LOVE BEGINS AT TWENTY (First National-Warner Brothers)
Screenplay by Dalton Trumbo (jointly with one other writer).

1936 — THE PRESIDENT'S MYSTERY (Republic)
Screenplay by Lester Cole (jointly with one other writer).

1936 — ROAD GANG (First National-Warner Brothers)
Story by Dalton Trumbo (jointly with two other writers).

April, 1936 — MEET NERO WOLFE (Columbia)
Director, Herbert Biberman.
    (Film released July, 1936.)

December, 1936 — TUGBOAT PRINCESS (Columbia)
Original screen story by Dalton Trumbo (jointly with one other writer).

1937 — DEVIL'S PLAYGROUND (Columbia)
Screenplay by Dalton Trumbo (jointly with two other writers).

1937 — A DOCTOR'S DIARY (Paramount)
Story by Samuel Ornitz (jointly with one other writer).

1937 — THE HIT PARADE (Republic)
Screenplay by Samuel Ornitz (jointly with one other writer).

1937 — IT COULD HAPPEN TO YOU (Republic)
Adapted by Samuel Ornitz (jointly with one other writer).

1937 — THE MAN IN BLUE (Universal)
Screenplay by Lester Cole.

1937 — PORTIA ON TRIAL (Republic)
Screenplay by Samuel Ornitz.

1937 — TWO WISE MAIDS (Republic)
Screenplay by Samuel Ornitz.

June, 1937 — AFFAIRS OF CAPPY RICKS (Republic)
Original screenplay by Lester Cole.

November, 1937 — SOME BLONDES ARE DANGEROUS (Universal)
Screenplay by Lester Cole.

1938 — THE CRIME OF DR. HALLET (Universal)
Original screen story by Lester Cole (jointly with one other writer).
Screenplay by Lester Cole (jointly with one other writer).

1938 — MIDNIGHT INTRUDER (Universal)
Screenplay by Lester Cole (jointly with one other writer).

1938 — THE JURY'S SECRET (Universal)
Story by Lester Cole. Screenplay by Lester Cole (jointly with one other writer).

February, 1938 — KING OF THE NEWSBOYS (Republic)
Developed from an original screen story by Samuel Ornitz (jointly with one other writer).
    (Film released March, 1938.)

255

March, 1938 — BLOCKADE (Wanger-United Artists)
Original screenplay by John Howard Lawson.
(Film released June, 1938.)

March, 1938 — SINNERS IN PARADISE (Universal)
Screenplay by Lester Cole (jointly with two other writers).
(Film released April, 1938.)

May, 1938 — ARMY GIRL (Republic)
Screenplay by Samuel Ornitz (jointly with one other writer).
(Film released July, 1938.)

July, 1938 — ALGIERS (Wanger-United Artists)
Screenplay by John Howard Lawson.
(Film released August, 1938.)

July, 1938 — FUGITIVES FOR A NIGHT (RKO)
Screenplay by Dalton Trumbo.
(Film released September, 1938.)

August, 1938 — A MAN TO REMEMBER (RKO)
Screenplay by Dalton Trumbo.
(Film released October, 1938.)

October, 1938 — KING OF CHINATOWN (Paramount)
Developed from an original screen story by Herbert Biberman.
(Film released March, 1939.)

October, 1938 — SECRETS OF A NURSE (Universal)
Screenplay by Lester Cole (jointly with one other writer).
(Film released December, 1938.)

December, 1938 — THE FLYING IRISHMAN (RKO)
Screenplay by Dalton Trumbo (jointly with one other writer).
(Film released March, 1939.)

December, 1938 — LITTLE ORPHAN ANNIE (Colonial-Paramount)
Story by Samuel Ornitz (jointly with one other writer). Screenplay by Samuel Ornitz (jointly with one other writer).
(Film released December, 1938.)

January, 1939 — THE KID FROM KOKOMO (Warners)
Developed from original screen story by Dalton Trumbo. Contributor to treatment, Ring Lardner, Jr.
(Film released June, 1939.)

March, 1939 — EVERYTHING HAPPENS TO ANN (Arcadia-Grand National)
Adapted from story by Dalton Trumbo.
(Film released February, 1939.)

March, 1939 — SORORITY HOUSE (RKO)
Screenplay by Dalton Trumbo.
(Film released May, 1939.)

April, 1939 — FIVE CAME BACK (RKO)
Screenplay by Dalton Trumbo (jointly with two other writers).
(Film released June, 1939.)

May, 1939 — CAREER (RKO)
Screenplay by Dalton Trumbo.
(Film released July, 1939.)

June, 1939 — TELEVISION SPY (Paramount)
Director, Edward Dmytryk.
(Film released October, 1939.)

July, 1939 — HEAVEN WITH A BARBED WIRE FENCE (20th Century-Fox)
Developed from original screen story by Dalton Trumbo. Screenplay by Dalton
Trumbo (jointly with two other writers).
(Film released November, 1939.)

July, 1939 — I STOLE A MILLION (Universal)
Developed from an original screen story by Lester Cole.
(Film released July, 1939.)

July, 1939 — WINTER CARNIVAL (Wanger-United Artists)
Screenplay by Lester Cole (jointly with two other writers).
(Film released July, 1939.)

3. Films Completed During the Period of the Nazi-Soviet Pact
(August, 1939-June, 1941)

August, 1939 — THEY SHALL HAVE MUSIC (Goldwyn-United Artists)
Screenplay by John Howard Lawson (jointly with one other writer).
(Film released August, 1939.)

September, 1939 — EMERGENCY SQUAD (Paramount)
Director, Edward Dmytryk.
(Film released January, 1940.)

October, 1939 — MEET DR. CHRISTIAN (Stephens-Lang-RKO)
Screenplay by Ring Lardner, Jr. (jointly with two other writers).
(Film released November, 1939.)

November, 1939 — THE BIG GUY (Universal)
Screenplay by Lester Cole.
(Film released November, 1939.)

November, 1939 — THE INVISIBLE MAN RETURNS (Universal)
Screenplay by Lester Cole (jointly with one other writer).
(Film released January, 1940.)

November, 1939 — THE MIRACLE ON MAIN STREET (Columbia)
Developed from an original screen story by Samuel Ornitz (jointly with one
other writer).
(Film released October, 1939.)

257

December, 1939 — GOLDEN GLOVES (Paramount)
Director, Edward Dmytryk.
(Film released August, 1940.)

December, 1939 — THE LONE WOLF STRIKES (Columbia)
Developed from an unpublished story by Dalton Trumbo.
(Film released January, 1940.)

January, 1940 — A BILL OF DIVORCEMENT (RKO)
Screenplay by Dalton Trumbo.
(Film released May, 1940.)

January, 1940 — THE HOUSE OF SEVEN GABLES (Universal)
Dialogue Director, Lester Cole. Screenplay by Lester Cole.
(Film released April, 1940.)

February, 1940 — CURTAIN CALL (RKO)
Screenplay by Dalton Trumbo.
(Film released April, 1940.)

February, 1940 — EARTHBOUND (20th Century-Fox)
Screenplay by John Howard Lawson (jointly with one other writer).
(Film released June, 1940.)

March, 1940 — THE COURAGEOUS DR. CHRISTIAN (Stephens-Lang-RKO)
Original screenplay by Ring Lardner, Jr. (jointly with one other writer).
(Film released April, 1940.)

March, 1940 — HALF A SINNER (Universal)
Developed from an original screen story by Dalton Trumbo.
(Film released April, 1940.)

April, 1940 — THREE FACES WEST (Republic)
Original screenplay by Samuel Ornitz (jointly with two other writers).
(Film released July, 1940.)

May, 1940 — FOUR SONS (20th Century-Fox)
Screenplay by John Howard Lawson.
(Film released June, 1940.)

June, 1940 — MYSTERY SEA RAIDER (Paramount)
Director, Edward Dmytryk.
(Film released August, 1940.)

June, 1940 — WE WHO ARE YOUNG (M-G-M)
Original screenplay by Dalton Trumbo.
(Film released July, 1940.)

November, 1940 — FOOTSTEPS IN THE DARK (Warners)
Screenplay by Lester Cole (jointly with one other writer).
(Film released March, 1941.)

November, 1940 — KEEPING COMPANY (M-G-M)
Screenplay by Adrian Scott (jointly with two other writers).
(Film released December, 1940.)

November, 1940 — KITTY FOYLE (RKO)
  Screenplay by Dalton Trumbo.
    (Film released December, 1940.)

December, 1940 — ARKANSAS JUDGE (Republic)
  Adapted by Ring Lardner, Jr. (jointly with two other writers).
    (Film released January, 1941.)

December, 1940 — THE DEVIL COMMANDS (Columbia)
  Director, Edward Dmytryk.
    (Film released February, 1941.)

December, 1940 — HER FIRST ROMANCE (Chadwick-Monogram)
  Director, Edward Dmytryk.
    (Film released December, 1940.)

February, 1941 — UNDER AGE (Columbia)
  Director, Edward Dmytryk.
    (Film released April, 1941.)

April, 1941 — SWEETHEART OF THE CAMPUS (Columbia)
  Director, Edward Dmytryk.
    (Film released June, 1941.)

April, 1941 — ACCENT ON LOVE (20th Century-Fox)
  Developed from an original screen story by Dalton Trumbo.
    (Film released July, 1941.)

4. Films Completed During the Period of Soviet-United Nations
   Collaboration in World War II (June, 1941-May, 1945)

June, 1941 — AMONG THE LIVING (Paramount)
  Author, Lester Cole (jointly with one other writer). Screenplay, Lester Cole
  (jointly with one other writer).
    (Film released December, 1941.)

June, 1941 — THE BLONDE FROM SINGAPORE (Columbia)
  Director, Edward Dmytryk.
    (Film released October, 1941.)

June, 1941 — THE PARSON OF PANAMINT (Sherman-Paramount)
  Screenplay by Adrian Scott (jointly with one other writer).
    (Film released June, 1941.)

June, 1941 — WE GO FAST (20th Century-Fox)
  Screenplay by Adrian Scott (jointly with one other writer).
    (Film released September, 1941.)

August, 1941 — THE REMARKABLE ANDREW (Paramount)
  Adapted from novel by Dalton Trumbo. Screenplay by Dalton Trumbo.
    (Film released January, 1942.)

August, 1941 — SECRETS OF THE LONE WOLF (Columbia)
  Director, Edward Dmytryk.
    (Film released November, 1941.)

259

August, 1941 — You Belong to Me (Columbia)
Developed from an unpublished story by Dalton Trumbo.
(Film released October, 1941.)

September, 1941 — Confessions of Boston Blackie (Columbia)
Director, Edward Dmytryk.
(Film released January, 1942.)

September, 1941 — Pacific Blackout (Paramount)
Screenplay by Lester Cole (jointly with one other writer).
(Film released January, 1942.)

October, 1941 — Woman of the Year (M-G-M)
Original screenplay by Ring Lardner, Jr. (jointly with one other writer).
(Film released February, 1942.)

December, 1941 — This Gun for Hire (Paramount)
Screenplay by Albert Maltz.
(Film released March, 1942.)

January, 1942 — Counter Espionage (Columbia)
Director, Edward Dmytryk.
(Film released September, 1942.)

August, 1942 — Seven Miles from Alcatraz (RKO)
Director, Edward Dmytryk.
(Film released January, 1943.)

September, 1942 — Night Plane from Chunking (Paramount)
Screenplay by Lester Cole (jointly with two other writers).
(Film released January, 1943.)

October, 1942 — Hitler's Children (RKO)
Director, Edward Dmytryk.
(Film released March, 1943.)

December, 1942 — Action in the North Atlantic (Warners)
Screenplay by John Howard Lawson.
(Film released June, 1943.)

January, 1943 — Mr. Lucky (RKO)
Screenplay by Adrian Scott (jointly with one other writer).
(Film released May, 1943.)

February, 1943 — The Falcon Strikes Back (RKO)
Director, Edward Dmytryk.
(Film released May, 1943.)

April, 1943 — Hostages (Paramount)
Screenplay by Lester Cole (jointly with one other writer).
(Film released August, 1943.)

April, 1943 — Sahara (Columbia)
Screenplay by John Howard Lawson (jointly with one other writer).
(Film released October, 1943.)

260

May, 1943 — BEHIND THE RISING SUN (RKO)
   Director, Edward Dmytryk.
      (Film released July, 1943.)

July, 1943 — THE CROSS OF LORRAINE (M-G-M)
   Screenplay by Ring Lardner, Jr. (jointly with three other writers).
      (Film released January, 1944.)

July, 1943 — NORTHERN PURSUIT (Warners)
   Screenplay by Alvah Bessie (jointly with one other writer).
      (Film released November, 1943.)

September, 1943 — DESTINATION TOKYO (Warners)
   Screenplay by Albert Maltz (jointly with one other writer).
      (Film released January, 1944.)

September, 1943 — A GUY NAMED JOE (M-G-M)
   Screenplay by Dalton Trumbo.
      (Film released March, 1944.)

October, 1943 — THE MAN IN HALF MOON STREET (Paramount)
   Contributor to screenplay construction, Albert Maltz (jointly with one other writer).
      (Film released October, 1944.)

October, 1943 — NONE SHALL ESCAPE (Columbia)
   Screenplay by Lester Cole.
      (Film released February, 1944.)

October, 1943 — TENDER COMRADE (RKO)
   Director, Edward Dmytryk. Original screen story by Dalton Trumbo. Screenplay, Dalton Trumbo.
      (Film released December, 1943.)

December, 1943 — ACTION IN ARABIA (RKO)
   Developed from an original screen story by Herbert Biberman (jointly with one other writer). Screenplay by Herbert Biberman (jointly with one other writer).
      (Film released February, 1944.)

December, 1943 — CAPTIVE WILD WOMAN (Universal)
   Director, Edward Dmytryk.
      (Film released June, 1943.)

March, 1944 — THEY LIVE IN FEAR (Columbia)
   Screenplay by Samuel Ornitz (jointly with one other writer).
      (Film released June, 1944.)

May, 1944 — THE VERY THOUGHT OF YOU (Warners)
   Screenplay by Alvah Bessie (jointly with one other writer).
      (Film released November, 1944.)

June, 1944 — THE MASTER RACE (Edward A. Golden Production-RKO)
   Director, Herbert Biberman. Developed from an original screen story by

261

Herbert Biberman. Screenplay by Herbert Biberman (jointly with two other writers).
(Film released September, 1944.

June, 1944 — THIRTY SECONDS OVER TOKYO (M-G-M)
Screenplay by Dalton Trumbo.
(Film released January, 1945.)

July, 1944 — MURDER, MY SWEET (RKO)
Producer, Adrian Scott. Director, Edward Dmytryk.
(Film released December, 1944.)

July, 1944 — MY PAL WOLF (RKO)
Producer, Adrian Scott.
(Film released November, 1944.)

August, 1944 — LITTLE DEVILS (Monogram)
Screenplay, Samuel Ornitz.
(Film released December, 1944.)

August, 1944 — OBJECTIVE BURMA (Warners)
Developed from an original screen story by Alvah Bessie. Screenplay by Lester Cole (jointly with one other writer).
(Film released February, 1945.)

August, 1944 — TOMORROW THE WORLD (United Artists)
Screenplay by Ring Lardner, Jr. (jointly with one other writer).
(Film released December, 1944.)

October, 1944 — TOGETHER AGAIN (Columbia)
Developed from an original screen story by Herbert Biberman (jointly with one other writer).
(Film released December, 1944.)

November, 1944 — CIRCUMSTANTIAL EVIDENCE (20th Century-Fox)
Adaptation, Samuel Ornitz.
(Film released March, 1945.)

November, 1944 — MISS SUSIE SLAGLE'S (Paramount)
Adaptation by Adrian Scott (jointly with one other writer).
(Film released March, 1946.)

December, 1944 — BLOOD ON THE SUN
(Cagney Productions, Inc.-United Artists)
Screenplay by Lester Cole.
(Film released June, 1945.)

December, 1944 — COUNTER-ATTACK (Columbia)
Screenplay by John Howard Lawson.
(Film released April, 1945.)

December, 1944 — OUR VINES HAVE TENDER GRAPES (M-G-M)
Screenplay by Dalton Trumbo.
(Film released September, 1945.)

262

January, 1945 — HOTEL BERLIN (Warners)
Screenplay by Alvah Bessie (jointly with one other writer).
(Film released March, 1945.)

February, 1945 — BACK TO BATAAN (RKO)
Director, Edward Dmytryk.
(Film released May, 1945.)

February, 1945 — PRIDE OF THE MARINES (Warners)
Screenplay by Albert Maltz.
(Film released September, 1945.)

March, 1945 — MEN IN HER DIARY (Universal)
Adaptation by Lester Cole.
(Film released September, 1945.)

5. Films Completed Since the Beginning of "The Cold War"
(May, 1945-   .)

June, 1945 — JEALOUSY (Republic)
Based on an original idea by Dalton Trumbo.
(Film released July, 1945.)

July, 1945 — DEADLINE AT DAWN (RKO)
Producer, Adrian Scott.
(Film released March, 1946.)

August, 1945 — CORNERED (RKO)
Producer, Adrian Scott. Director, Edward Dmytryk.
(Film released December, 1945.)

January, 1946 — STRANGE CONQUEST (Universal)
Story by Lester Cole (jointly with one other writer).
(Film released May, 1946.)

January, 1946 — TILL THE END OF TIME (RKO)
Director, Edward Dmytryk.
(Film released August, 1946.)

April, 1946 — FIESTA (M-G-M)
Original screenplay by Lester Cole (jointly with one other writer).
(Film released July, 1947.)

June, 1946 — CLOAK AND DAGGER (United States Pictures, Inc.-Warners)
Screenplay by Albert Maltz and Ring Lardner, Jr.
(Film released September, 1946.)

August, 1946 — SMASH-UP (Universal)
Screenplay by John Howard Lawson.
(Film released March, 1947.)

October, 1946 — NEW ORLEANS (Jules Levy-United Artists)
Associate Producer, Herbert J. Biberman. Original screen story by Herbert J.
Biberman (jointly with one other writer).
(Film released April, 1947.)

December, 1946 — THE ROMANCE OF ROSY RIDGE (M-G-M)
   Screenplay by Lester Cole.
      (Film released August, 1947.)

March, 1947 — CROSSFIRE (RKO)
   Producer, Adrian Scott. Director, Edward Dmytryk.
      (Film released August, 1947.)

March, 1947 — FOREVER AMBER (20th Century-Fox)
   Screenplay by Ring Lardner, Jr. (jointly with one other writer).
      (Film released October, 1947.)

August, 1947 — HIGH WALL (M-G-M)
   Screenplay by Lester Cole (jointly with one other writer).
      (Film released February, 1948.)

September, 1947 — THE NAKED CITY (Universal)
   Written by Albert Maltz (jointly with one other writer).
      (Film released March, 1948.)

November, 1947 — SMART WOMAN (Allied Artists)
   Screenplay by Alvah Bessie (jointly with two other writers).
      (Film released April, 1948.)

October, 1948 — THE FORBIDDEN STREET (20th Century-Fox)
   Screenplay by Ring Lardner, Jr.
      (Film released June, 1949.)

APPENDIX I-C

Films of "The Hollywood Ten," 1929–1949:
Statistical Tables: Production and Release Data.

TABLE 1

TOTAL PRODUCING, DIRECTING AND WRITING SCREEN CREDITS
RECEIVED BY "THE HOLLYWOOD TEN"
1929–1949

	Number	Percent
Producing Credits	6	3.4
Directing Credits	28	15.6
Writing Credits	145	81.0
TOTAL SCREEN CREDITS	179	100.0

265

TABLE 2

(*Totals and Percentages*)
1929–1949

	Number	Percent	Total	Percent
Producer	5	2.8		
Associate Producer	1	.6		
Total Producer Credits			6	3.4
Director	27	15.0		
Dialogue Director	1	.6		
Total Director Credits			28	15.6
Original screen story	15	8.4		
Joint original screen story	12	6.7		
Joint original screen play	3	1.6		
Original screen play	3	1.6		
Novel (basis of a film)	1	.6		
Play (basis for a film)	1	.6		
Joint Play (basis for a film)	1	.6		
Original story idea	1	.6		
Total Original story credits			37	20.7
Adaptation	2	1.1		
Joint adaptation	2	1.1		
Contributor to treatment	1	.6		
Total Adaptation credits			5	2.8
Sole screen play	34	18.9		
Joint screen play (collaborating with one other writer)	50	27.9		
Joint screen play (collaborating with two or more writers)	15	8.4		
Contributor to screen play construction	1	.6		
Dialogue	1	.6		
Collaborated on dialogue	2	1.1		
Total Screen play Credits			103*	57.5
Grand Total	179	100.0	179	100.0

* This figure does not include Original Screen Play credits, which are included above under Original Story credits.

TABLE 3

TYPES OF SCREEN CREDITS RECEIVED BY EACH OF "THE HOLLYWOOD TEN"
1929–1949

	Bessie	Biberman	Cole	Dmytryk	Lardner, Jr.	Lawson	Maltz	Ornitz	Scott	Trumbo
Producer	—	—	—	—	—	—	—	—	5	—
Associate Producer	—	1	—	—	—	—	—	—	—	—
Director	—	3	—	24	—	—	—	—	—	—
Dialogue Director	—	—	1	—	—	—	—	—	—	—
Original screen story	1	2	2	—	—	1	—	2	—	7
Joint original screen story	—	2	3	—	—	—	—	5	—	2
Joint original screen play	—	—	1	—	1	—	—	1	—	—
Original screen play	—	—	1	—	—	1	—	—	—	1
Novel (basis for a film)	—	—	—	—	—	—	—	—	—	1
Play (basis for a film)	—	—	—	—	—	1	—	—	—	—
Joint Play (basis for a film)	—	—	—	—	—	—	1	—	—	—
Original story idea	—	—	—	—	—	—	—	—	—	1
Adaptation	—	—	1	—	—	—	—	1	—	—
Joint Adaptation	—	—	—	—	—	1	—	—	1	—
Contributor to treatment	—	—	—	—	—	1	—	—	—	—
Sole screen play	—	—	8	—	1	6	1	6	—	12
Joint screen play with one collaborator	3	2	18	—	2	7	4	9	3	2
Joint screen play with two or more collaborators	1	1	4	—	4	—	—	1	1	3
Contributor to screen play construction	—	—	—	—	—	—	1	—	—	—
Dialogue	—	—	—	—	—	—	—	1	—	—
Collaborated on dialogue	—	—	—	—	—	2	—	—	—	—
TOTAL NUMBER OF SCREEN CREDITS	5	11	39	24	10	18	7	26	10	29

TABLE 4

FILMS ON WHICH "THE HOLLYWOOD TEN" RECEIVED WRITER CREDITS,
1929–1949
Showing the Total Number of Writers Credited per Picture

	Number	Percent
1 writer only credited	4*	2.9
2 writers credited	38	27.3
3 writers credited	51	36.7
4 writers credited	31	22.3
5 writers credited	8	5.8
6 writers credited	4	2.9
7 writers credited	1	.7
9 or more writers credited	2	1.4
TOTAL FILMS ON WHICH "THE HOLLYWOOD TEN" RECEIVED WRITING CREDIT	139	100.0

* These solo writer credits were as follows:

BLOCKADE (Wanger–United Artists) 1938. Original screenplay by John Howard Lawson.

WE WHO ARE YOUNG (M-G-M) 1940. Original screenplay by Dalton Trumbo.

THE REMARKABLE ANDREW (Paramount) 1941. Adapted from the novel by Dalton Trumbo. Screenplay by Dalton Trumbo.

TENDER COMRADE (RKO) 1943. Screen story by Dalton Trumbo. Screenplay by Dalton Trumbo.

TABLE 5

	Number	Percent
The "New Revolutionary Era" (1929–August, 1935)	24	15.1
The Period of the "Popular Front" (1935–August, 1939)	43	27.0
The Period of the Nazi–Soviet Pact (August, 1939–June, 1941)	27	17.0
The Period of Soviet–United Nations Collaboration (June, 1941–May, 1945)	49	30.8
Since the beginning of "The Cold War"	16	10.1
TOTAL	159	100.0

1. Films from the years 1929–1938 are classified by release date rather than date of completion of the film, as this latter information (obtained from Academy records) is not available on films released prior to 1938.

TABLE 6

A-Features Credited to "The Hollywood Ten" During the Five
Successive Periods of Reorientation of Communist Party
Policy and Propaganda Since 1929

	Number of A-Features	Percent of total films credited during the period	Percent of total A-Features credited 1929–1949
The "New Revolutionary Era" (1929–August, 1935)	10	41.7	17.9
The Period of the "Popular Front" (August, 1935–August, 1939)	10	23.3	17.9
The Period of the Nazi–Soviet Pact (August, 1939–June, 1941)	4	14.8	7.1
The Period of Soviet–United Nations Collaboration (June, 1941–May, 1945)	23	46.9	41.1
Since beginning "The Cold War" (May, 1945–to date)	9	56.4	16.0
TOTAL	56		100.0

270

TABLE 7

Year of Release of Films Credited to Each of "The Hollywood Ten," 1929–1949

	Bessie	Biberman	Cole	Dmytryk	Lardner, Jr.	Lawson	Maltz	Ornitz	Scott	Trumbo
1929	—	—	—	—	—	1	—	2	—	—
1930	—	—	—	—	—	3	—	1	—	—
1931	—	—	—	—	—	1	—	—	—	—
1932	—	—	1	—	—	—	1	2	—	—
1933	—	—	1	—	—	—	—	2	—	—
1934	—	—	3	—	—	1	—	1	—	—
1935	—	1	3	1	—	1	—	2	—	—
1936	—	1	2	—	—	—	—	2	—	3
1937	—	—	3	—	—	—	—	5	—	1
1938	—	1	5	—	—	2	—	3	—	2
1939	—	—	3	1	2	1	—	1	—	7
1940	—	—	2	4	1	2	—	1	1	6
1941	—	—	2	5	1	—	—	—	2	2
1942	—	—	1	2	1	—	1	—	—	1
1943	1	—	2	6	—	2	—	—	1	1
1944	1	3	1	1	2	—	2	2	2	1
1945	2	—	3	2	—	1	1	1	1	3
1946	—	—	1	1	1	—	1	—	2	—
1947	—	1	2	1	1	1	—	—	1	—
1948	1	—	1	—	—	—	1	—	—	—
1949	—	—	—	—	1	—	—	—	—	—
Total Number Films Credited	5	7	36	24	10	16	7	25	10	27

TABLE 8

FILMS OF "THE HOLLYWOOD TEN" BY PERIOD OF RELEASE AND PICTURE TYPE
(1929–1949)

	1929 to Aug. 1935	Aug. 1935 to Aug. 1939	Aug. 1939 to June 1941	June 1941 to May 1945	May 1945 to date	Total 1929 to 1949
Biographical	—	1	—	—	—	1
Historical	—	—	—	—	—	—
Period Pictures	—	—	1	—	1	2
Social Theme (or psychological)	5	8	5	—	4	22
War and Service Films	—	1	1	21	—	23
Prison Pictures	1	2	1	—	—	4
Crooks	1	—	—	1	—	2
Gangster	—	—	—	—	—	—
Racketeer	1	2	3	1	—	7
Criminal	—	2	—	—	—	2
Murder	—	—	—	—	—	—
Murder-Mystery	3	3	2	5	3	16
Mystery	—	1	—	—	—	1
Spy or Espionage	—	2	—	7	2	11
Horror	—	—	1	2	—	3
Fantasy	—	—	2	—	—	2
Juvenile	—	2	1	1	—	4
Domestic	1	1	1	2	—	5
Love Story or Romance	4	2	1	2	2	11
Career	2	4	4	2	1	13
Musical	—	2	1	—	1	4
Situation Comedy	—	—	—	—	—	—
Sport	—	3	1	—	1	5
Western	2	—	—	1	—	3
Action and Adventure	4	7	1	1	1	14
Not Classified	—	—	1	3	—	4
TOTAL	24	43	27	49	16	159

272

APPENDIX II

Films of Writers, Directors and Producers who Declared Themselves to Have Been Former Communists.

Dates in parentheses indicate the period of Communist Party membership.

A. WRITERS

HAROLD J. ASCHE (1933–1939)
  No screen credits during this period

LEOPOLD ATLAS (1944–1947)
  1944 — TOMORROW THE WORLD (Cowan-UA) Joint screenplay
  1945 — HER KIND OF MAN (Warners) Joint screenplay
  1945 — G. I. JOE (Cowan-UA) Joint screenplay
  1946 — CHILD OF DIVORCE (RKO) Play basis "Wednesday's Child"
  1948 — RAW DEAL (Reliance-Eagle-Lion) Joint screenplay

GEORGE BECK (1938–1947)
  1938 — EVERYBODY'S DOING IT (RKO) Story
  1940 — FORGOTTEN GIRLS (Republic) Contributor to screenplay
  1940 — HIRED WIFE (Universal) Original story
  1942 — TAKE A LETTER, DARLING (Paramount) Sole original story

MAX BENOFF (1944)
  1944 — TAKE IT OR LEAVE IT (20th Century-Fox) Joint screenplay

MARTIN BERKELEY (1936–1943)
  1942 — SHADOW OF A DOUBT (Universal) Joint screenplay

SIDNEY BUCHMAN (1938–1945)
  1938 — HOLIDAY (Columbia) Joint screenplay
  1939 — MR. SMITH GOES TO WASHINGTON (Columbia) Sole screenplay
  1940 — THE HOWARDS OF VIRGINIA (Lloyd-Columbia) Sole screenplay
  1941 — HERE COMES MR. JORDAN (Columbia) Joint screenplay
  1942 — THE TALK OF THE TOWN (Columbia) Joint screenplay
  1944 — A SONG TO REMEMBER (Columbia) Sole screenplay
  1945 — OVER 21 (Sidney Buchman-Columbia) Sole screenplay

RICHARD COLLINS (1938–1947)
  1939 — RULERS OF THE SEA (Paramount) Joint original screen story
      and joint screenplay

---

* Credits are also given for films released during the year following the termination of Communist Party membership to allow for possible time lag in the release of pictures.

1940 — One Crowded Night (RKO) Joint screenplay
1940 — Hudson Bay (20th Century-Fox) Joint treatment to story
1941 — Lady Scarface (RKO) Joint original screenplay
1943 — Private Miss Jones (M-G-M) Joint story
1943 — Thousands Cheer (M-G-M) Joint screenplay
1943 — Song of Russia (M-G-M) Joint screenplay
1945 — Little Giant (Universal) Joint original story

LILLIAN HELLMAN (before 1949*)

1935 — The Dark Angel (United Artists) Collaborated on screenplay
1936 — These Three (Goldwyn-United Artists) Screenplay based on her play "The Children's Hour"
1937 — Dead End (United Artists) Screenplay
1937 — Spanish Earth (Prometheus Pictures) Collaborated on Spanish Earth
1941 — The Little Foxes (Goldwyn-RKO) Play and sole screenplay
1942 — Watch on the Rhine (Warners) Play basis of and additional scenes and dialogue
1943 — The North Star (Crescent-RKO) Original screen story and sole screenplay
1946 — The Searching Wind (Hal Wallis Prod.-Paramount) Play basis of and sole screenplay
1947 — Another Part of the Forest (Univ.-Int.) Play basis

ROY HUGGINS (1940–1947)

1947 — The Fuller Brush Man (Edward Small) Based on short story "Now You See It"
1947 — I Love Trouble (Cornell Productions) Based on novel "The Double Take" and sole screenplay
1948 — Too Late for Tears (Hunt Stromberg-UA) Based on serial basis of and sole screenplay

ROLAND W. KIBBEE (1937–1939)

No screen credits during this period (First record of Hollywood screen credit in 1946)

DAVID LANG (1942–1946)

1942 — Northwest Rangers (M-G-M) Joint original screenplay
1944 — Midnight Manhunt (Pine-Thomas-Paramount) Sole original screenplay
1945 — People Are Funny (Pine-Thomas-Paramount) Original screen story and joint screenplay

---

* Lillian Hellman declined to give the exact dates of membership, but indicated that it was prior to 1949. Thus we have included all credits prior to this date, since there is no way of knowing the date when her membership began.

1946 — Traffic in Crime (Republic) Sole original screenplay
1946 — Queen of the Burlesque (Producers Releasing Corporation)
    Sole original screenplay
1946 — Jungle Flight (Pine-Thomas-Paramount) Original screen story
1947 — Caged Fury (Pine-Thomas-Paramount) Sole original screenplay

ISOBEL LENNART (1938–1946)

1942 — A Stranger in Town (M-G-M) Joint original screenplay
1942 — The Affairs of Martha (M-G-M) Joint original screenplay
1943 — Lost Angel (M-G-M) Sole original screenplay
1944 — Anchors Aweigh (M-G-M) Sole screenplay
1945 — Holiday in Mexico (M-G-M) Sole screenplay
1946 — It Happened in Brooklyn (M-G-M) Sole screenplay
1947 — The Kissing Bandit (M-G-M) Joint original screenplay

MELVIN LEVY (1933 and 1944–1947)

1944 — Sunday Dinner for a Soldier (20th Century-Fox)
    Joint screenplay
1944 — She's a Soldier Too (Columbia) Sole screenplay
1945 — Renegades (Columbia) Joint screenplay
1945 — The Bandit of Sherwood Forest (Columbia) Joint screenplay

BART LYTTON (1936–1937)

No credits in the period 1936–1938.
First screen credit in 1942.

CLIFFORD ODETS (1934–1935)

1936 — The General Died at Dawn (Paramount) Sole screenplay

GERTRUDE PURCELL (1939–1942)

1939 — Lady and the Mob (Columbia) Joint screenplay
1939 — Destry Rides Again (Universal) Joint screenplay
1939 — First Love (Universal) Joint original screen story
1940 — Arkansas Judge (Republic) Joint adaptation of novel
    "False Witness"
1940 — One Night in the Tropics (Universal) Joint screenplay
1940 — The Invisible Woman (Universal) Joint screenplay
1940 — A Little Bit of Heaven (Universal) Joint screenplay
1941 — Ellery Queen and the Murder Ring (Darmour-Columbia)
    Joint screenplay
1941 — A Close Call for Ellery Queen (Darmour-Columbia)
    Contributor to special sequence
1942 — Ice Capades Revue (Republic) Joint screenplay
1942 — In Old California (Republic) Joint screenplay
1943 — Follow the Boys (C. K. Feldman Group Production-Universal)
    Joint original screenplay

SYLVIA RICHARDS (1937–1946)
  1946 — POSSESSED (Warners) Joint screenplay
  1947 — SECRET BEYOND THE DOOR (Djana Prod. Inc.-Universal-
    International) Sole screenplay

STANLEY ROBERTS (1945–1948)
  1947 — SONG OF THE THIN MAN (M-G-M) Unpublished story basis
  1949 — CURTAIN CALL AT CACTUS CREEK (Universal-International)
    Joint story

BERNARD SCHOENFELD (1945–1948)
  1946 — THE DARK CORNER (20th Century-Fox) Joint screenplay

BUDD SCHULBERG (1937–1940)
  1938 — LITTLE ORPHAN ANNIE (Colonial-Paramount) Joint screenplay
  1939 — WINTER CARNIVAL (Wanger-UA) Story and joint screenplay
  1941 — WEEK END FOR THREE (RKO) Unpublished story basis

SOL SHOR (1938–1949)
  1938 — THE FIGHTING DEVIL DOGS (Republic) Joint original screenplay
  1938 — DICK TRACY RETURNS (Republic) Joint original screenplay
  1939 — THE LONE RANGER RIDES AGAIN (Republic)
    Joint original screenplay
  1939 — DAREDEVILS OF THE RED CIRCLE (Republic)
    Joint original screenplay
  1939 — DICK TRACY'S G-MEN (Republic) Joint screenplay
  1939 — ZORRO'S FIGHTING LEGION (Republic) Joint original screenplay
  1940 — DRUMS OF FU MANCHU (Republic) Joint screenplay
  1940 — ADVENTURES OF RED RYDER (Republic) Joint original screenplay
  1940 — KING OF THE ROYAL MOUNTED (Republic)
    Joint original screenplay
  1940 — MYSTERIOUS DOCTOR SATAN (Republic) Joint original screenplay
  1941 — ADVENTURES OF CAPTAIN MARVEL (Republic)
    Joint original screenplay
  1942 — THE YUKON PATROL (Republic) Joint original screenplay
  1942-1946 — In U. S. Armed Forces
  1946 — THE CRIMSON GHOST (Republic) Joint original screenplay
  1946 — SON OF ZORRO (Republic) Joint original screenplay
  1947 — JESSE JAMES RIDES AGAIN (Republic) Serial
    Joint original screenplay
  1947 — THE BLACK WIDOW (Republic) Serial. Joint original screenplay
  1947 — DANGERS OF THE CANADIAN MOUNTED (Republic)
    Joint original screenplay
  1947 — G-MEN NEVER FORGET (Republic) Serial
    Joint original screenplay

1948 — Sons of Adventure (Republic) Sole original screenplay
1948 — Adventures of Frank and Jesse James (Republic)
    Joint original screenplay
1948 — Federal Agents vs. the Underworld Inc. (Republic) Serial
    Joint original screenplay
1948 — Daughter of the Jungle (Republic) Original screen story
1949 — Ghost of Zorro (Republic) Joint original screenplay
1949 — King of the Rocket Men (Republic) Joint Screenplay
1949 — Radar Patrol vs. Spy Ring (Republic) Serial
    Joint original screenplay

LEO TOWNSEND (1943–1948)
1943 — Chip Off the Old Block (Universal) Joint screenplay
1944 — Can't Help Singing (Universal) Joint original screen story
1945 — Night and Day (Warners) Joint screenplay
1946 — That Way with Women (Warners) Sole screenplay

PAULINE SWANSON TOWNSEND (1943–1948)
No screen credits during this period.

FRANK TUTTLE (1937–1947)
No writer credits during this period. See below under DIRECTORS.

ELIZABETH WILSON (1937–1947)
No writer credits during this period.

B. DIRECTORS

EDWARD DMYTRYK (1944–1945)
1944 — Murder, My Sweet (RKO)
1945 — Back to Bataan (RKO)
1945 — Cornered (RKO)
1946 — Till the End of Time (RKO)

ELIA KAZAN (1934–1936)
No screen credits during this period. (First Hollywood film credit in 1946.)

FRANK TUTTLE (1937–1947)
1937 — Dr. Rhythm (Paramount)
1937 — Waikiki Wedding (Paramount)
1938 — Paris Honeymoon (Paramount)
1939 — Charlie McCarthy Detective (Universal) Also producer
1939 — I Stole A Million (Universal)
1941 — This Gun for Hire (Paramount)
1942 — Lucky Jordan (Paramount)
1943 — Rainbow Island (Paramount) co-director
1943 — The Hour Before Dawn (Paramount)

277

1943 — HOSTAGES (Paramount)
1944 — THE GREAT JOHN L (Bing Crosby Productions-UA)
1945 — SUSPENSE (King Bros.-Monogram)
1945 — DON JUAN QUILLIGAN (TW)
1946 — SWELL GUY (Mark Hellinger-Universal-International)

C. PRODUCERS

WILLIAM L. ALLAND   (1946–1949)
No screen credits during this period.

SIDNEY BUCHMAN   (1938–1945)
See above, under WRITERS.

HAROLD A. HECHT   (1936–1940)
No screen credits during this period.

FRANK TUTTLE   (1937–1947)
See above, under DIRECTORS.

APPENDIX III-A

Changes in the Content of Hollywood Motion Pictures 1947-1954:
Statistical Tables.

TABLE 9

DOMESTIC AND FOREIGN FEATURE-LENGTH MOTION PICTURES
Approved by
The Production Code Administration of the MPPA
(*Shown in Percentages*)
1947[1]–1954

	1947[1]	1948	1949	1950	1951	1952	1953	1954
Domestic Companies	92.3	94.6	89.8	91.6	89.8	90.8	88.1	87.8
Foreign Companies	7.7	5.4	10.2	8.4	10.2	9.2	11.9	12.2
TOTAL	100.0	100.0	100.0	100.0	100.0	100.0	100.0	100.0

1. Includes the last half of 1947 only.

TABLE 10

FEATURE-LENGTH MOTION PICTURES WHICH WERE FILMED ENTIRELY IN THE
UNITED STATES, IN THE UNITED STATES AND ABROAD, OR ENTIRELY ABROAD
Approved by
The Production Code Administration of the MPPA[1]
(*Shown in Percentages*)
1947[2]–1954

	1947[2]	1948	1949	1950	1951	1952	1953	1954
Filmed entirely in the United States	89.6	93.1	83.0	83.7	81.7	80.2	75.4	70.7
Filmed in the United States and Abroad	1.1	.5	3.6	3.7	3.7	4.3	4.8	6.9
Filmed entirely Abroad	9.3	6.4	13.4	12.6	14.6	15.5	19.8	22.4
TOTAL	100.0	100.0	100.0	100.0	100.0	100.0	100.0	100.0

1. Includes all films having major release in this country and many which are released by smaller distributors. Productions of foreign companies comprise an average of about 10% for the period shown (for annual figures giving the percentage foreign films, see Table 9).
2. Includes the last half of 1947 only.

TABLE 11

NEGATIVE COSTS OF FEATURE-LENGTH MOTION PICTURES
Approved by
The Production Code Administration of the MPPA[1]
(*Shown in Percentages*)
1947–1954

Negative Cost	1947	1948	1949	1950	1951	1952	1953	1954
More than $500,000	58.4	46.3	53.9	48.3	54.2	56.5	46.6	47.1
$200,000-$500,000	16.5	10.3	8.7	11.0	10.9	10.6	20.3	24.0
$150,000-$200,000	22.7	14.5	3.6	5.1	4.4	5.0	4.0	4.6
$100,000-$150,000	1.6	12.3	7.5	7.7	7.1	5.4	6.5	4.9
$ 50,000-$100,000	.8	13.0	17.1	18.4	13.2	13.3	11.0	8.2
Less than $50,000	—	3.6	8.7	9.5	10.2	9.2	11.6	11.2
No Information	—	—	.5	—	—	—	—	—
TOTAL	100.0	100.0	100.0	100.0	100.0	100.0	100.0	100.0

1. Includes all films having major release in this country, and many which are released by smaller distributors. Productions of foreign companies comprise an average of about 10% for the period shown (for annual figures giving the percentage foreign films, see Table 9).

TABLE 12

COLOR, BLACK-AND-WHITE, AND TONED FEATURE-LENGTH MOTION PICTURES
Approved by
The Production Code Administration of the MPPA[1]
(*Shown in Percentages*)
1947[2]–1954

	1947[2]	1948	1949	1950	1951	1952	1953	1954
Black and White	87.9	83.2	82.0	81.5	76.2	60.2	57.0	41.6
Black and White and Color	—	—	—	—	.2	—	—	—
Color	12.1	16.8	18.0	18.5	23.4	38.8	42.1	58.1
Color and Toned	—	—	—	—	.2	—	—	—
Toned	—	—	—	—	—	1.0	.6	.3
Black and White and Toned	—	—	—	—	—	—	.3	—

1. Includes all films having major release in this country, and some which do not. Productions of foreign companies comprise an average of about 10% for the period shown (for annual figures giving the percentage foreign films, see Table 9).
2. Includes the last half of 1947 only.

TABLE 13
SOURCE MATERIAL OF FEATURE-LENGTH MOTION PICTURES
Approved by
The Production Code Administration of the MPPA[1]
(*Shown in Percentages*)[2]
1947–1954

Source	1947	1948	1949	1950	1951	1952	1953	1954
Original screen stories	57.7	56.1	68.0	73.4	67.3	66.9	64.1	58.4
Stage plays	4.2	6.0	4.3	4.2	5.8	4.6	5.4	3.7
Novels	21.5	17.5	18.1	15.6	16.2	17.4	20.3	20.1
Biographies	—	.4	1.0	.7	.5	—	.9	.3
Short stories	1.2	5.3	3.8	2.4	5.8	5.7	4.8	4.0
Source unknown	2.5	2.3	—	—	—	—	—	—
Miscellaneous	12.9	12.4	4.8	3.7	4.4	5.4	4.5	13.5

1. Includes all films having major release in this country, and many which are released by smaller distributors. Productions of foreign companies comprise an average of about 10% for the period shown (for annual figures giving the percentage foreign films, see Table 9).
2. Figures taken from the *1954 Annual Report*, Motion Picture Association of America, Inc.

TABLE 14
TYPES OF FEATURE-LENGTH MOTION PICTURES
Approved by
The Production Code Administration of the MPPA[1]
(*Shown in Percentages*)
1947[2]–1954

	1947[2]	1948	1949	1950	1951	1952	1953	1954
Drama	22.5	18.3	14.6	14.5	15.1	13.0	12.1	18.1
Melodrama	55.5	60.7	60.8	64.2	58.1	62.0	67.4	65.1
Comedy	19.2	16.1	16.6	13.6	12.3	13.6	14.0	9.5
Farce	1.7	3.2	6.1	4.9	7.6	8.0	3.7	3.0
Documentary or semi-documentary	—	.2	1.2	2.3	2.8	1.0	2.5	3.3
Fantasy	1.1	1.5	.7	.5	3.9	1.9	—	1.0
Variety	—	—	—	—	.2	.5	—	—
Featurette	—	—	—	—	—	—	.3	—

1. Includes all films having mjaor release in this country, and some which do not. Productions of foreign companies comprise an average of about 10% for the period shown (for annual figures giving the percentage foreign films, see Table 9).
2. Includes the last half of 1947 only.

TABLE 15

PREDOMINANT CLASSIFICATIONS OF FEATURE-LENGTH MOTION PICTURES
Approved by
The Production Code Administration of the MPPA[1]
(*Shown in Percentages*)
1947[2]–1954

	1947[2]	1948	1949	1950	1951	1952	1953	1954
Western	25.2	23.7	26.3	27.1	18.0	20.3	17.7	22.1
Social Problems and Psychological	28.0	20.2	17.7	11.7	12.5	12.7	9.2	9.2
Crime and Crime Investigations	12.6	15.3	16.3	20.3	16.2	12.1	13.2	16.3
Romantic	10.4	13.6	8.8	11.0	14.6	17.6	15.7	7.3
Musical	5.0	3.7	4.9	4.2	4.9	5.2	3.9	5.9
Adventure	5.0	5.7	5.6	4.0	4.4	4.6	7.6	10.0
Mystery, Spy and Espionage	4.4	6.7	2.2	2.6	3.0	1.5	4.2	3.0
Historical, Biographical and Autobiographical, and Historical Fiction	2.2	2.2	2.9	4.4	3.3	4.3	5.3	6.2
War and Military	1.7	1.7	1.5	3.7	7.6	7.0	7.1	6.3
Total	94.5	92.8	86.2	89.0	84.5	85.3	83.9	86.3
All Other Classifications[3]	5.5	7.2	13.8	11.0	15.5	14.7	16.1	13.7
GRAND TOTAL	100.0	100.0	100.0	100.0	100.0	100.0	100.0	100.0

1. Includes all films having major release in this country, and many which are released by smaller distributors. Productions of foreign companies comprise an average of about 10% for the period shown (for annual figures giving the percentage foreign films, see Table 9).
2. Includes the last half of 1947 only.
3. For detailed figures, see Table 16.

TABLE 16

Detailed Breakdown on Classification of Feature-Length
Motion Pictures
Approved by
The Production Code Administration of the MPPA[1]
(*Shown in Percentages*)
1947[2]–1954

	1947[2]	1948	1949	1950	1951	1952	1953	1954
Western	25.2	23.7	26.3	27.1	18.0	20.3	17.7	22.1
Adventure	5.0	5.7	5.6	4.0	4.4	4.6	7.6	10.0
Crime	12.6	15.3	16.3	8.6	11.6	6.9	6.7	8.7
Crime Investigation	—	—	—	11.7	4.6	5.2	6.5	7.6
Mystery	4.4	6.7	2.2	2.6	3.0	.5	4.2	1.7
Spy and Espionage	—	—	—	—	—	1.0	—	1.3
Suspense	—	—	—	—	—	.8	—	—
Horror	—	.5	.2	—	.7	1.4	.6	.3
Science Fiction	—	—	—	—	—	.8	—	3.0
Science	—	—	—	—	—	1.0	4.5	1.3
Romantic	10.4	13.6	8.8	11.0	14.6	17.6	15.7	7.3
Domestic	—	—	—	5.4	5.1	3.5	1.6	1.0
Sports	1.1	2.0	2.7	1.2	1.6	2.0	2.8	1.7
Musical	5.0	3.7	4.9	4.2	4.9	5.2	3.9	5.9
Cartoon	—	.5	.2	—	.2	.3	—	—
Juvenile	.6	.2	.5	.7	1.2	1.0	2.0	1.0
Travelogue	—	—	.2	—	—	—	.8	—
Historical	1.1	1.7	2.9	1.2	.5	—	.8	.3
Biography and Autobiography	1.1	.5	—	.4	1.4	2.7	2.0	1.3
Historical Fiction	—	—	—	2.8	1.4	1.6	2.5	4.6
Economic	—	—	—	—	.2	—	—	—
Governmental	—	—	.2	—	—	—	—	—

TABLE 16 — Continued

	1947[2]	1948	1949	1950	1951	1952	1953	1954
Military	—	.2	1.5	3.7	7.6	6.0	6.8	6.3
War	1.7	1.5	—	—	—	1.0	.3	—
Social Problem	20.9	16.5	16.5	8.9	9.0	12.2	8.1	9.2
Psychological	7.1	3.7	1.2	2.8	3.5	.5	1.1	—
Religious and Biblical	1.1	.5	—	.4	1.4	2.7	2.0	1.3
Miscellaneous	3.8	4.0	9.3	2.3	5.3	3.8	2.6	4.3
TOTAL	100.0	100.0	100.0	100.0	100.0	100.0	100.0	100.0

1. Includes all films having major release in this country, and many which are released by smaller distributors. Productions of foreign companies comprise an average of about 10% for the period shown (for annual figures giving the percentage foreign films, see Table 9).
2. Includes last half of 1947 only.

TABLE 17

TYPES OF ENDINGS ON FEATURE-LENGTH MOTION PICTURES
Approved by
The Production Code Administration of the MPPA[1]
(*Shown in Percentages*)
1947[2]–1954

	1947[2]	1948	1949	1950	1951	1952	1953	1954
Happy	87.4	88.6	90.8	85.5	83.9	87.0	86.2	84.9
Unhappy	4.9	5.7	3.9	6.5	4.7	1.6	3.9	5.9
Moral	5.5	3.7	2.9	6.1	6.7	5.4	6.2	8.9
Other	2.2	2.0	2.4	1.9	4.7	6.0	3.7	.3
TOTAL	100.0	100.0	100.0	100.0	100.0	100.0	100.0	100.0

1. Includes all films having major release in this country, and some which do not. Productions of foreign companies comprise an average of about 10% for the period shown (for annual figures giving the percentage foreign films, see Table 9).
2. Includes last half of 1947 only.

APPENDIX III-B

Changes in the Content of Hollywood Motion Pictures 1947–1954: Award-Winning Films.[1]

AWARD-WINNING HOLLYWOOD FILMS

	New York Film Critics Award — Best Picture	Nat. Board of Review Ten Best	Film Daily Ten Best	Academy — Nominated as Best Production
1. 1947 RELEASES:				
*THE BISHOP'S WIFE (Goldwyn-RKO)		X	X	X
BOOMERANG (20th Century-Fox)		X	X	
CROSSFIRE (RKO)		X	X	X
DESIGN FOR DEATH (Documentary) (RKO)				Best[2]
*GENTLEMAN'S AGREEMENT (20th Century-Fox)	Best	X	Best	Best
KISS OF DEATH (20th Century-Fox)		X		
THE LATE GEORGE APLEY (20th Century-Fox)		X		
LIFE WITH FATHER (Warner Brothers)		X	X	
MIRACLE ON 34TH STREET (20th Century-Fox)		X	X	X

---

1. There is sometimes an overlapping of awards from one year to another: studios frequently hold some of their best pictures for initial release in the holiday season at the close of the year. Thus a film may not receive an award until the following year (this is never true of Academy awards, which are always given strictly according to year of release). The above awards are for the year of release or the year following release, as the case may be. This accounts for any apparent duplication of awards in the above list.
2. Won Academy Award as the best feature-length Documentary.

* Also a Box Office Champion.

	New York Film Critics Award — Best Picture	Nat. Board of Review Ten Best	Film Daily Ten Best	Academy — Nominated as Best Production
MONSIEUR VERDOUX (Chaplin-United Artists)		Best		
*THE YEARLING (M-G-M)		X	X	

2. 1948 RELEASES:[3]

CALL NORTHSIDE 777 (20th Century-Fox)			X	
*I REMEMBER MAMA (RKO Radio)		X	X	
JOAN OF ARC (Sierra Pictures-RKO)		X		
*JOHNNY BELINDA (Warner Brothers)		X	X	X
*THE NAKED CITY (Universal-International)			X	
*SITTING PRETTY (20th Century-Fox)		X	X	
*THE SNAKE PIT (20th Century-Fox)		X	Best	X
THE TREASURE OF THE SIERRA MADRE (Warner Brothers)	Best	X	X	X
*STATE OF THE UNION (M-G-M)			X	

3. 1949 RELEASES:

ALL THE KING'S MEN (Columbia)	Best			Best
*BATTLEGROUND (M-G-M)				X
THE CHAMPION (Screen Plays Corp.-United Artists)			X	

3. Both the Academy of Motion Picture Arts and Sciences and the National Board of Review named the British production HAMLET (Rank-U.I.) as the best picture of the year.

	New York Film Critics Award — Best Picture	Nat. Board of Review Ten Best	Film Daily Ten Best	Academy — Nominated as Best Production
COME TO THE STABLE (20th Century-Fox)			X	
*COMMAND DECISION (M-G-M)			X	
THE HEIRESS (Paramount)		X	X	X
HOME OF THE BRAVE (Screen Plays Corp.-United Artists)		X	X	
INTRUDER IN THE DUST (M-G-M)		X		
*A LETTER TO THREE WIVES (20th Century-Fox)		X	X	X
*PINKY (20th Century-Fox)			X	
*THE STRATTON STORY (M-G-M)			X	
*TWELVE O'CLOCK HIGH (20th Century-Fox)		X		X

4. 1950 RELEASES:

	New York Film Critics Award — Best Picture	Nat. Board of Review Ten Best	Film Daily Ten Best	Academy — Nominated as Best Production
*ALL ABOUT EVE (20th Century-Fox)	Best	X		Best
*BORN YESTERDAY (Columbia)			X[4]	
EDGE OF DOOM (Goldwyn-RKO)		X		
*FATHER OF THE BRIDE (M-G-M)				X
*KING SOLOMON'S MINES (M-G-M)				X
THE MEN (Kramer-United Artists)		X		

4. This film was named as one of the Ten Best by *The Film Daily* for 1951. The ten best of 1950 were never announced by *The Film Daily*.

287

	New York Film Critics Award — Best Picture	Nat. Board of Review Ten Best	Film Daily Ten Best	Academy — Nominated as Best Production
No Way Out (20th Century-Fox)		X		
Panic in the Streets (20th Century-Fox)		X		
Stage Fright (Warners)		X		
*Sunset Boulevard (Paramount)		Best		X
5. 1951 RELEASES:				
*An American in Paris (M-G-M)		X	X	Best
Bright Victory (Universal-International)			X	
Cyrano de Bergerac (Kramer-United Artists)		X	X	
Death of a Salesman (Kramer-Columbia)		X	X	
*Decision Before Dawn (20th Century-Fox)		X		X
*Detective Story (Paramount)		X	X	
Fourteen Hours (20th Century-Fox)		X		
*The Great Caruso (M-G-M)			X	
I Was a Communist for the FBI (Warner Brothers)				X[5]
*A Place in the Sun (Paramount)		Best	Best	X
*Quo Vadis (M-G-M)		X	X	X
The Red Badge of Courage (M-G-M)		X		

5. Nominated by the Academy as best feature-length documentary.

	New York Film Critics Award – Best Picture	Nat. Board of Review Ten Best	Film Daily Ten Best	Academy – Nominated as Best Production
Strangers on a Train (Warner Brothers)		X		
*A Streetcar Named Desire (Warner Brothers)	Best	X	X	X

6. 1952 RELEASES:

*African Queen (Horizon-United Artists)			X	
Above and Beyond (M-G-M)		X		
*The Bad and the Beautiful (M-G-M)		X		
*Come Back, Little Sheba (Paramount)			X	
Five Fingers (20th Century-Fox)		X	X	
*The Greatest Show on Earth (Paramount)			X	Best
*High Noon (Kramer-United Artists)	Best	X	Best	X
The Hoaxsters (Documentary) (M-G-M)				X⁵
Ivanhoe (M-G-M)			X	X
Limelight (Chaplin-United Artists)		X		
*Moulin Rouge (Romulus-United Artists)			X	X
My Son John (Paramount)		X		
Navajo (Bartlett-Foster Production-Lippert)				X⁵
*The Quiet Man (Argosy-Republic)		Best	X	

---

5. Nominated by the Academy as best feature-length documentary.

AWARD-WINNING HOLLYWOOD FILMS — Continued

	New York Film Critics Award — Best Picture	Nat. Board of Review Ten Best	Film Daily Ten Best	Academy — Nominated as Best Production
THE SEA AROUND US (Documentary) (RKO Radio)				Best
*SINGIN' IN THE RAIN (M-G-M)		X	X	
*THE SNOWS OF KILIMANJARO (20th Century-Fox)		X		
THE THIEF (Fran Productions-United Artists)		X		
WITH A SONG IN MY HEART (20th Century-Fox)			X	

7. 1953 RELEASES:

	New York Film Critics Award — Best Picture	Nat. Board of Review Ten Best	Film Daily Ten Best	Academy — Nominated as Best Production
*FROM HERE TO ETERNITY (Columbia)	Best	X	Best	Best
JULIUS CAESAR (M-G-M)		Best		X
LILI (M-G-M)		X	X	
*LITTLE BOY LOST (Paramount)			X	
THE LIVING DESERT (Documentary) (Disney-Buena Vista)				Best
*MOGAMBO (M-G-M)		X		
THE MOON IS BLUE (Preminger-Herbert-United Artists)			X	
*THE ROBE (20th Century-Fox)		X	X	X
*ROMAN HOLIDAY (Paramount)			X	X
*SHANE (Paramount)		X	X	X
*STALAG 17 (Paramount)		X	X	

	New York Film Critics Award — Best Picture	Nat. Board of Review Ten Best	Film Daily Ten Best	Academy — Nominated as Best Production
8. 1954 RELEASES:				
BEAT THE DEVIL (Santana-United Artists)		X		
*THE CAINE MUTINY (Kramer-Columbia)			Best	X
THE COUNTRY GIRL (Paramount)		X	X	X
*EXECUTIVE SUITE (M-G-M)		X	X	
*THE GLENN MILLER STORY (Universal-International)			X	
*THE HIGH AND THE MIGHTY (Warners)			X	
*ON THE WATERFRONT (Columbia)	Best	Best	X	Best
*REAR WINDOW (Paramount)			X	
SABRINA (Paramount)		X	X	
SEVEN BRIDES FOR SEVEN BROTHERS (M-G-M)		X	X	X
A STAR IS BORN (Warners)		X		
THREE COINS IN A FOUNTAIN (20th Century-Fox)			X	X
20,000 LEAGUES UNDER THE SEA (Disney-Buena Vista)		X		
THE VANISHING PRAIRIE (Documentary) (Disney-Buena Vista)		X		Best

APPENDIX III-C

Changes in the Content of Hollywood Motion Pictures 1947–1954:
Box-Office Successes.*

1. BOX-OFFICE SUCCESSES OF 1946–1947

BACHELOR AND THE BOBBY-SOXER
  (RKO)
THE BEST YEARS OF OUR LIVES
  (Goldwyn-RKO)
BLUE SKIES
  (Paramount)
CALIFORNIA
  (Paramount)
DEAR RUTH
  (Paramount)
DUEL IN THE SUN
  (Selznick Releasing Organization)
THE FARMER'S DAUGHTER
  (RKO)
GONE WITH THE WIND
  (Selznick-M-G-M)
THE HUCKSTERS
  (M-G-M)
HUMORESQUE
  (Warners)
I WONDER WHO'S KISSING HER NOW
  (20th Century-Fox)
IT'S A WONDERFUL LIFE
  (Liberty-RKO)
THE JOLSON STORY
  (Columbia)
LIFE WITH FATHER
  (Warners)

MARGIE
  (20th Century-Fox)
MY FAVORITE BRUNETTE
  (Paramount)
NO LEAVE, NO LOVE
  (M-G-M)
NORA PRENTISS
  (Warners)
THE PERILS OF PAULINE
  (Paramount)
POSSESSED
  (Warners)
THE RAZOR'S EDGE
  (20th Century-Fox)
TILL THE CLOUDS ROLL BY
  (M-G-M)
THE TIME, THE PLACE AND THE GIRL
  (Warners)
TWO YEARS BEFORE THE MAST
  (Paramount)
VARIETY GIRL
  (Paramount)
WELCOME STRANGER
  (Paramount)
THE YEARLING
  (M-G-M)

---

* These Box-Office "Champions" are based on key city grosses for the period
October 1 of the first year to September 30 of the succeeding year, and reported
annually in *Fame* (Quigley Publications, New York).

292

2. BOX-OFFICE SUCCESSES OF 1947–1948

ABBOTT & COSTELLO
MEET FRANKENSTEIN
  (Universal-International)
THE BISHOP'S WIFE
  (Goldwyn-RKO)
BODY AND SOUL
  (Enterprise-United Artists)
CAPTAIN FROM CASTILE
  (20th Century-Fox)
CASS TIMBERLANE
  (M-G-M)
A DATE WITH JUDY
  (M-G-M)
THE EASTER PARADE
  (M-G-M)
THE EMPEROR WALTZ
  (Paramount)
A FOREIGN AFFAIR
  (Paramount)
FOREVER AMBER
  (20th Century-Fox)
FORT APACHE
  (Argosy-RKO)
THE FOXES OF HARROW
  (20th Century-Fox)
THE FULLER BRUSH MAN
  (Small-Columbia)
GENTLEMEN'S AGREEMENT
  (20th Century-Fox)
GREEN DOLPHIN STREET
  (M-G-M)

HOMECOMING
  (M-G-M)
I REMEMBER MAMA
  (RKO)
KEY LARGO
  (Warners)
MR. BLANDING BUILDS
HIS DREAM HOUSE
  (Selznick Releasing Office)
MY WILD IRISH ROSE
  (Warners)
THE NAKED CITY
  (Hellinger-Universal-International)
THE PARADINE CASE
  (Selznick Releasing Office)
ROAD TO RIO
  (Paramount)
SECRET LIFE OF WALTER MITTY
  (Goldwyn-RKO)
SITTING PRETTY
  (20th Century-Fox)
STATE OF THE UNION
  (Liberty-M-G-M)
TAP ROOTS
  (Wanger-Universal-International)
UNCONQUERED
  (De Mille-Paramount)
VOICE OF THE TURTLE
  (Warners)

3. BOX-OFFICE SUCCESSES OF 1948–1949

APARTMENT FOR PEGGY
(20th Century-Fox)

THE BARKLEYS OF BROADWAY
(M-G-M)

COMMAND DECISION
(M-G-M)

CONNECTICUT YANKEE IN
KING ARTHUR'S COURT
(Paramount)

EVERY GIRL SHOULD BE MARRIED
(RKO)

FAMILY HONEYMOON
(Universal-International)

FLAMINGO ROAD
(Warners)

HAMLET
(Rank-Universal-International)

JOAN OF ARC
(Sierra-RKO)

JOHNNY BELINDA
(Warners)

JULIA MISBEHAVES
(M-G-M)

A LETTER TO THREE WIVES
(20th Century-Fox)

LITTLE WOMEN
(M-G-M)

LOOK FOR THE SILVER LINING
(Warners)

MR. BELVEDERE GOES TO COLLEGE
(20th Century-Fox)

NEPTUNE'S DAUGHTER
(M-G-M)

THE PALEFACE
(Paramount)

RED RIVER
(Monterey-United Artists)

THE RED SHOES
(Rank-Universal-International)

THE SNAKE PIT
(20th Century-Fox)

SORROWFUL JONES
(Paramount)

THE STRATTON STORY
(M-G-M)

TAKE ME OUT TO THE BALL GAME
(M-G-M)

THE THREE MUSKETEERS
(M-G-M)

WAKE OF THE RED WITCH
(Republic)

WHEN MY BABY SMILES AT ME
(20th Century-Fox)

WHISPERING SMITH
(Paramount)

WORDS AND MUSIC
(M-G-M)

YELLOW SKY
(20th Century-Fox)

4. BOX-OFFICE SUCCESSES OF 1949–1950

ADAM'S RIB
  (M-G-M)
ANNIE GET YOUR GUN
  (M-G-M)
BATTLEGROUND
  (M-G-M)
THE BLACK ROSE
  (20th Century-Fox)
BROKEN ARROW
  (20th Century-Fox)
CHEAPER BY THE DOZEN
  (20th Century-Fox)
CINDERELLA
  (Disney-RKO)
COLT .45
  (Warners)
FANCY PANTS
  (Paramount)
FATHER OF THE BRIDE
  (M-G-M)
THE FLAME AND THE ARROW
  (Norma-Warners)
FRANCIS
  (Universal-International)
I WAS A MALE WAR BRIDE
  (20th Century-Fox)
JOLSON SINGS AGAIN
  (Columbia)

MY FRIEND IRMA
  (Wallis-Paramount)
ON THE TOWN
  (M-G-M)
OUR VERY OWN
  (Goldwyn-United Artists)
PINKY
  (20th Century-Fox)
SAMSON AND DELILAH
  (DeMille-Paramount)
SANDS OF IWO JIMA
  (Republic)
SHE WORE A YELLOW RIBBON
  (Argosy-RKO)
SUMMER STOCK
  (M-G-M)
SUNSET BOULEVARD
  (Paramount)
TASK FORCE
  (Warners)
TEA FOR TWO
  (Warners)
THREE LITTLE WORDS
  (M-G-M)
TWELVE O'CLOCK HIGH
  (20th Century-Fox)
WINCHESTER '73
  (Universal-International)

5. BOX-OFFICE SUCCESSES OF 1950–1951

ALICE IN WONDERLAND
(Disney-RKO)

ALL ABOUT EVE
(20th Century-Fox)

AT WAR WITH THE ARMY
(Paramount)

BORN YESTERDAY
(Columbia)

BRANDED
(Paramount)

CAPTAIN HORATIO HORNBLOWER
(Warners)

DAVID AND BATHSHEBA
(20th Century-Fox)

FATHER'S LITTLE DIVIDEND
(M-G-M)

FRANCIS GOES TO THE RACES
(Universal-International)

GO FOR BROKE
(M-G-M)

THE GREAT CARUSO
(M-G-M)

HALLS OF MONTEZUMA
(20th Century-Fox)

HARVEY
(Universal-International)

HERE COMES THE GROOM
(Paramount)

KIM
(M-G-M)

KING SOLOMON'S MINES
(M-G-M)

THE LEMON DROP KID
(Paramount)

ON MOONLIGHT BAY
(Warners)

ON THE RIVIERA
(20th Century-Fox)

OPERATION PACIFIC
(Warners)

ROYAL WEDDING
(M-G-M)

SHOW BOAT
(M-G-M)

THAT'S MY BOY
(Wallis-Paramount)

6. BOX-OFFICE SUCCESSES OF 1951–1952

AFFAIR IN TRINIDAD
  (Columbia)
AFRICAN QUEEN
  (Horizon-United Artists)
AN AMERICAN IN PARIS
  (M-G-M)
BEND OF THE RIVER
  (Universal-International)
CLASH BY NIGHT
  (Wald-Krasna-RKO)
DECISION BEFORE DAWN
  (20th Century-Fox)
DETECTIVE STORY
  (Paramount)
THE GREATEST SHOW ON EARTH
  (Paramount)
HIGH NOON
  (Kramer-United Artists)
JUST FOR YOU
  (Paramount)
THE MERRY WIDOW
  (M-G-M)
THE MIRACLE OF FATIMA
  (Warners)

PAT AND MIKE
  (M-G-M)
A PLACE IN THE SUN
  (Paramount)
THE QUIET MAN
  (Argosy-Republic)
QUO VADIS
  (M-G-M)
SAILOR BEWARE
  (Paramount)
SINGIN' IN THE RAIN
  (M-G-M)
SON OF PALEFACE
  (Paramount)
STORY OF ROBIN HOOD
  (Disney-RKO)
A STREETCAR NAMED DESIRE
  (Warners)
SUDDEN FEAR
  (RKO)
WITH A SONG IN MY HEART
  (20th Century-Fox)

7. BOX-OFFICE SUCCESSES OF 1952–1953

THE BAD AND THE BEAUTIFUL
   (M-G-M)
THE BAND WAGON
   (M-G-M)
BWANA DEVIL
   (United Artists)
CALL ME MADAM
   (20th Century-Fox)
THE CHARGE AT FEATHER RIVER
   (Warners)
COME BACK LITTLE SHEBA
   (Paramount)
FORT TI
   (Columbia)
FROM HERE TO ETERNITY
   (Columbia)
GENTLEMEN PREFER BLONDES
   (20th Century-Fox)
HANS CHRISTIAN ANDERSEN
   (Goldwyn-RKO)
HOUSE OF WAX
   (Warners)
IVANHOE
   (M-G-M)
MILLION DOLLAR MERMAID
   (M-G-M)

THE MISSISSIPPI GAMBLER
   (Universal-International)
MOULIN ROUGE
   (United Artists)
THE NAKED SPUR
   (M-G-M)
NIAGARA
   (20th Century-Fox)
PETER PAN
   (Disney-RKO)
ROAD TO BALI
   (Paramount)
ROMAN HOLIDAY
   (Paramount)
SALOME
   (Columbia)
SCARED STIFF
   (Paramount)
SHANE
   (Paramount)
THE SNOWS OF KILIMANJARO
   (20th Century-Fox)
STALAG 17
   (Paramount)
TITANIC
   (20th Century-Fox)

8. BOX-OFFICE SUCCESSES OF 1953–1954

APACHE
(United Artists)

THE CAINE MUTINY
(Columbia)

DEMETRIUS AND THE GLADIATORS
(20th Century-Fox)

DIAL M FOR MURDER
(Warners)

EXECUTIVE SUITE
(M-G-M)

GLENN MILLER STORY
(Universal-International)

HIGH AND THE MIGHTY
(Warners)

HONDO
(Warners)

HOW TO MARRY A MILLIONAIRE
(20th Century-Fox)

JOHNNY GUITAR
(Republic)

KNIGHTS OF THE ROUND TABLE
(M-G-M)

KNOCK ON WOOD
(Paramount)

LITTLE BOY LOST
(Paramount)

LONG, LONG TRAILER
(M-G-M)

MAGNIFICENT OBSESSION
(Universal-International)

MOGAMBO
(M-G-M)

MONEY FROM HOME
(Paramount)

ON THE WATERFRONT
(Columbia)

REAR WINDOW
(Paramount)

THE ROBE
(20th Century-Fox)

SASKATCHEWAN
(Universal-International)

SEVEN BRIDES FOR SEVEN BROTHERS
(M-G-M)

SUSAN SLEPT HERE
(RKO)

THIS IS CINERAMA
(Cinerama)

THREE COINS IN THE FOUNTAIN
(20th Century-Fox)

APPENDIX III-D

Changes in the Content of Hollywood Motion Pictures 1947–1954: The Anti-Communist Films, 1947–1954, and a Partial List of Earlier Anti-Communist Features.

1. THE ANTI-COMMUNIST FILMS, 1947–1954*

Nov., 1947 — NINOTCHKA (M-G-M) — Social Theme (Comedy) Re-Issue

May, 1948 — THE IRON CURTAIN (20th Century-Fox) — Spy (Melodrama) — Documentary approach

Aug., 1948 — SOFIA (Film Classics) — Spy (Melodrama)

Sept., 1948 — WALK A CROOKED MILE (Columbia) — Spy (Melodrama)

Jan., 1949 — ROSE OF THE YUKON (Republic) — Spy (Melodrama)

May, 1949 — THE RED MENACE (Republic) — Social Theme (Melodrama)

Sept., 1949 — THE WOMAN ON PIER 13 (RKO) — Spy (Melodrama)

Sept., 1949 — THE RED DANUBE (M-G-M) — Social Theme (Drama)

Nov., 1949 — PROJECT X (Film Classics) — Spy (Melodrama)

Dec., 1949 — GUILTY OF TREASON (Eagle Lion Classics) — Social Theme (Drama) — Documentary approach

Jan., 1950 — THE FLYING SAUCER (Film Classics) — Adventure (Melodrama)

Jan., 1950 — BELLS OF CORONADO (Republic) — Western (Melodrama)

Feb., 1950 — THE CONSPIRATOR (M-G-M) Spy (Drama)

May, 1951 — I WAS A COMMUNIST FOR THE FBI (Warners) — Social Theme (Melodrama) — Documentary approach

June, 1951 — PEKING EXPRESS (Paramount) — Spy (Melodrama)

Oct., 1951 — WHIP HAND (RKO) — Spy (Melodrama)

Feb., 1952 — THE STEEL FIST (Monogram) — Social Theme (Melodrama)

Mar., 1952 — MY SON JOHN (Paramount) — Domestic (Drama)

Apr., 1952 — THE ATOMIC CITY (Paramount) — Spy (Melodrama)

Apr., 1952 — WALK EAST ON BEACON (RD-DR Corp.-Columbia) — Spy (Melodrama) — Documentary approach

May, 1952 — RED PLANET MARS (Seiller-United Artists) — Adventure (Melodrama)

June, 1952 — DIPLOMATIC COURIER (20th Century-Fox) — Spy (Melodrama)

July, 1952 — ARCTIC FLIGHT (Monogram) — Spy (Melodrama)

---

* This list, compiled from many sources, is probably not a complete one although it does include all of the important anti-Communist films of the 1947-1954 period.

July, 1952 — RED SNOW (All-American Film Corp.-Columbia) — Adventure (Melodrama)

Sept., 1952 — BIG JIM MCLAIN (Warners) — Spy (Melodrama)

Sept., 1952 — ASSIGNMENT — PARIS (Columbia) — Action (Melodrama)

Oct., 1952 — THE THIEF (Fran Prod.-UA) — Spy (Melodrama)

Dec., 1952 — THE HOAXTERS (M-G-M) — Social Theme (Documentary)

Dec., 1952 — TARGET HONG KONG (Columbia — Spy (Melodrama)

Feb., 1953 — SAVAGE MUTINY (Esskay Pic. Co.-Columbia) — Action (Melodrama)

Mar., 1953 — NEVER LET ME GO (M-G-M) — Action (Melodrama)

Apr., 1953 — MAN ON A TIGHTROPE (20th Century-Fox) — Social Theme (Drama)

July, 1953 — SAVAGE DRUMS (Lippert) — Action (Melodrama)

May, 1954 — PRISONER OF WAR (M-G-M) — War (Drama) — Documentary approach

Sept., 1954 — NIGHT PEOPLE (20th Century-Fox) — Spy (Melodrama)

2. PARTIAL LIST OF EARLIER ANTI-COMMUNIST FEATURES (prior to 1947)

July, 1923 — RED RUSSIA REVEALED (Fox)

April, 1935 — TOGETHER WE LIVE (Columbia)

Sept., 1935 — FIGHTING YOUTH (Universal)

Sept., 1935 — SOAK THE RICH (Paramount)

Sept., 1935 — THE RED SALUTE (Reliance-United Artists)

Jan., 1939 — HERO FOR A DAY (Warners)

Aug., 1939 — CAMPUS WIVES (Paramount)

Aug., 1939 — THE BIGGER THEY ARE (Columbia)

Aug., 1939 — MAY DAY (Borris Morros Productions)

Aug., 1939 — OUR LEADING CITIZEN (Paramount)

Oct., 1939 — NINOTCHKA (M-G-M)

Dec., 1940 — COMRADE X (M-G-M)

Aug., 1940 — HE STAYED FOR BREAKFAST (Columbia)

Sept., 1940 — PUBLIC DEB NUMBER ONE (20th Century-Fox)

APPENDIX IV

Summary of Shifts in the Communist Party Line, 1929–1949.*

1929–AUGUST, 1935: During the "New Revolutionary Period" the Communist Party strove internationally primarily for the preservation of the world *status quo* as a means of protecting the Russian oligarchy. During this period the Communists

1. Promoted a strongly revolutionary-sounding type of propaganda, intended to harry capitalism, not to destroy it.
2. Branded the Socialists as "twins" of the Fascists, and singled them out as the main enemy of the Communists.
3. Called for "A Soviet America" as the only way out of the depression, and for the defense of the Soviet Union as "the Fatherhood of the workers of the whole world."
4. Demanded social insurance, free rent, free use of gas, electricity, water and public transportation for the unemployed during the depression.
5. Followed an independent trade union policy, setting up separate Communist unions in the United States through the Trade Union Unity League.

AUGUST, 1935–AUGUST, 1939: Communist strategy was dominated by fear of the growing power of the Nazi State. During this period the Communists

1. Revived the "People's Front" or *"Popular Front"* policy of the Comintern. This was announced in 1935 at the 7th Congress of the Communist International, and called for a coalition of Communist, Socialist, democratic and progressive elements against fascist and reactionary elements.
2. Supported the idea of *collective security* — joined the League of Nations — and urged the United States to enter into a system of collective security along with the Soviet Union.

---

* This summary is based primarily upon the following sources: *Primer on Communism* prepared by the Anti-Defamation League of B'nai B'rith as one of the Freedom Pamphlet Series (New York: Anti-Defamation League of B'nai B'rith, 1951); "The Report of the Executive Board Committee appointed by President Murray to Investigate Charges Against the International Longshoremen's and Warehousemen's Union," prepared by the C.I.O. and read into the U. S. Congressional Record; *Left, Right and Center* by Sidney Lens (New York: Henry Regnery Company, 1949), and *World Revolutionary Propaganda* by Harold D. Lasswell and Dorothy Blumenstock (New York, Knopf, 1939).

3. Sought to sharpen whenever possible existing differences among European powers.
4. Intervened on the side of the Republic government in Spain against the Fascists who were supported by Italy and Nazi-Germany.
5. Fought a short but full-scale war with Japan along the Soviet Manchurian border.
6. Urged the boycott of German, Japanese and Italian goods in the United States.
7. Favored changing the Neutrality Act to allow shipment of arms to countries who were the victims of Fascist attack.

AUGUST, 1939–JUNE, 1941: Communist strategy was built around the corner-stone of Nazi-Soviet collaboration (as embodied in the Nazi-Soviet Pact). During this period the Communists

1. Denounced the war as an "Imperialist" struggle — charging England and France with responsibility for the war.
2. Supported Hitler's proposals of October 8th, 1939 for ending the war, including settlement of the "Jewish problem."
3. In France, spoke of turning the "Imperialist" war into civil war.
4. In the United States, called the Defense Program a program fostered by Wall Street.
5. In the United States, sought to defeat all measures intended to aid the powers which were opposing Hitler, capitalizing on isolationist and pacifistic sentiments. Thus in the United States Communists
   a. opposed the draft
   b. opposed Lend-Lease
   c. promoted the slogan "The Yanks Are Not Coming."
6. In Asia, when Japanese preparations for war with the United States were well advanced (April, 1941), the Soviet Union signed a 5-year neutrality pact with Japan including Soviet recognition of the puppet state of Manchuria.

JUNE, 1941–JUNE, 1945: Communist strategy was dominated by concern for the military threat against the Soviet Union as a victim of Nazi aggression. During this period the Communists

1. Supported Soviet-American-British coalition against the Fascist Axis, and called for all-out aid to the Soviet Union and Great Britain.
2. Urged a "Second Front" in Europe (to aid the Soviet Armies) and sponsored the slogan "The Yanks Are Not Coming Too Late."
3. Dissolved the Comintern (in 1943), declaring it a "hindrance to the . . . national workers' parties." In the United States the Communist Party was dissolved (January, 1944), and the Communist Political

303

Association was formed which proclaimed its "acceptance of free enterprise," favoring a new policy of "progressive" coalition between capital and labor.

4. Gave all-out support to the "People's War" (in the previous period referred to as the "Imperialist War"), and advocated national service legislation.

5. Gave all-out support to the war effort in the United States
   a. pushed for all-out war production
   b. vigorously demanded a "No Strike" pledge for the duration and for the post-war period
   c. urged that there be no wage increases for the duration.

JUNE, 1945–1949 AND THEREAFTER: The period of the "Cold War." During this period the Communists

1. Attempted to weaken the economy and political life of the western countries — particularly France and Italy, but also western Germany.

2. Promoted armed uprisings and prolonged rebellions by guerillas, as in Greece 1946–1949, in French Indo-China, etc.

3. Demanded the withdrawal of American troops from China, and supported the Chinese Communists; demanded recognition of Red China, etc.

4. Opposed the Truman Doctrine.

5. Opposed the Marshall Plan.

6. Opposed the Atlantic Pact.

7. Conducted propaganda and diplomatic campaigns for peace and disarmament, to divert attention from the steadily mounting Soviet war preparations.

8. Conducted propaganda and diplomatic campaigns against "American Imperialism" as the aggressor in Korea against the peoples of Asia and as "instigator of atomic war to destroy the Soviet world."

9. Did everything possible to sharpen differences between the United States and its allies over such issues as negotiation of peace in Korea, disposition of Formosa, the seating of China in the United Nations, etc.

Index

305

307

308

312

The Arno Press Cinema Program

Dickinson, Thorold and Catherine De la Roche. **Soviet Cinema.** 1948.

Dickson, W. K. L., and Antonia Dickson. **History of the Kinetograph, Kinetoscope and Kinetophonograph.** 1895.

Forman, Henry James. **Our Movie Made Children.** 1935.

Freeburg, Victor Oscar. **The Art of Photoplay Making.** 1918.

Freeburg, Victor Oscar. **Pictorial Beauty on the Screen.** 1923.

Hall, Hal, editor. **Cinematographic Annual,** 2 vols. 1930/1931.

Hampton, Benjamin B. **A History of the Movies.** 1931.

Hardy, Forsyth. **Scandinavian Film.** 1952.

Hepworth, Cecil M. **Animated Photography: The A B C of the Cinematograph.** 1900.

Hoban, Charles F., Jr., and Edward B. Van Ormer. **Instructional Film Research 1918-1950.** 1950.

Holaday, Perry W. and George D. Stoddard. **Getting Ideas from the Movies.** 1933.

Hopwood, Henry V. **Living Pictures.** 1899.

Hulfish, David S. **Motion-Picture Work.** 1915.

Hunter, William. **Scrutiny of Cinema.** 1932.

Huntley, John. **British Film Music.** 1948.

Irwin, Will. **The House That Shadows Built.** 1928.

Jarratt, Vernon. **The Italian Cinema.** 1951.

Jenkins, C. Francis. **Animated Pictures.** 1898.

Lang, Edith and George West. **Musical Accompaniment of Moving Pictures.** 1920.

L'Art Cinematographique, Nos. 1-8. 1926-1931.

London, Kurt. **Film Music.** 1936.

Lutz, E [dwin] G [eorge]. **The Motion-Picture Cameraman.** 1927.

Manvell, Roger. **Experiment in the Film.** 1949.

Marey, Etienne Jules. **Movement.** 1895.

Martin, Olga J. **Hollywood's Movie Commandments.** 1937.

Mayer, J. P. **Sociology of Film: Studies and Documents.** 1946. New Introduction by J. P. Mayer.

Münsterberg, Hugo. **The Photoplay: A Psychological Study.** 1916.

Nicoll, Allardyce. **Film and Theatre.** 1936.

Noble, Peter. **The Negro in Films.** 1949.

Peters, Charles C. **Motion Pictures and Standards of Morality.** 1933.

Peterson, Ruth C. and L. L. Thurstone. **Motion Pictures and the Social Attitudes of Children.** Shuttleworth, Frank K. and Mark A. May. **The Social Conduct and Attitudes of Movie Fans.** 1933.

Phillips, Henry Albert. **The Photodrama.** 1914.

Photoplay Research Society. **Opportunities in the Motion Picture Industry.** 1922.

Rapée, Erno. **Encyclopaedia of Music for Pictures.** 1925.

Rapée, Erno. **Motion Picture Moods for Pianists and Organists.** 1924.

Renshaw, Samuel, Vernon L. Miller and Dorothy P. Marquis. **Children's Sleep.** 1933.

Rosten, Leo C. **Hollywood: The Movie Colony, The Movie Makers.** 1941.

Sadoul, Georges. **French Film.** 1953.

Screen Monographs I, 1923-1937. 1970.

Screen Monographs II, 1915-1930. 1970.

Sinclair, Upton. **Upton Sinclair Presents William Fox.** 1933.

Talbot, Frederick A. **Moving Pictures.** 1912.

Thorp, Margaret Farrand. **America at the Movies.** 1939.

Wollenberg, H. H. **Fifty Years of German Film.** 1948.

RELATED BOOKS AND PERIODICALS

Allister, Ray. **Friese-Greene: Close-Up of an Inventor.** 1948.

Art in Cinema: A Symposium of the Avant-Garde Film, edited by Frank Stauffacher. 1947.

The Art of Cinema: Selected Essays. New Foreword by George Amberg. 1971.

Balázs, Béla. **Theory of the Film.** 1952.

Barry, Iris. **Let's Go to the Movies.** 1926.

de Beauvoir, Simone. **Brigitte Bardot and the Lolita Syndrome.** 1960.

Carrick, Edward. **Art and Design in the British Film.** 1948.

Close Up. Vols. 1-10, 1927-1933 (all published).

Cogley, John. **Report on Blacklisting. Part I: The Movies.** 1956.

Eisenstein, S. M. **Que Viva Mexico!** 1951.

Experimental Cinema. 1930-1934 (all published).

Feldman, Joseph and Harry. **Dynamics of the Film.** 1952.

Film Daily Yearbook of Motion Pictures. Microfilm, 18 reels,
35 mm. 1918-1969.

Film Daily Yearbook of Motion Pictures. 1970.

Film Daily Yearbook of Motion Pictures. (Wid's Year Book).
3 vols., 1918-1922.

The Film Index: A Bibliography. Vol. I: The Film as Art. 1941.

Film Society Programmes. 1925-1939 (all published).

Films: A Quarterly of Discussion and Analysis. Nos. 1-4, 1939-1940
(all published).

Flaherty, Frances Hubbard. **The Odyssey of a Film-Maker:
Robert Flaherty's Story.** 1960.

General Bibliography of Motion Pictures, edited by Carl Vincent,
Riccardo Redi, and Franco Venturini. 1953.

Hendricks, Gordon. **Origins of the American Film.** 1961-1966. New
Introduction by Gordon Hendricks.

Hound and Horn: Essays on Cinema, 1928-1934. 1971.

Huff, Theodore. **Charlie Chaplin.** 1951.

Kahn, Gordon. **Hollywood on Trial.** 1948.

New York Times Film Reviews, 1913-1968. 1970.

Noble, Peter. **Hollywood Scapegoat: The Biography of Erich
von Stroheim.** 1950.

Robson, E. W. and M. M. **The Film Answers Back.** 1939.

Weinberg, Herman G., editor. **Greed.** 1971.

Wollenberg, H. H. **Anatomy of the Film.** 1947.

Wright, Basil. **The Use of the Film.** 1948.